Baja Legends

The Historic Characters, Events, and Locations That Put Baja California on the Map

GREG NIEMANN

Sunbelt Publications

San Diego, California

BAJA LEGENDS

Copyright © 2002 by Sunbelt Publications, Inc.
All rights reserved. First edition 2002, fourth printing 2014.
Edited by Jennifer Redmond
Cover, maps, and book design by Michael Schrauzer
Project management by Deborah Young
Printed in the United States of America

Sunbelt Publications, Inc.
P.O. Box 191126
San Diego, CA 92159-1126
(619) 258-4911, fax: (619) 258-4916
www.sunbeltpub.com

"Sunbelt Cultural Heritage Books"
A Series Edited by Lowell Lindsay

18 17 16 15 14   8 7 6 5 4

Library of Congress Cataloging-in-Publication Data

Niemann, Greg, 1939–
    Baja Legends : the historic characters, events, and locations that put Baja
California on the map / by Greg Niemann.
        p. cm.
    Includes bibliographical references and index.
    ISBN 0-932653-47-2 (pbk.)
        1. Baja California (Mexico : Peninsula)--Description and travel. 2. Baja California
(Mexico : Peninsula)--History. 3. Baja California (Mexico : Peninsula)--Biography. 4.
Business enterprises--Mexico--Baja California (Peninsula)--History. 5. Baja California
(Mexico : Peninsula)--Folklore.

F1246 .N54 2002
972'.2--dc21
                                                                2001049564

Dedication

This book is dedicated to my Baja fishing buddy Don Lund, who passed away in 2000,

... and to the many big-hearted gringo residents in Baja's remote regions who have given much to their adopted land. An outstanding example was Deborah Lucero of San Ignacio, who lost her life in 2000 in a Flying Doctors plane crash,

... and to the selfless and dedicated professional men and women of the Flying Samaritans who volunteer their time and talent to help those in need,

... and to all of the good and gentle *bajacalifornios* who, regardless of their station in life, are the warmest hosts on earth.

Acknowledgements

Thanks to Anne Batty, first draft editor of *Baja Legends*, for her candor in helping me improve the project.

Thanks to reviewers Gene Kira, Graham Mackintosh, David Kier, Lynn Mitchell, and especially Shirley Miller, for all their great and constructive comments. I also appreciate the input offered by Judy Botello.

Thanks to Jennifer Redmond, Diana Lindsay, and others at Sunbelt Publications for their encouragement and direction.

All photos are by or from the collection of Greg Niemann, except where noted.

Cover map and vintage maps for chapters 1–4 are from *Loreto: Capital de las Californias*, by Miguel León-Portilla, published by Fonatur.

Contents

CONTENTS

Epilogue 245

Selected Bibliography 247

Index 253

Maps

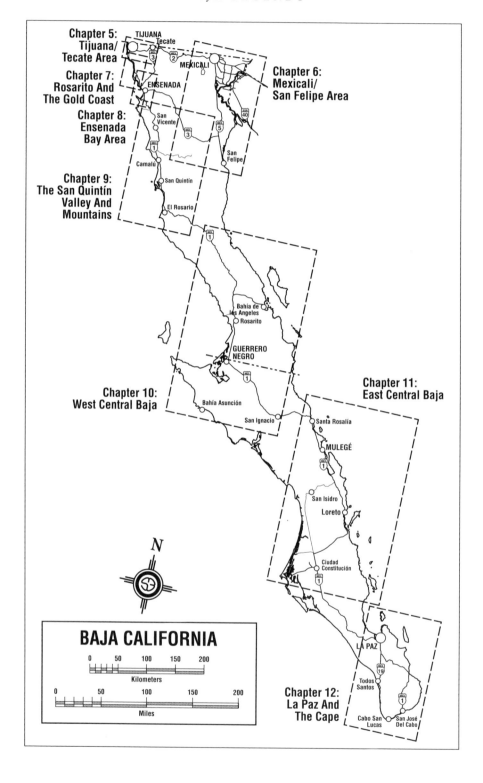

Introduction

....

What Is Baja, Anyway?

"*Baja,*" which means "Lower" in Spanish, refers to an 800-mile long peninsula separated from Mexico's mainland by the Gulf of California — or the Sea of Cortez, if you prefer. The peninsula is comprised of two Mexican states, Baja California (Norte), with Mexicali as capital, and Baja California Sur, whose capital city is La Paz. To make it easy, *Norte* means "North" and *Sur* means "South."

The peninsula is important, as it served as a stepping stone to the colonization of the U.S. state of California. Once the Spaniards left the Baja California peninsula to expand their efforts northward, the remote and arid peninsula was left to languish, virtually unpeopled and almost completely ignored by Mexico and the United States alike.

Baja California (Norte) did not become a Mexican state until 1952. The southern half of the peninsula, Baja California Sur, entered statehood in 1974, less than a year after the first paved road linking north to south (Highway 1) was completed.

What Do We Mean by Baja Legends?

This book's *Baja Legends* fit into three broad categories:

Legendary Tales and Stories

The "Legends" of Baja California began with the first people who entered the Americas from the Asian land-bridge. To this day much of their culture, best evidenced by cave art, remains a mystery.

Then the first Europeans arrived, inspired by legends of a fictional island peopled by beautiful women, where pearls and jewels lay about in abundance. These stories fired the fertile imaginations of a generation of seamen, creating more legends and wonderful stories of early visitors.

One of the most enduring legends about Baja California is that for 140 years most of the world thought the place was an island, even though several explorations had concluded otherwise.

I

The legendary tales and stories run the gamut from true to false to mysterious or questionable, and include wishful thinking and dreaming, lost missions and graves, and the perennial search for riches. *Baja Legends* looks into many of these stories to determine fact from fancy.

Legendary Characters

The development of Baja California required hardy people with an equal abundance of vision and willingness to overcome obstacles. This was true of the pirates, the pearlers, the padres, the miners, the settlers, the carpetbaggers, and those who created and maintained remote outposts and resorts for a growing legion of tourists.

Many of the colorful people and characters who have inhabited Baja and developed Baja over the years have themselves become legendary, and their presence has added to the folklore of Baja. In this book, we'll meet many of these individuals who, by themselves, deserve to be called *Baja Legends*.

Legendary Establishments (Past and Present)

Some of Baja's business establishments, from small ranchos and historic restaurants and cantinas to certain fly-in fishing resorts and upscale hotels, have thrived for 40, 50, 75, and even 100 years and more. Many of these landmarks are still in business today. Rather than featuring only the oldest using a strict cut-off year, we have rather attempted to base our selection on their importance in Baja. What's a few years in a timeless land?

There are a handful of others, including old casinos that no longer offer gambling and fly-in ranches that no longer have airstrips, which have served their purpose and are now but memories of a time gone by. These now defunct establishments once held the spotlight and attracted celebrities and sportsmen to that wondrous land called Baja. These legendary places helped pave the way for others.

Along with the tales, stories, and characters, much of this book visits many of these businesses, most still around today, as they too have earned the distinction of being called *Baja Legends*.

Part 1:
Early Legends

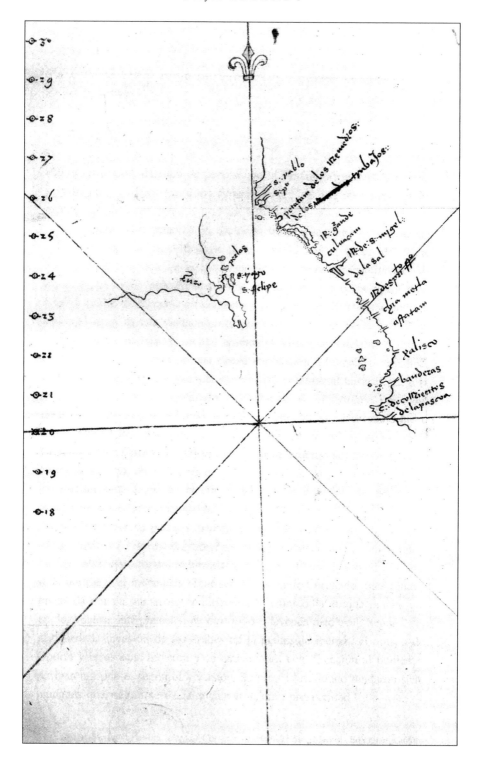

Chapter 1: Pre-Colonization

THE LEGENDS OF BAJA'S EARLY PEOPLE

Primitive Artists or Primitive People?

The legends of Baja California began with the early people, those first visitors to the rocky and arid peninsula — predecessors of the nomadic Indians found by the Europeans.

To this day much of their culture remains a mystery, chiefly visible to us in the wondrous cave paintings and petroglyphs etched upon desolate mountain caves dating from 1,000 to 3,000 years ago. Where did these ancient people come from? How did they exist in such a hostile environment? Where did they go?

Almost certainly they originally crossed over the Bering Strait land bridge from Asia, as did the other North American tribes. By following a natural route south along the coast, they reached the Baja California peninsula from 7,000 to 10,000 years ago.

Cave paintings (pictographs) and etchings (petroglyphs) found in mountain regions throughout Baja remind us of their presence. Some early groups, especially those who settled in Baja's northern reaches, even developed sophisticated weapons and pottery along with their art.

Much of the art depicts humans with hands raised, either monochromatic, half-black and half-red, or striped. The art at most sites, which varies slightly in technique, also features animals such as mountain lions, deer, sheep, fish, and birds. One rock painting even highlights the winter solstice, indicating a startling knowledge of astronomy. Who were these early groups who vanished a millennium ago, leaving only their artistic legacy?

The later indigenous Indians, the Guaycura, Pericú, and Cochimí, who were inhabiting the peninsula when the Spaniards arrived, were too busy eking out a simple existence to engage in artful endeavors. They told the Europeans that the rock art was created by a race of giants who had preceded them.

As some of the major rock sites extend hundreds of feet in length and are 30 feet high, the local Cochimí concluded that only giants could have done them.

More recent explorers indicate that materials in the areas could have been used to create scaffolding. There goes the giant theory. Even so, little is known about the artists to this day.

The native Indians found living in the central and southern reaches of Baja California when the first Europeans arrived bore little resemblance to their more sophisticated predecessors, who left their amazing and memorable marks upon the caves.

About the most primitive

The later groups encountered by the European explorers were about the most primitive of peoples ever encountered. They lived off the land and slept naked out in the open. They were neither great hunters nor farmers, but gathered their sustenance from plants, small animals, grubs, and insects.

The *pitahaya* cactus, from which blossomed a sweet bright red fruit each fall, was cause for celebration. During the *pitahaya* season, the natives gorged themselves on the succulent fruit. They would get so fat that the padres who came to enlighten them reported that some were hardly recognizable. Then they would eke out a meager existence during the rest of the year, rapidly losing weight in the process.

One of the most memorable, if not gross, legends of Baja concerns the *pitahaya*. It was reported by the padres that the natives enjoyed *pitahaya* so much they cultivated a "second harvest," so to speak.

To maximize the feast, they would defecate upon flat rocks, where once their stool dried they could gather all the *pitahaya* seeds and grind them up for grain, from which flat breads could be made! This legend found its way into print by the early padres themselves, but at least one contemporary Baja expert sheds doubt because of the soft seeds of the fruit.

One person obviously not impressed with the Baja natives was the German Johann Jakob Baegert, who spent the years 1751–1768 as a Jesuit missionary in the rocky mountains midway between Loreto and La Paz. He opens his 1771 book *Observations in Lower California* by criticizing his former charges:

> "Everything concerning [Baja] California is of such little importance that it is hardly worth the trouble to take a pen and write about it. Of poor shrubs, useless thorn bushes and bare rocks, of piles of stone and sand without water or wood, of a handful of people who, besides their physical shape and ability to think, have nothing to distinguish themselves from animals, what shall or what can I report?"

It appears Baegert didn't run into any giants, nor artists either for that matter.

BAJA CAVE ART

Museums in the Mountains

They're considered the finest examples of cave art in the Western Hemisphere. Yet the centuries-old paintings in Baja California have been available to westerners only for the past half-century or so. It wasn't until several explorers, writers, and adventurers (among them Erle Stanley Gardner, who wrote the *Perry Mason* series, and Harry Crosby), documented and analyzed these significant finds that the public learned much about them.

Central Baja California abounds in remote mountain sites where predecessors of the indigenous Cochimí Indians used sheer mountain cliffs as their palettes. There, applying substances ground from plants and minerals to create black, red, and ochre

Cave painting near Cataviña

inks, they gave us clues of their existence. They drew the animals they hunted, the arrows they crafted, and their victorious celebrations.

The gallery walls of Baja are a far cry from traditional somber museums, cordoned-off building wings, stern guards, and spotlights shining on glass protective coverings. Baja's walls are instead smooth sections of sandstone cliffs, ceilings, and overhangs of caves.

Visiting most of these "Museums in the Mountains" requires considerably more effort than buying a ticket at a kiosk and walking around a few flights of stairs. The most picturesque caves, including those considered the grandest, the Cueva Pintada (Painted Cave, also called Gardner Cave) and the Cueva Flecha (Arrow Cave) require a journey of several days down into steep canyons on the backs of sure-footed mules.

Cataviña

Some caves have easier access, including the small one in the Cataviña area. Less than a mile north of the La Pinta Hotel, Highway 1 fords a stream. While you can hike from that junction, it's easier to drive north up the hill to the first clearing off the highway. These days there's a little *palapa* there.

Drive in to the base of a hill overlooking the junction of two streams. Park at the end of the clearing and look up; you should see a sign announcing the small cave. The sign now visible from the highway wasn't there years ago, and you had to find the cave by trial and error.

After a short scramble up a trail, you'll find a cave formed by large boulders. It's not much, just a crawl space, actually a kind of boy's hideout. But there are some colorful

7

paintings on the ceiling, a sunray and a few circles and other markings. For accessibility, you can't beat it. A 15-minute detour from the highway and you've experienced some cave art.

Cueva Ratón

You can drive to other sites, but they're not so near the main highway as Cataviña. Probably the most outstanding cave you can drive to is Cueva Ratón, up in the Sierra San Francisco. The little community of San Francisco is the take-off point for mule rides to the major cave sites.

From Highway 1, about halfway between the towns of Vizcaíno and San Ignacio, a graded dirt road takes off to the east. A sign reading *"Cuevas Rupestres"* signifies that it indeed is the road to the cave art area.

The 23-mile road begins wide and straight (although rocky), and then starts winding up a ridge. The road continues up a plateau and follows the crest of a mountain spur even when it narrows; there are huge drop-off canyons on either side. Before the road vanishes into the mountains, an incredible panorama extends back, way out across the Vizcaíno Desert from San Ignacio to Guerrero Negro.

You can see the dusty village of San Francisco hugging the top of a barren plateau as you near, but first the road makes a few precipitous bends around the deep canyon. Way down below, palm trees and pools appear dwarfed by the deep, sheer canyon walls. More remarkable, you can see the mule trail heading down into that abyss.

You actually drive past Cueva Ratón a mile and a half before entering town, but you will need permission to visit it.

A few lazy cows and small herds of goats with tinkling bells welcomed my entrance to the village, which sits atop the world on a barren saddle at the canyon's head. It was not hard to imagine that this is a harsh, windy place in winter.

An old cowboy sat by a building near some tethered burros and children playing. He pointed out the house of the government coordinator, Enrique Arce of the ubiquitous Arce family. After I signed Arce's book, he sent his brother-in-law Jorge Guadalupe Arce, a younger, leathered cowboy who was in dire need of dental work, as a guide.

Jorge and I drove back to Cueva Ratón, where he unlocked the gate. We climbed the few stairs put in by the government during the mid-1990's. There are now signs explaining the paintings. Viewing platforms extend the length of the cave.

The paintings are massive. I shot plenty of film, both wide angle and close-ups, prints and slides, showing details of deer, cougars, and hunters. Much of the black and red drawings are covered over by newer paintings, and sometimes it takes a few minutes to figure out just what is what. But it is remarkable and gives one a feeling of awe and being in the presence of the past.

For those who wish to view Cueva Ratón, be sure to register with the coordinator. It only costs a few pesos for the guide. The 23 miles to San Francisco takes about an hour and a half each way. Or you might just go on into San Ignacio and inquire about a guided trip. If you can, take the burro ride to the most significant sites.

Cave art, Cañon de Trinidad

Cañon de Trinidad, Mulegé

Farther to the south are numerous cave paintings in the mountains west of Mulegé. Local guides, Salvador Castro or Ciro Cuesta to name two, can be arranged through Mulegé hotels. Preferring to do it myself, I set off one Sunday morning to visit some caves in the Cañon de Trinidad. Heading west, unsettling rain clouds lingered on the mountaintops, providing occasional sprinkles and some spectacular rainbows.

A good graded dirt road heads out through the inland suburbs of the tropical village of Mulegé past palm groves, farms, orchards, and ranches, up through desert into the mountains on a marked road to San Eustancio. Just past a compact little rancho, a small sign points left to "Rancho Trinidad." That's the side road to the caves.

That last mile or so of the 17-mile journey from town is rougher and requires high-clearance vehicles. There is one cattle gate, which you must open and then close behind you. Soon you arrive at a rustic rancho nestled on a bluff with a magnificent view off to the south, across a verdant valley and up into mountains. In every direction are high rocky peaks dappled with green and white *palo blanco* trees perched on improbable overhangs and looking like white-stemmed bunches of broccoli clinging tenaciously to steep hillsides.

At road's end, Rancho Trinidad has plenty of water, including a large cistern you could swim in, numerous trees, and cattle. It is owned by a Santa Rosalía doctor and managed by Placido Castro and his wife, Armida Arce de Castro, who raised four children during the 22 years they've been there.

The official register is provided by the Castros, who collect the fee of approximately $3.50 U.S. and will take you to the caves. There are two cave painting sites in the Cañon de Trinidad behind the rancho; one is about a one-and-a-half-mile round-trip on a good trail with some boulder hopping, and the other is about a three-hour round-trip from the rancho.

To get to the closer site, the trail crosses a makeshift dam and numerous pools of water. The steep canyon walls speckled with greenery give the place an ethereal look, like a set out of the movie *Lost Horizon*. Rounding a bend, a cave the early people had obviously used for lodging comes into view. Across the creek from it, in a couple of locations, are some outstanding examples of cave art. Placido, who had given the tour many times, pointed out the significance of the art.

The murals included outlines of hands and many animals, including fish, deer, and smaller game. One scene looks like a stag mounting a doe, denoting the early people's attention to animal husbandry. There is a hunter dancing in jubilation over the slain deer at his feet. There are even arrows protruding from a human figure, reminding current viewers of humankind's affinity for warfare.

Out in the center of the canyon rest large boulders, which through the years have come tumbling down from above. Much of the rock art is buried beneath the rubble at the foot of the caves, as you can see where the smooth art-covered rock palettes abruptly end and looser dirt prevails. At your feet an occasional drawing pokes through the rubble. The site is much more natural than those of the Sierra San Francisco, as it has yet to be fenced off.

On the trail back and around the rancho are other reminders of early dwellers in the area. There are several wonderful petroglyphs etched or pecked through the dark exterior of boulders, leaving the image on the lighter interior, as well as metates used for grinding grain.

Armida had been busy in her detached and open kitchen while we were gone. In true Baja hospitality, she asked if I would like some *machaca* (dried beef). Imagine the contrast of stepping out of the New York Metropolitan Museum of Art and being accosted by a vendor of overpriced hot dogs.

Forget the Louvre, the Prado, the Getty, and the Met. The cave paintings of Baja California are wonderfully displayed in nature's own magnificent art gallery, the Museums of the Mountains.

TALL TALES ATTRACT EUROPEANS

Women and Riches — Fact or Fancy?

Throughout history, few subjects have fired up man's imagination more than the prospect of instant riches. And if you throw in a legend about beautiful women, you've got a box office hit. In the case of "California" in the early 16th century, you've got the ingredients for the intrigue that surrounded that mythical "island."

Following the discovery of great wealth in Mexico and Peru, the Spaniards were willing to believe anything. Fancy was so attractive it became fact.

The popular Spanish novel *Las Sergas* (The Exploits of) *de Esplandián* talked of Amazon women with "beautiful robust bodies" on an island where gold was the only metal. The unknown land had to be out there somewhere, and Mexico became filled with adventurers who sought it, further spreading tall tales in their pursuit. Even Mexico's conqueror Hernán Cortés was taken in by the myth and wrote the King of Spain that he would seek its truth.

In addition, an old European legend about seven cities of gold in a place called Cíbola was resurrected by Cabeza de Vaca and his handful of men, who wandered lost for eight years throughout what is now the southwest United States. They claimed to have seen the cities shimmering in the sunlight from a distance. Over the next century adventurers searched for both legends and settled for the reality that the seven cities were yellow clay Indian pueblos, and that the "island" of California had neither Amazons nor the riches they sought.

MUTINY AND DEATH MARK FIRST BAJA LANDING
Violence Is As Violence Gets

Mexico's conqueror, Hernán Cortés, sent ships to seek the land inspired by legend, that mythical "island of riches" that became California. In 1532 his first two ships didn't get far, landing back on the east side of the gulf. One ship turned back in a storm and the crew of the other, commanded by Cortés' cousin, were all killed by natives on the mainland.

Hernan Cortés

He sent two more ships late in 1533, but they separated and the first one returned to Acapulco. The other ship, the *Concepción*, was commanded by another Cortés relative, Diego Becerra de Mendoza, who was not well liked. The crew mutinied, killing him in his sleep, and established the Basque pilot Fortún Jiménez in command. They stopped on the mainland coast north of Acapulco, sent Becerra's sympathizers ashore, and set about fleeing to the north.

A storm blew the fugitives west into what is now La Paz, making them the first Europeans to set foot on (Baja) California. Unfortunately, most of the men didn't live to tell about it, as local Indians killed Jiménez and 20 of his men. The 18 survivors fled, sailing back across the gulf only to fall into the hands of Cortés' arch-rival, Nuño de

11

Guzmán. Most were killed, but at least one escaped to relate to Cortés the tale of landing in the new "island" to the west where there were many pearls. Thus the actual discovery of California by Europeans was an ignoble result of treachery, storms, mistakes, mutiny, and counter-mutiny, all shrouded in violence perpetrated by both the fugitive visitors and those whose homes and cultures, primitive as they may have been, were endangered.

Hardships Thwart Mexico's Conqueror

Cortés' Colony Short-Lived

After hearing tales of pearls and wealth in this "island" to the west, Cortés used some of his own wealth to take three ships and about 100 Spanish colonists, setting out to colonize the new land. On May 3, 1535, the party landed in what Cortés called Santa Cruz, the northeast corner of La Paz Bay, on what they called the Isle of Pearls. The Cortés party found evidence of the earlier Jiménez landing and also found pearls in great abundance — at least 30 pearl oyster beds, but most were deep and would require diving.

From the start, Cortés had problems supporting the colony. Not only were they harassed by the hostile Pericú natives, but they found the land too arid to support them. Cortés sent the ships back to the mainland to pick up additional colonists and supplies, but they had such bad luck that only one returned, and without any provisions at that.

Cortés himself took off with the remaining ship and found one vessel that had run aground on the mainland coast of Sinaloa, which they were able to release, and the other severely damaged upon a reef. Using the somewhat seaworthy ship, they had a hard time getting supplies. To further complicate matters, the pilot died on the journey back, so Cortés himself had to take the wheel. When they finally arrived back in Santa Cruz (La Paz) they found that 23 of the colonists had starved to death. A few others soon died from gorging themselves when food arrived.

The colony built a church and housing, but could not sustain themselves from the land nor count on consistent supplies. Cortés abandoned the colony, and the last of the colonists returned to the mainland in 1536. Cortés spent a fortune on this yearlong enterprise and had nothing to show for it other than a few nice pearls, including one that was allegedly valued at 5,000 ducats (a ducat was a gold coin).

The Naming of California

"Very Near the Terrestrial Paradise"

The word "California" first began appearing on maps without a reference as to the origin of the word. Naturally this led to speculation, and several theories proliferated. It wasn't until 1862 that someone suggested that the name had come from a novel. That soon became the most widely accepted explanation of the name.

One popular earlier theory, since discarded, suggests that the word "California" might have come from the Latin *Calida Fornax* meaning "hot furnace," referring to the blistering temperatures often encountered in the deserts of Baja California.

Another not quite popular theory suggested a corruption of a combination of a Latin and Spanish word. It was proffered that the Spanish word *Cala*, meaning "little bay," was combined with the Latin word *Fornix*, which means "arch." This reference would be about the arch at Cabo San Lucas, but the early explorers hardly even stopped there.

In 1862, a New England clergyman and writer, Edward Everett Hale, came across the Spanish novel *Las Sergas* (The Exploits of) *de Esplandián*, first published in 1510, and suddenly it became clear. The novel that was very popular (five printings) at the time of Spain's conquest of Mexico contained the word "California." How the word was used left no doubt that the name originated there.

"On the right hand of the Indies"

The author, Garcí Ordóñez de Montalvo, wrote about a faraway fictional island "on the right hand of the Indies very near the terrestrial Paradise." He called that island "California."

It has been suggested that Ordóñez originally chose that name because it was so far away. Writers at the time were well aware that the word "colophon" meant the "end" of a book: title, name of publisher, and other notes. Colophon was the name of a Greek city in Iona whose people were proverbially at the end, the farthest away, the least civilized. In Spanish, the term became "Colophonia." The German spelling was very similar to California or Kalifornia. It could have been a play on words with California signifying "the end place."

In any event, the application of that name to new world territory was attributed to the journal of Francisco Preciado, a seaman who traveled with Francisco de Ulloa in 1539 and 1540 as they looped the Sea of Cortez and then explored the Pacific Coast up to about the San Quintín Bay area. In his diary, which was later published in Europe, he obviously recalled the book and referred to the newly discovered lands as "California."

What is California?

The term "California," prior to the 1769 exploration into what is now the U.S. state, only meant the peninsula. Then the practice began of calling the north (now U.S.) "Alta California" (Upper California) and the peninsula "Baja California" (Lower California). "The Californias" referred to it all.

The words "Alta California" were used even up to the late 19th century. To those in the U.S., "Baja California" was more commonly called by its English name "Lower California" up until the mid-20th century.

The northern half of the peninsula became the Mexican state of Baja California. The southern state, Baja California Sur (South), is south of the 28th parallel. People sometimes call the northern Mexican state Baja California Norte (BCN) to differentiate north from south, but the official name is simply Baja California.

Now one of the most recognizably named places on the planet, it seems fitting that the paradise we call California began "very near the terrestrial paradise."

VIZCAÍNO'S PERSEVERANCE PAID OFF

The Names Are Changed

Sebastián Vizcaíno is responsible for naming more places along the California and Baja California coasts than any other. On a major exploration in 1602 he defied direct orders to assure that his names, rather than those of his predecessors, would survive. In spite of his earlier failure at La Paz, he was still the logical person to get that 1602 command.

At La Paz in 1596, Vizcaíno had set up a colony at Cortés' old colony site of Santa Cruz. Vizcaíno called it La Paz (Peace) because at first he found the natives so peaceful.

Back in mainland Mexico, he told stories of pearls, rich salt deposits, gold and silver, and of many natives all begging to be converted to Spain's Catholic religion. His embellished propaganda convinced the viceroy that another voyage should be attempted.

Sebastián Vizcaíno
(Photo: San Diego Historial Society Collection)

Hoping to exercise more control, Spain gave Vizcaíno specific instructions to explore only the coastline to Cape Mendocino. He was not to explore large bays, only note their entrances. He was to establish no settlements and keep out of trouble with the Indians. He was to stay out of the gulf, except for possibly on the return trip, assuming California was an island, and under no circumstances was he to change the names of landmarks already firmly established.

But Vizcaíno had aboard a cartographer and three Carmelite friars, one of whom he charged with writing an official diary of the journey. The Carmelite made many erroneous and fantastic claims, adding further confusion to the prevailing geographical ideas about California.

Vizcaíno also renamed everything in sight, his reason being that Rodríguez Cabrillo's earlier observations on his historic voyage were so inaccurate that he could not find the localities mentioned. Thus Cabrillo's "San Miguel" in 1542 became Vizcaíno's "San Diego" in 1602, both names honoring the specific saints on their day. And the "Desert Islands" of Cabrillo became the "Coronados" under Vizcaíno.

On Nov. 5, 1602, Vizcaíno arrived at the future site of Ensenada. It was the feast of All Saints and Vizcaíno was to declare, "By God's sweet wounds! It is so beautiful we will name it after all the saints. Take possession of it in the name of His Most Catholic Majesty, the King of Spain, and call it Bahía Todos Santos."

He arrived at Monterey Bay on Dec. 16, 1602 and was astute enough to name that place after his boss, the Viceroy of New Spain, Don Gaspar de Zúñiga, Conde de Monterrey.

In a letter Vizcaíno sent to Zúñiga 12 days later from Monterey, Vizcaíno also claims he also put into the port of "Francisco," leading some to believe he sailed through the Golden Gate. Historians doubt it mainly because even though he was ordered not to, he could not have completely resisted exploring the bay, searching for the Strait of Anián, in the process learning of its size and possible importance. He did not elaborate about the bay in his letter, yet he was profuse in his praise for the smaller bays at San Diego and Monterey.

Most of Vizcaíno's names are the ones that endured, and he himself, with a monumental ego that matched his sense of adventure, became a legend.

Ironically, the only town named after Vizcaíno is the small, dusty agricultural hamlet of 2,339 in the middle of Baja's Vizcaíno Desert.

CALIFORNIA BELIEVED AN ISLAND FOR OVER 200 YEARS

The Island of California

One of the oldest and longest-enduring legends about the land called California is that (Baja) California was an island. Mostly it was a case of wishful thinking and people ignoring facts that ran counter to accepted beliefs.

When you consider that the entire American continent was but a "speed bump" to those Europeans who wanted to sail to the Orient and back with ships laden with riches, you understand. For years mariners and explorers searched in vain for a "Northwest Passage" or the fabled "Strait of Anián" to bypass North America.

The Spanish under Cortés had already crossed the continent and were to establish Acapulco on the South Sea (Pacific Ocean) as the departure point to Manila in the Philippines. The long gulf to the north, separating Baja California from the mainland, lent itself as a possible entrance to a more direct route and could perhaps even tie in with the Northwest Passage. This wishful thinking lasted almost two centuries, even though numerous explorers had proved it was a peninsula.

A few years after Cortés' first ship made landfall at La Paz and Cortés tried to establish a colony there, the conqueror of Mexico sent Francisco de Ulloa to explore the gulf in 1539 and 1540. Ulloa's two ships looped the Vermilion Sea (later to be called the Sea of Cortez). They reached the mouth of the Colorado River, proving that California was in fact an island.

But only one ship returned to Cortés to report the news, and the flagship bearing Ulloa was never heard from again. While chroniclers aboard reported their findings to Cortés, he was not anxious to believe them and died thinking Baja California was an island. Neither Ulloa's ship nor log was ever found, but his narrative of the trip surfaced in Seville, Spain well over 100 years later.

The mouth of the Colorado

The year after Ulloa's journey, Hernando de Alarcón headed up the gulf in search of the legendary seven cities of gold. He noted the tidal bore at the mouth of the Colorado River and proceeded upriver some distance. A map from this expedition, drawn by seaman Castillo, showed California to be a peninsula. Most of the maps drawn by explorers and cartographers of the 16th century also accurately depicted California as a peninsula, but some continued to depict it as an island.

Sebastián Vizcaíno was not only a fine sailor and a brave explorer, but also his own P.R. man. To continue his popularity and assure future commands, Vizcaíno exaggerated the success of his 1602 trip up the west coast. He even claimed to have reached the very mouth of the Strait of Anián, but could not explore it fully as his men were sick. This report begat another round of "island fever," convincing some Europeans that California was indeed an island, even though most mariners based in the new world knew otherwise.

In 1615, a Spanish pearler named Juan de Iturbe also advanced the island myth when he entered the gulf to escape Dutch pirates and proceeded north. He claimed that he could see the sea widen to a point where it was about 10 to 12 leagues (30 to 36 miles) coast to coast. He ordered a sailor to climb the mast to confirm the sightings. The sailor stated that he could see that both littorals were not united and that navigation could be continued toward the northwest. Yet by Iturbe's own admission, he had only reached Latitude 30 (about Gonzaga Bay). His sailor in the crow's nest needed eyes like a hawk to see about 120 miles to the mouth of the Colorado River. Another explorer whose poor knowledge of the local geography helped perpetuate the "island" legend.

Baja California was drawn as an island on numerous of maps, including one by Dutch pirates in 1625, and on another one drawn in 1648. Many other maps created in that century, however, correctly portrayed Baja California to be a peninsula.

Jesuit explorations put theory to rest

The Jesuit padres who were successful in colonizing the Baja California peninsula for Spain were also instrumental in its exploration. While based in Sonora on the mainland in 1684, Padre Eusebio Kino explored to the mouth of the Colorado River. In 1701, after the first few peninsular missions were established, Kino and Padre Juan Salvatierra made an expedition by land to link the missions of the northern Sonora region with those of the peninsula. They were successful in proving conclusively that Baja California was indeed a peninsula.

The Jesuit Juan de Ugarte had also reached the Colorado River in a 1721 expedition, thus confirming that the gulf did not go through.

However, it wasn't until after the exploration of another Jesuit in 1746 that the King of Spain finally decreed the "Island of California" to be a peninsula. The adventurous Padre Consag made a journey to the Colorado River and produced a map that finally squelched the dreams and wishes of the insularists.

Things move slowly in Baja, and taking 200 years to decide whether the place is an island or a peninsula set the pace for the next 200 years.

SWASHBUCKLING ADVENTURES ON THE HIGH SEAS

The Treasure of the *Santa Ana*

Among the most enduring and romantic of old legends are those of pirates on the high seas. Romanticized in operas, novels, movies, and even adventure rides at Disneyland, those sword-dueling adventurers of another era created a sense of excitement and drama. The reality, of course, is that where there were riches in vulnerable ships, there were thieves lying in wait, and the grim brutality of the pirates was a matter of record.

Baja California became an important piece of land when Spanish galleons in the year 1565 began rounding the cape as they crossed the Pacific to the Philippines and the Far East. Called "Manila Galleons," these richly laden ships returned to Acapulco on their eventual journey to European ports.

Over 1,000 ships followed the same sea-road for a period of 250 years, and the Spanish exchanged cochineal, cocoa, copper, and other products for silk, fans, ivory, articles of jasper and jade, carved furniture, urns, bronzes, chinaware, pearls, gold, rubies, and diamonds from the Orient. Where such wealth was handled by sea, piracy was a real and common threat.

Over the years seamen from other nations made a habit of taking on the Spanish ships. Sir Francis Drake was the first major English pirate to challenge the Spanish in their Pacific domain. In 1578, Drake and his three ships attacked and sacked ports all over the Pacific, bearing the colors of the excommunicated Queen Elizabeth with whom he was associated.

Their booty was so great that the little *Golden Hind*, at only 120 tons, had to limit its cargo to just silver and gold. Called the *Scourge of God* by his Spanish victims, Drake may have stopped at the tip of Baja to take on water and then proceeded north.

Raids embarrassed Spanish Crown

Emboldened by Drake's success, other English and Dutch pirates attacked the Spanish ships. Their raids not only embarrassed the Spanish crown, but also caused a serious financial drain on the country's wealth. Not only that, Spaniards were forced to hide out in Baja's coves, bays, and harbors, most notably those at La Paz and Cabo San Lucas.

Between 1586 and 1588 another English pirate, Thomas Cavendish, caused considerable damage to the Spanish fleet all along the Pacific Coast. Cavendish, who later claimed he burned 119 vessels large and small, had committed every type of crime imaginable. But he never hit the jackpot in terms of gold or silver until he decided to take on the 700-ton Spanish galleon *Santa Ana* at Cabo San Lucas in 1587. It was described by the Bishop of the Philippines as "the richest ship to ever leave these isles."

Cavendish and his two small ships, the 120-ton *Desire* and 80-ton *Content*, lay in wait at Cabo San Lucas. He had scuttled one smaller ship of 40 tons.

According to English seaman Francis Pretty, "The 14 of November we fell with the cape of S. Lucas, which cape is very like the Needles at the Isles of Wight; and within the said cape is a great bay called by the Spaniards Aguada Segura...."

On the morning of November 14, the *Desire* and *Content* were "beating up and down the headland of California" and spotted a sail. They gave chase, and the smaller, faster English ships caught up to the larger vessel in about four hours.

"We gat up unto them..."

Pretty continued,

> "In the afternoone we gat up unto them, giving them the broad side with our great ordinance and a volee of small shot, and presently layed the ship abo-ord, whereof the King of Spain was owner, which was Admiral of the south sea, called the S. Anna, & thought to be 700 tunnes in burthen. Now as we were ready on their ships side to enter her, being not past 50 or 60 men at the uttermost in our ship, we perceived that the Captaine of the said ship had made fights fore and after, and layd their sailes close on their poope, their mid ship, with their fore castle, and having not one man to be seene, stood close under their fights, with lances, javelings, rapiers, and targets, & an innu-merable sort of great stones, which they threw overboard upon our heads and into our ship so fast and there being so many of them, that they put us off the ship againe, with the losse of 2 of our men which were slaine, & with the hurting of 4 or 5...."

Aboard the *Santa Ana* was seaman Antonio de Sierra. He reported,

> "Those of us on our ship, the *Santa Ana*, as soon as we saw the said English on board with swords and iron bucklers, went at them and we killed five Eng-lish and wounded six. When they saw that the battle was against them, the wounded and the others threw themselves into the water, leaving three of our men dead. The English general accepted this, and, then in full earnest, began to ram us cruelly. During this encounter, an Englishman climbed into our rig-ging; and, since we did not see him, he was able to cut the mainsail retainers. Our Captain then loaded two balls in an arquabus and fired at the man on the mainmast. He killed him and the man fell dead on the upper deck of the ship...."

"A young man of little age"

The *Santa Ana*'s Captain, Tomás de Alzola, called Cavendish "An English corsair and thief ... a young man of little age" (Cavendish was only 27 years old at the time). Captain Alzola then described the continuing battle. "A third time the said English ship turned to come alongside the *Santa Ana* on the inside of the prow where Diego Meléndez Flores was accompanied by the Captain and this squad of men. Although the enemy fired artillery and small arms, and boarded men over the fender-beam and side, they were resisted with great force and made to jump into the sea and onto their ship. Thus, they retired again, and standing off, they began to batter the said ship with their artillery, which later appeared to be twenty-nine heavy pieces of finished bronze and iron, and two stone projectile lombards. This damaged the said ship, and its men brought down masts and tackle and struck two or three times at the water-line where the sea entered...."

The galleon *Santa Ana* was a veritable fortress, but it was so heavily loaded that it could not maneuver, and the cannons were below the waterline, rendering them useless. Sinking and without artillery, Captain Alzola arranged for a surrender, sparing the lives of his remaining crew and passengers.

Captain Alzola continued, "On the third day, the seventeenth of November, they went to the Port of San Lucas where they anchored with their ships and the ship *Santa Ana*. There, on the eighteenth, the General and officers of the aforesaid fleet gathered together, called all of the people of the said ship *Santa Ana*, and ordered them that, under the threat of death, they should turn over all the keys to the boxes as well as deliver up all the gold they carried. In compliance with this ... everyone brought forth the gold, perfume, musk and pearls which was a great deal and of great value. All of this was received by the said English General, and he put it away in a box. This entire day was spent at this task."

Survivors put ashore

The following day, 190 survivors from the *Santa Ana*, including four women, were put ashore. Cavendish had de Alzola remove the treasure of the ship as noted in the registry. Cavendish then piled all the gold and treasure and made three piles, keeping two for himself and letting his crew divide one pile.

Before leaving, the Englishmen took out all the chests and bundles and opened them with axes, searching for more gold. Captain Alzola reported, "In sacking the said ship *Santa Ana*, they committed great harm and insolence until the twenty-ninth when they had no more space to load. In the manner of infidels and enemies of the Catholic Faith, they cut the masts and tackle of the said ship and then set fire to it."

The survivors in San José del Cabo, headed by Vizcaíno, who was traveling as a merchant, extinguished the fire, repaired the *Santa Ana* as best they could, and were able to sail it to the mainland.

The English pirates loaded the *Desire* and the *Content* with as much booty as they dared carry and set off. That very night they separated, and the richly laden *Content* was never heard from again. Cavendish, aboard the *Desire*, arrived in Plymouth, England in September 1588.

A dream of pirate treasure

The legend of the *Content* is a dream of pirate treasure that endures through the ages. Could it be the same vessel referred to in an old Baja California Indian legend about a wooden ship found stranded in a bay with the dried-up corpses of men on board? On shore were bones of other men in tattered clothing. When the Indians built a fire on the ship's deck to cook their food, as they did on land, the ship burned and sank.

The riches of the *Content*, which allegedly had millions in silver pesos in addition to the plunder from the *Santa Ana*, have never been found. The Indian legend puts the vessel in a sheltered bay on the Pacific north of Cabo San Lucas. Over 300 years of storms and rising coastlines could have buried any protruding evidence.

The brave pirates who served under the young and daring Cavendish were not able to enjoy the spoils of their adventures.

DUTCH PIRATES IN LA PAZ

The Legend of Pichilingue

The Spanish domination of the coast of Baja California was challenged in the late 16th and early 17th centuries, not only by the English, but by Dutch pirates as well. Both Protestant countries delighted in avenging their Catholic enemies by ambushing the Spanish fleet.

The first wave of Dutch pirates in 1598 was not very successful in its hunt for Spanish riches along the coast of New Spain. A second armada in 1600 had such moderate success it decided to "capture the goose where its eggs were being laid" and crossed the Pacific to the Philippines. Commanded by Olivier van Noort, the Dutch fleet was soundly thumped by the Spanish and forced to flee.

The third armada, commanded by Admiral Joris van Spilbergen, was equipped with larger and better armed ships. This third Dutch fleet earned respect from the sailors of New Spain. The Spanish, who had looked forward to the 1615 confrontation, were cocky and boastful, even insulting their enemy by calling them "Dutch hens." They really "ate their words," as the Spanish fleet was destroyed in only one day.

The Spanish began calling the formidable Dutch enemy "Pichilingues" a name considered by some to be a mispronunciation of an area of The Netherlands where most of the pirates hailed from.

Spilbergen, while sailing around the area, discovered the Revillagigedo Islands southeast of the tip of Baja California. Other Dutch pirates continued to harass the Spanish from Baja coves and shelters for years.

In the ensuing years so many Spanish ships were ravaged by the Dutch in the Bay of La Paz alone that the name Pichilingue was affixed to the area. To this day, the ferry departs from that area of La Paz known as Pichilingue.

PIRATE WAS MAROONED ON ISLAND

Robinson Crusoe in Baja?

Yes, it's true that the real Robinson Crusoe, hero of Daniel Defoe's timeless 1719 novel, spent time in Baja California. But what is not true is the rumor that Baja was the setting for the fictional island. Alexander Selkirk, later immortalized as Crusoe, was a seaman born in Fife, Scotland in 1676 and later shipwrecked on the island of Más a Tierra, part of the Juan Fernández group of islands some 400 miles off the coast of Chile.

He was rescued in 1709 by English buccaneers led by Captain Woodes Rogers, who put in at the island for fresh goat meat. Finding Selkirk, who had been marooned there for four years, Rogers described him as having the appearance of "a wild man, clothed all in goatskin, who seemed wilder than the original owners of his apparel."

The pirate Rogers took Selkirk, who then served his rescuer as shipmaster, with him to the tip of Baja California, where they continued to pillage Spanish ships. Rogers's second mate at the time was the infamous pirate William Dampier. Among other misdeeds, Rogers and his crew captured the extremely valuable Manila galleon *Encarnación* at Cabo San Lucas in what was described as a sharp contest, continuing more than 100 years of pirates harassing the Spanish fleet.

Selkirk's incredible story of survival became Defoe's inspiration. Defoe's book went on to become the inspiration for generations of young people who dream of far-off adventure.

In 1996 Chile attempted to attract tourists by renaming Más a Tierra Island, changing its name to Robinson Crusoe Island.

TERRA ANTI
REGIS GAST
INVETA: AXP
ROCOLVBO:i
VÊSi

Chapter 2: Legends of the Padres

A Blessing or a Curse?

Few Americans realize how significant the exploration of the Baja California peninsula was to the development of California and its eventual U.S. statehood.

The chain of California missions actually began in Baja California in 1697, and over the next 150 years, it stretched all the way to northern California, with 25 missions established in Baja and 21 more in Alta California.

The Spanish soldiers and their accompanying padres developed the overland route to California by establishing settlements and missions throughout the (Lower) California peninsula. The Baja missions were integral in the colonization of the harsh, semi-arid peninsula. The colonization of Baja California did not begin until the Catholic Jesuits in their zeal made it happen.

The missions they established became the center of settlements in which the indigenous Indians could learn agriculture, ranching, and social skills. In addition they received heavy doses of what Spain determined to be the one true religion, and, of course, the forced cultural adaptations to make the vanquished more like the Europeans.

Some historians see the Spanish padres in the altruistic light in which they saw themselves (saving the lost souls of heathens). Others noted that they were brutal, dominating masters who enslaved the natives, subjecting them to European diseases and forcing an alien culture upon them.

On all accounts, it appears the newly acquired agricultural skills and improved living conditions came with a price. The local tribes had to relinquish their time-honored traditions, their beliefs, and their identity. In addition, they were subjected to diseases unknown to their culture.

In most cases it appears the intrusion of the padres was both a blessing and a curse upon the indigenous tribes. Whatever their reasons or methods, the padres who colonized under the Spanish flag truly made an impact on all that could be called California.

WHITE MAN'S WAYS RAVAGE PEOPLE
What Killed the Indians?

It is estimated that the native Indian population in Baja California declined from more than 20,000 when Loreto was settled in 1697 to only about 5,000 by 1777, and continued on the decline from then.

An example would be that of Mission San Borja. At its peak there were more than 3,000 Indians, yet when the last resident padre departed in 1818, there were fewer than 100 remaining. It was much the same at many of the missions.

The padres knew how to save the souls, not the bodies of "heathens." They desperately wanted to convert and baptize them before the diseases of dysentery, smallpox, measles — or the most widespread, syphilis — wiped the Indians out.

Ironically, those diseases were unknown among the susceptible Indian tribes in California and only arrived with the European conquerors. Yet the padres often saw the diseases as God's way to punish the local tribes for their evil heathen ways.

To pinpoint one disease, Don Pedro Fages, Governor of both Californias in the 1770s, stated, "That the Missions have deteriorated is beyond question. ...The reason is so clear that it cannot be doubted. The disease syphilis ravages both sexes and to such an extent that the mothers no longer conceive, and if they do conceive, the young are born with little hope of surviving."

There were other problems, too. In 1722 there was a plague of locusts. As their crops were wiped out, many natives were forced to eat locusts, from which they got ulcers and died. Next there was a plague of dysentery. Most of the Indians were killed in three major epidemics, in 1742, 1744, and 1748, which killed five out of six local Baja California Indians.

PADRE JUAN DE UGARTE
The Paul Bunyan of Baja

That the mission system under Spain played a significant role in the settlement and development of Baja California is a matter of historic record. Like all endeavors, those of some Catholic padres were more instrumental than others. One of them, a bear of a man, became a legend in his own time. Jesuit Padre Juan de Ugarte was as real to Baja in the early 18th century as Paul Bunyan was to the U.S. More real, in fact — Ugarte really existed!

In fact, his former boss, Padre Juan Salvatierra, president of the California missions, wrote of Ugarte: "...he was the Atlantic, the Pillar of California, to whom after God is due the conversion of the Indians of these Missions." How's that for a job review, to be rated number two to the Deity himself?

While several Baja mission padres were significant in the development of Baja California and eventually the U.S. (Alta) California, many historians feel that Ugarte was the greatest of the missionary pioneers, and that his contributions were crucial for the success of the missions.

Others made very important contributions, including Padre Eusebio Kino, who explored the area first and established a temporary settlement, and Salvatierra, who founded the first mission at Loreto in 1697 and was an influential president of the missions. Later, Franciscan Padre Junípero Serra became widely known, primarily for his work in Alta California.

When it comes to individual effort and results in getting the job done, Ugarte's name heads the list. And he wasn't even Spanish! Padre Juan de Ugarte, a former professor of philosophy at the Jesuit College in Mexico City, was Honduran. Of the New World himself, Ugarte was born in the capital city of Tegucigalpa in 1660.

A distinguished theologian, Ugarte was educated in Guatemala City and had become chair of philosophy at the esteemed Colegio de San Pedro y San Pablo in Mexico City. He also served as rector of San Gregorio. He and his brother, Padre Pedro de Ugarte, both served as missionaries in Baja California.

Juan de Ugarte was involved in everything. He successfully solicited funds in mainland Mexico to sustain the missionary effort; he established missions; he related with the Indians better than his fellow missionaries and squelched their fears and superstitions. He served as president of the missions after Salvatierra and even constructed the first boat ever built in Baja California.

A bear of a man

By all accounts, Juan de Ugarte was a bear of a man. He was enormously strong, large in stature — perhaps over six feet tall — larger in bearing, and even larger in legend.

While Kino and Salvatierra were planning the California occupation like military strategists, they desperately needed funds to get the enterprise off the ground. Ugarte, as treasurer of the Pious Fund, was named Procurator of the Missions in Mexico City. He spent several years banging on doors to obtain donations and promises of support. He was joined for a while by Salvatierra. With donations secured, Salvatierra was sent to establish the mission at Loreto in 1697; Padre Francisco Piccolo received the second one at San Javier (Xavier) in 1699.

Ugarte was "champing at the bit" to get into the action himself. He rode overland from Mexico City to meet with then Mission President Padre Kino in Sonora. He got the approval to enter the fray in California, but needed transportation, so he repaired a shipwrecked longboat and, with seven Yaqui Indians and provisions for the missions, crossed the gulf in a storm, arriving at Loreto on Apr. 1, 1701 at the age of 41.

A colleague of Ugarte's second-guessed his decision by writing, "I cannot think of this without being moved to compassion and without recognizing the power of God, the sight of a gentleman, raised amid comforts of a wealthy home, now reduced to a tedious and burdensome life, and buried in obscure and remote solitude, a man of letters and highly esteemed in the schools and pulpits of Mexico, a man of sublime genius, voluntarily condemned to associate for thirty years with stupid savages."

At Loreto, Ugarte studied the Cochimí language for a few months and then headed up into the mountains to take over Mission San Javier, which was deserted because of a threatened revolt. After he arrived with his escort of soldiers, he found the Indians

Mission San Javier

would not come around because of the presence of the soldiers. So in an act of faith, he sent the soldiers back to Loreto and confronted the Indians alone. Soon he had them coming in large numbers to hear him preach about his God.

Threats and deception

But all was not easy. There were murderous threats from those natives who were unwilling to become docile converts to this new religion. There were thefts and deceptions.

At the beginning, the natives who sat for catechism classes used to howl with laughter when Ugarte mispronounced a word. When he saw how they made fun of his attempts to speak Cochimí, he asked some about a correct word or pronunciation. They intentionally answered him with absurdities so they would have something to laugh about during their lessons. He learned quickly to only ask children, for they proved to be more sincere.

Once, his scantily-clad natives gathered about him on a cold winter's day, and he began preaching about the hellfires of damnation that awaited those who did not live the good life. His sermon was quickly disrupted by hordes of bone-chilled natives as they crowded around him, wanting to know how they could go to this warm place. The fires of hell sounded pretty comforting to them.

When he got too exasperated with the natives, it is recorded that he resorted to corporal punishment. He would jerk them about by the hair or grab a couple of them and bump their heads together.

Ugarte commanded respect among his charges. He earned it. In one incident, the natives confessed to being so terrified of mountain lions that they had determined the animals were gods. This made it tough when Ugarte tried to convince them that his was the only true God.

The mountain lion god

One day he was out with some of his Indians when they came across a mountain lion. The Indians wanted to flee, but Ugarte picked up some rocks and stoned the lion, dazing him. He then walked over and choked it to death with his bare hands. He threw it over the saddle of his burro, and amid the chatter of the startled natives, returned to the village. To complete the symbolism, while the village watched, he skinned a portion of the meat, cooked it, and ate it. That night the Indians removed the carcass and ate the rest of the meat. There was never another argument about the godliness of the mountain lion.

Ugarte was practical as well as theological. While the fires of hell were tempting to his neophytes, warm clothing was better. He planted cotton and brought over sheep and goats from the Mexican mainland. He hired a weaver from the mainland, paying him 500 pesos to come over and teach Ugarte's disciples to weave cloth to cover themselves. The clothing served two purposes. In addition to providing warmth for winter's chill, it appeased the missionaries' aversion to seeing people in their natural naked state.

Ugarte cleared land and planted corn, wheat, and beans. He even established orchards of olives, pomegranates, figs, citrus, grapes, and dates. He was the Padre who first introduced the "mission" variety of figs, citrus, grapes, and olives to the Californias, spawning what would be the leading crops of a major U.S. state 300 years later.

He had to dig and hew from rocks an elaborate irrigation system and build dams and canals to nurture the newly-planted crops (portions of that system are still in evidence today).

With zeal and skill he administered his Mission San Javier. He established the first school for Indian children in the Californias, a seminary to teach boys; girls were taught in a separate building by an Indian woman. He established another building as California's first hospital and for the care of the aged. He journeyed to neighboring Indian settlements, further spreading his belief in Christianity.

Ugarte traveled widely, exploring the area and establishing visiting chapels. In 1706, Ugarte, Padre Jaime Bravo, 12 Spanish soldiers, and 40 Yaqui Indians made an expedition to the west to the South Sea (Pacific Ocean). While most Indians they encountered were friendly, as they neared the ocean, they were threatened by some 200 Guaycuras and had to be on constant vigilance for fear of being ambushed. Their search for consistent supplies of fresh water on that trip proved fruitless.

In 1719, a popular choice among the Indians, Juan de Ugarte succeeded Salvatierra as president of the California missions. Earlier, he had saved the entire California mission project by convincing Salvatierra not to give up during some very trying times.

Ugarte had long dreamed of establishing a land route from Sonora, Mexico, past the Colorado River and down to the Baja missions. But he needed a ship and none was available for exploration. Small matter to an overachiever like Ugarte. He'd build one!

Those of you who know the explored regions of Baja California at that time (just the southern part) realize that the chances of finding wood big enough and sturdy enough to build a ship would be nonexistent, but Ugarte found some. Indians told him that about 50 leagues (150 miles) northwest of Loreto were some large trees of a hard wood called by the natives *guëribo* or *güiribo*. (A later mission named Guadalupe was established on this site.)

So the resourceful Ugarte hired a shipbuilder to come over from the mainland, grabbed some soldiers and some Indians, and headed off into the mountains. They not only had to hew the timbers, they had to cut a trail through the mountains so that oxen could haul the wood down to the estuary at Mulegé where the *balandra* (bark), was built.

California's first ship builder

Ugarte called the ship *Triunfo de le Cruz* or *Triumph of the Cross* and launched it on Sept. 14, 1719. That first ship built in the Californias was immediately considered the most beautiful, the sturdiest, and the best constructed sailing vessel ever known in California. It was used many times to cross the Sea of Cortez to the mainland for provisions.

In 1720 Ugarte sailed his new ship from Loreto to La Paz, taking Padre Bravo with him to establish a mission there. Also aboard were three Guaycura Indians from La Paz whom Ugarte had rescued from a pearling ship that had put in at Loreto. They had been imprisoned by the pearlers, and Ugarte wanted to return them.

A large group of Guaycura Indians greeted Ugarte and Bravo in a hostile manner, aiming their bows and arrows at them. The Guaycura had reason, having constantly been at war with the pearl fishermen, but when they saw only two padres and their mission comrades, they immediately put down their arms and sat down to talk.

Among the gifts the Padres brought were woolen clothing which was undoubtedly woven at the Mission San Javier. Ugarte stayed at La Paz three months, making friends with many Indians, even those of Cerralvo and Espíritu Santo Islands, who were normally hostile. The mission secure, he returned to Loreto in January 1721.

Later in 1721 Ugarte took his *Triunfo de la Cruz* on an exploratory trip, heading northward up Baja's Sea of Cortez coast to Bahía de los Angeles and Angel de la Guarda Island. From there he crossed over to the mainland and continued north to the upper reaches of the gulf. The ship there encountered the tidal bore that enters the Colorado River but avoided being capsized by the wave of rushing water. Ugarte then continued south along the Baja California coastline, making note of places for shelter, water, and anchorage along the way.

Brother Pedro served five years

While Juan de Ugarte's exploits affected so many so profoundly, his brother Pedro served in a less conspicuous manner. Padre Pedro de Ugarte ended up in charge of Mission San Juan Bautista Ligüí, where he spent five years. There he showed his Indians how to make mud for adobe, cut timbers for rafters, and thatch the ceiling of the chapel and other quarters.

With assistance from his early converts, Pedro roamed the Sierra de la Giganta, searching out Indians so that he might bring them to his mission for indoctrination. He, like so many of the Padres, was energized by zeal and stoicism and made the extremely difficult a daily endeavor. Because of poor health, he left California for Sinaloa in 1710.

Pedro's legendary brother, the indefatigable Juan de Ugarte, had boundless energy and rarely rested, even though he constantly suffered from an asthmatic cough and fever in the last years of his life. When urged to slow down and retire, he said, "Rest and quiet make me suffer more, and from this you may judge that travel and labor is for me a relief."

The legendary president of the missions was absent much of the time from San Javier, but continued to be in charge there. He died in his bed in 1730 at the age of 69, and was buried on the land he loved so much. The current Mission San Francisco Javier de Viggé, which was not completed until after Ugarte's death, boasts a stone belfry, Moorish spires, and is considered the best-preserved mission in Baja California.

How one's contemporaries view one's contribution can be very telling indeed. If we are to believe a couple of Jesuit historians, Juan de Ugarte should be in line for Catholic sainthood ahead of Serra.

In 1757 Jesuit Padre Miguel Venegas wrote, "Not without reason did Salvatierra name Ugarte 'The Apostle.' Untiring, he led in everything, did everything, undertook and succeeded in everything, because he was so thoroughly prepared. At one moment he would be at the presidio counseling the soldiers, confessing them; soon he would be away looking for new areas for planting or pasturing, now baptizing children, now teaching adults, now administering the last sacraments to the dying, or laboring in the Mission workshop; or in the fields, irrigating, seeding, cultivating; or at the port, taking charge of the loading or unloading of ships, or seeing that they were properly kept in repair...."

The accolades continue

Continuing in the same vein, 30 years later, in 1787, the Jesuit historian Francisco Xavier Clavijero wrote about Ugarte, "...nature blessed him with an illustrious birth, a phenomenal physique, a sublime mentality, keen ingenuity, a facility for arts and sciences, rare industry, prudence in economic matters, great magnanimity, a man superior to all obstacles and dangers, with meekness of spirit, while zealous in saving souls for God."

The Mexican historian Pablo L. Martínez, in his 1960 landmark work *A History of Lower California*, continued to highlight Ugarte's eminence: "Ugarte raised the first regular crops. And this was not achieved with great facility; the water spring in that place was far from being something that was worth the trouble. But this enterprising man ... exerted himself to remove stones and more stones to clear the space needed for planting. He planted the first vines and produced the wine that was consumed in the missions. When he had wool from his sheep he proceeded to teach the Indians how to make yarn and weave. He cultivated wheat and other cereals, although not in sufficient quantity to supply the needs of the conquistadores and natives. The date, the fig, the olive, lemons and oranges were brought there by this indefatigable man.

"Lower California would do well to proclaim as a type of public spirited citizen the venerable Padre Juan de Ugarte, because men like him are indispensable even today to subdue the terrain of the peninsula and cultivate useful crops in what for the greater part is a desert of stone," continued Martínez.

It appears there really was a Paul Bunyan in Baja — he was larger than life and his name was Padre Juan de Ugarte.

THE LEGENDARY JUNÍPERO SERRA

Serra Heads for the Border

When the U.S. Capitol building lined a hallway with statues of each state's historic personalities, California had no trouble deciding that Padre Junípero Serra, the legendary Franciscan priest who founded several missions, should represent the Golden State.

While Serra is known for establishing the first nine of California's 21 missions, what is not as well known are his endeavors to the south, in Baja California.

Serra founded the Baja California Mission of San Fernando Velicatá in 1769. Later that same year he was credited with establishing Alta California's first mission in San Diego. Why did Serra literally "head for the border" from San Fernando, leaving the remaining nine Baja missions to be established later by the Dominican order of Catholic padres?

The answers are mostly political and are based on Spain's decision at the time to claim as much land as possible.

Previously, Spain had allowed its clergy in the form of the Jesuit order to establish settlements in California, where they established 15 missions in Baja, from San José Del Cabo in the south to Santa María in the north.

The Jesuits enjoyed power and authority and were the settlement leaders, even dispensing discipline and pay to the soldiers who accompanied them for protection. Reports reached the king, citing resentment and jealousies over the Jesuits' alleged accumulated wealth and power, so Spain's King Charles III abruptly expelled the Jesuit order from the New World. On Feb. 3, 1768, 16 Jesuits had to depart for Europe after seven decades of difficult efforts in establishing a physical as well as spiritual foothold in Baja California.

Up to that time the Franciscan order had been responsible for missionary activity in northwest mainland Mexico. They were hastily ordered to Baja California. Fifteen Franciscan priests, under the leadership of Padre Junípero Serra, landed at Loreto on Apr. 1, 1768 and were duly assigned to take over the existing missions.

Serra's timing was providential

Their timing was providential, because Spain had finally decided to establish settlements in Alta California. It appears that Russian fur trappers and explorers were working their way down the northwest Pacific Coast, establishing outposts as far south as San Francisco. Spain had to challenge their intrusion. An ambitious Spanish politician named José de Gálvez was sent to New Spain (Mexico) in 1765 by King Charles III specifically to do so.

The Jesuits didn't benefit from that decision, as Gálvez played a large part in their expulsion. The king gave him broad powers and also royal orders to organize an expedition that would head north and colonize Alta California, thwarting the Russian advance.

Serra and the incoming Franciscan padres found that, largely because of Gálvez' influence, they did not enjoy the theocratic authority that the Jesuits had enjoyed for 70 years. They were pushed aside, and their efforts were secondary to the political and military leaders.

Gálvez arrived at Loreto from the Mexican mainland on July 12, 1768 and planned the expedition north; it would be in four units, two by land and two by sea. For the sea journey, he had secured the two largest and strongest brigantines in western Mexico, the *San Carlos* and the *San Antonio*.

Now instead of the religious leaders calling the shots, it was Gálvez who directed what the Franciscans would do. He informed Serra that the padres would accompany the troops and initially establish missions at San Diego, Monterey, and one place in between, with others to follow.

He wanted to use Baja's then northernmost Jesuit mission, Santa María, as a convenient place to supply the future missions to the north.

The two land expeditions would be under the command of Captain Gaspar de Por-

Padre Junípero Serra

tolá, with the advance party led by Captain Fernando Javier de Rivera y Moncada, then commander of the Loreto Presidio.

Gálvez himself ordered Rivera y Moncada to stop at each mission on his way north and round up as many supplies as each mission could afford in the way of cattle, horses, and other provisions. The missions were duly stripped as the advance party made its way north to Santa María, many never fully recovering from such a ransacking.

As Santa María had insufficient pastureland for the livestock, Rivera y Moncada was forced to relocate. He and the advance party, which included Padre Juan Crespí, went north to a place the Indians called Velicatá. He sent a report back as to his new location in December 1768. The main party with Portolá and Padre Serra would later leave Loreto to make the journey.

The advance party, with Rivera y Moncada, Padre Crespí, 25 soldiers, a guide, three mule drivers, and a large number of Indians armed with bows and arrows left the Velicatá valley on Mar. 25 and arrived in San Diego on May 14, 50 days later. Meanwhile, the main party of Portolá and Serra took different routes north and reunited in Santa María on May 5, 1769.

A life's preparation

Serra, then 56 years old, had spent his life preparing for the tasks that lie ahead. Born in 1713 on the Spanish island of Mallorca, he was a small and sickly child who entered the seminary at age 16. He overcame his illnesses, but as an adult, at only 5'2" or 3", this man, small in stature, became an historical giant.

He was ordained in 1739, received his doctorate in 1742, and taught philosophy. He then decided to leave his career to enter the missionary field and help convert the heathens of the new world. He wore a foot-long crucifix on a chain around his neck. So sincere was his dedication that he never took off the chain, even while sleeping. He never complained about hardships and seemed to need very little sleep.

When he first arrived in Mexico, he made the 270-mile walk from Veracruz to Mexico City during the rainy season. His foot began to swell from mosquito bites, and plagued him the rest of his life. Before he was called to Baja California, Serra had become president of five mainland Mexican missions.

When he and Portolá arrived at Santa María, they took the mission priest, Padre Miguel de la Campa y Cos, and headed for Velicatá, a place also called "the well of the sweet water," arriving on May 13, 1769. The country around Velicatá made such a favorable impression that Portolá and Serra resolved to establish a presidio and a mission in order to facilitate later communication with Alta California.

In his diary, Padre Serra described the event by writing: "On the 14th of May, the day of the feast of the Holy Pentecost, in the morning a little hut of palisades was cleaned out and adorned. It was one that the advance party had left standing.

"In that hut the altar was arranged, the soldiers were drawn up under arms in their leather jackets and shields, and with all the neatness of holy poverty I celebrated the Mass of that great day with the consolation that this was the first of those Masses which must be continued with permanency at this new Mission of San Fernando, which dated from this day.

"The Mass was solemnized by the oft-repeated discharge of the muskets of the soldiers, the fumes of the powder in this instance substituting for incense, which we did not have because we could not afford it..."

Mission San Fernando became important, as it was situated nearly midway between the missions on the gulf and those on the Pacific. It became home to approximately 1,500 Indians, who helped raise sheep and cattle in the small valley. The mission flourished until an epidemic in 1777–1780 wiped out the population. By 1818 the mission was abandoned entirely.

It is a remote location now, but accessible (only three miles) from the Transpeninsular Highway #1, some 40 miles south of El Rosario. The mission ruins are today grotesque pillars of weathered adobe, now protected by cyclone fencing. Palm trees and the ancient irrigation system grace the valley floor.

His leg began to worsen

Serra and Portolá then continued north to fulfill Gálvez's order and establish the presidios and missions of Alta California. Serra's leg began to worsen.

According to an account by Franciscan Padre Francisco Paloú, "...the joy and distraction of the founding [of the mission] made him forget about his pain, but it was not so afterwards, for on the first journey of three leagues [9 miles] the leg and foot became so inflamed that it appeared there was a cancerous condition there. They were so painful that they gave him no rest. Nevertheless without complaining to anyone, he traveled another day, also of three leagues duration, until he came to a place called San Juan de Dios. There he felt so burdened with his infirmity that he could neither stand nor sit but had to lie down in bed, suffering such pain that it was impossible for him to sleep."

When Portolá suggested they construct a litter to have him carried by Indians, Serra decided to take the matter into his own hands. He approached the muleteer who healed the sores of animals, begging him to treat his leg as he would an animal. The muleteer balked, but finally mixed the tallow and herbs and applied it to the wounds.

The poultice worked well enough for Serra to continue the journey, but it did not alleviate the pain he endured for the rest of his life.

Portolá went on to become a legend in the annals of California history, but no less than Serra, who went on to establish nine missions, finally passing away at the age of 71 at his favorite one, San Carlos de Carmelo (Carmel), where he is buried. The Catholic Church is currently conducting the canonization process to recognize the sainthood of a real legend who didn't let obstacles get in his way.

SEÑORA BORJA DONATES FOR MISSIONS

The Legend of the Duchess

The very remoteness and inaccessibility of the rugged area around the Mission of San Francisco de Borja Adac was precisely the reason the mission was founded there. And the person who made that decision not only never set foot in Baja, but lived in luxury as a duchess in Spain.

Señora María de Borja, the Duchess of Gandía, might seem an unlikely benefactor to the peninsula's progress, but it was her donation that established three of the most remote and inaccessible missions of the New World.

She learned of the Baja California missionary efforts from a soldier who returned to Spain and became a servant in her household. The servant, who had served in Loreto, told her of the ruggedness and sterility of the Baja peninsula. He related stories of the ordeals of the Jesuit padres among the Indians. He added that they were unable to help some Indians because they lived in far-off mountain valleys.

The duchess was so moved by these stories that she changed her will to donate a sizable amount to the Jesuit Pious Fund, stipulating that the funds be used to establish three missions in the most remote reaches of this isolated peninsula called California.

From a notable and notorious family

She came from a family that was both notable and notorious. As well as hereditary dukes from the Duchy of Gandía in Valencia, Spain, there were also two popes and one canonized saint (San Francisco de Borja, a third general in the Company of Jesus).

As Borja is the Spanish spelling of Italy's Borgia, it was the Italian ancestors who gained the most fame. Two of the seven children of Pope Alexander VI, Cesare and Lucretia Borgia, allegedly became a brother-and-sister poisoning act, dispatching notable guests

Mission San Francisco de Borja Adac

with pharmaceutical adroitness. Keeping power in the family, Cesare and another uncle were made cardinals in the church.

Señora María de Borja died in 1747. From the original 60,000 Spanish pesos donated, with interest the amount had grown to over 70,000 by the time the three missions were established. Among the stipulations Señora Borja specified when donating the funds was that one of the new missions be named for her canonized ancestor, San Francisco de Borja.

From her funds, Mission San Borja was founded in 1759, the short-lived Mission Calamagué (Calamaguet) in 1766, and Mission Santa María in 1767.

The San Borja mission opened in a remote mountainous area, rimmed by cliffs of red rock, where there were 300 Indians. Soon so many arrived the padres could barely support them, even with help from other missions.

At San Borja, figs, olives, grapes, and dates were planted and cattle and sheep were raised. The Indians who were attracted to the mission soon became dependent on the padres for their sustenance. Before that, in their native habitat, the Indians lived on insects, lizards, rodents, and other larger animals. The orchards, grain, and livestock soon became an important source of food for all.

An assortment of diseases almost wiped out the native population, which peaked at 3,000 Indians, and by 1818 when the last resident priest departed, there were fewer than 100 Indians remaining.

Among the handsomest missions

The stone edifice that still stands today, although never entirely completed, is considered one of the handsomest of the peninsula missions. This is remarkable, as it had not had formal maintenance. In recent years a group called the Baja California Missions Foundation has been instrumental in preserving both San Borja and Santa Gertrudis Mission to the south, the two finest examples of mission architecture in the northern state of Baja California.

The chapel is intact and still occasionally used by visiting priests. A circular stairwell of carved rock rises to a second level loft above the chapel. Remarkable stonework is visible everywhere. There's a water cistern with four-inch-thick walls carved from one rock. Detailed carvings grace window and door arches. Fallen statuary lies undisturbed amid a courtyard cactus garden.

This remote mission can be reached by either of two 22-mile dirt roads, one off the road to Bahía de Los Angeles, and the other from Highway 1 at a small village called Rosarito, some 350 miles south of Ensenada.

San Borja is desolate, serving as a proud monument and a reminder of those difficult times long ago. Visitors can enjoy the solitude and quiet dignity of a place that was once the cultural and social center of this mountainous area. Duchess Borja requested an inaccessible place and she would not be disappointed, even today — almost 250 years later.

Is There a Mission Santa Isabel?
The Legend of the Lost Mission

The Jesuit order of the Catholic Church had for over 70 years defied incredible physical odds in establishing a foothold in the forbidding land of Baja California. Wielding great power, they had, with the help of soldiers and Indians, established 15 missions and three "*visita*" missions in the southern half of the peninsula.

But their power appeared to be their downfall, as it inspired jealousies and wild stories, real or imagined, about how their main agenda was not to save souls but to acquire wealth.

José de Gálvez, who was sent by Spain's King Charles III to colonize Alta California, especially distrusted the Jesuits. He was convinced that they had "mismanaged potentially rich missions, or used them and the people as bases and tools to secretly hoard great wealth of pearls, gold, and silver."

Stories emerged in Europe, including one in which a chest of pearls, coral, and precious stones was shipped by the Jesuit padres in California to a Venetian merchant in Cádiz, Spain. This story made it to the court in Madrid. Rumors began that the Jesuits had vast treasures in that land called California.

The King obviously believed enough of the stories and decided to show the Jesuits just who was really boss. In 1768 he expelled the Jesuit order from the provinces of New Spain. And this expulsion set the stage for the Legend of the Lost Mission.

Allegedly, the Jesuits hastily established one last mission, called Santa Isabel, and this is where they hid all their accumulated wealth. One legend has it that shortly after the last Jesuit mission of Santa María was established, the padres received a confidential message from their superiors in Rome about the impending expulsion. They were instructed to submit peacefully to the Spanish Crown but leave no trace of their wealth.

Did they hide this wealth?

The legend says the Jesuits collected the treasure of gold, silver, pearls, and valuable objects from all the missions and transported it by burro to a deep gorge in the mountains some distance beyond Santa María, where they founded Mission Santa Isabel. When the order for their expulsion arrived, they closed off the entrance to the gorge by means of a landslide before submitting to the authorities at Loreto. Other legends say the gorge was at the site of a working gold mine that the Jesuits had kept secret.

One old Indian (himself a great-grandson of a mission Indian who served under Jesuit Padre Wenceslao Linck) who helped out at Mission San Borja, farther to the south of Santa María, told a story about Indians seeing golden objects in a nearby cave. He went on to describe how his ancestors had seen mule trains arriving from all the far-flung missions, their saddlebags laden with candelabras of gold and silver inset with precious stones, as well as other sacred vessels valued by the padres.

He then indicated that the booty was carefully hidden in a cave and a Mass was held. Shortly thereafter, a rockslide sealed the entrance, and because all the cliffs look so similar, no one has ever been able to find it.

A 1955 expedition from New York arrived at a white limestone cliff, where their metal detectors allegedly went crazy. They found an ancient compass, hundreds of years old. Directly above was a small cave with painted rock art of deer and mountain lions. They found no gold and decided to pursue it further on a later trip. On their return trip, they found the cave had been dynamited, leading them to speculate that they had been followed and perhaps their pursuers had found the lost gold.

Mystery writer Erle Stanley Gardner spent vast sums of money and launched several expeditions in his search for the Mission Santa Isabel. Some critics felt he searched too far to the north.

The efforts of Gastón Flourie

Perhaps the most dogged and persistent searcher for the lost Mission Santa Isabel was Gastón Eugenio René Flourie Sablaroles, who came to Baja California in 1924 at the age of 23. Flourie became a chemical engineer for the El Boleo Company at Santa Rosalía and during the 1930s enjoyed going out on desert forays searching for gold.

He became enamored with the story of the Lost Mission and spent much of his life looking for it. On an exploration in 1950 he discovered an old artesian well once used by the Jesuits, but no lost mission.

He moved to Ensenada and founded his own Mission Santa Isabel in 1951, the name he gave his new hotel at Blvd. Lázaro Cárdenas and Ave. Castillo. Naturally, he designed it in Mission style, and at one time the stately bell tower was a town landmark. His children still run the hotel.

But the hotel business didn't slake Flourie's craving for the treasure of the Lost Mission of Santa Isabel. In 1952, he undertook another trip, accompanied by guide Felipe Ortega from San Felipe, Mr. Charles B. Berry, Serge D'Blanc, and a writer and photographer for *National Geographic* magazine. They found hidden waterholes (*tinajas*), Indian petroglyphs, and some arrowheads, but no treasure.

In 1954, Flourie was part of another major expedition to find the lost mission when he accompanied Dana and Ginger Lamb of Corona del Mar, California on a search. The Lambs, who had considerable Baja experience, were the authors of *Enchanted Vagabonds*. The group combed a wide area south of Matomí Canyon in the southern San Pedro Mártir mountain range, using planes, trucks, and mules and guided by Don Santiago Espinosa. According to the *Los Angeles Times*, all they found on that journey were more Indian petroglyphs.

They keep searching for the Lost Mission

In 1967, a search party found the lost president of the Mountain Climbers Association of California, who claimed that in his wanderings, he had found a canyon with seven palms, above which on the cliff was a rock slide that responded to his metal detector. His rescuers made numerous trips in search of the elusive seven palms and the lost treasure of Santa Isabel. They never found it.

A scientific expedition conducted by Boston University in 1975 also involved Flourie. They were looking for any Jesuit books and papers, as well as the treasure, but found *nada*.

Unfortunately, the legend of the Lost Mission of Santa Isabel has not been confirmed by history. There were pearls in the La Paz area and some gold and silver to be found in Baja California, but most authorities note that the Jesuits were too busy trying to save the souls of the indigenous people to be bothered about collecting such a treasure. They had to devote far too much time just producing food for themselves and the Indians to really care about any treasure.

However, the legend persists even to this day, and many expeditions have spent considerable time searching for it. Some say it should be in a steep canyon off the eastern escarpment of the San Pedro Mártir. Others put it farther south, around Laguna Chapala, and others farther north in one of the barren ranges near the gulf.

Rumors that it was near Laguna Chapala were rampant for a few years; Arturo Grosso, the owner of Rancho Chapala, reported that many Americans used to camp near his ranch in search of the Mission Santa Isabel. He told them, "Forget it. If it exists, I would have found it already. I'm always climbing mountains, hunting wild sheep, deer, and antelope, and I have never seen a sign of a wall or a mission."

But the lure of finding lost treasure continued.

Hey, if you want to say you've actually been to Baja's famed Santa Isabel, just go and check in at Ensenada's Hotel Santa Isabel. It apparently is the only treasure realized by the hotel's founder Flourie. By virtue of his tenacity and zeal in searching for the original, his hotel, now a half-century old itself, has become a legend.

PADRE BEGETS MANY CHILDREN
The Good "Father" of Todos Santos

Dominican Padre Gabriel González was sent to minister the mission in the idyllic little valley of Todos Santos. There, among other nefarious activities, he single-handedly helped reverse the decline of the Indian population, which was caused by diseases brought by the Spaniard invaders. It is said that he fathered "a multitude of children."

At Todos Santos in 1838 Padre González was accused of retaining the personal profits of the mission even after the secularization of the missions and the absence of neophytes. He fought hard in opposing the colonization of the mission lands, even provoking a rebellion.

Padre González later became a popular leader in the Mexican-American War. Two of his sons served as officers, and the influential padre and his forces were a formidable foe against the American invaders.

González served as Dominican mission president (1840–1854) and had to leave to administer the northern missions, but returned to his beloved Todos Santos in 1854, where he lived out his life and was able to look after his children.

Padre Gabriel Gonzalez Pareyra of Spain died in Todos Santos on June 2, 1868 and was buried in the local cemetary. A vintage photo of him in the Todos Santos Cultural Center reveals a handsome young man with deep penetrating eyes.

Of his progeny, one of the most revered was his granddaughter Dionisia Villarino. Called "*La Coronela*" (The Colonel), she was an illustrious *todosanteña* who served with distinction in the Mexican Revolution. La Coronela's daughter, Amalia Salgado Villarino, then went on to become on the most prominent and influential citizens of Todos Santos.

According to historian Pablo L. Martínez in *A History of Lower California*, "...This priest (González) had carried his activities beyond the church and had been converted into a farmer, merchant, cattleman, politician, and father of a family."

Father González was not the only padre to succumb to the temptation of the flesh. Celibacy proved to be too much of an encumbrance to a young priest assigned to El Rosario in 1947. The handsome 32-year-old, who played the piano, cut hair, cooked, and taught school, found the charms of a *señorita* named Ramona too tempting, and they eloped.

It would be 18 years before another resident priest arrived to ring the church bells in El Rosario. And the townspeople were relieved when he proved to be an older fellow.

WEST OF SAN IGNACIO?
The Lost Mission of Santa Clara

Jutting vertically from the valley floor of the Vizcaíno peninsula are the arid and desolate Santa Clara Mountains, home to small herds of *berrendos*, a type of pronghorn antelope. I've never seen one in the area, but when there I wondered about another old Baja legend, since the barrenness of the location screamed doubts of its veracity.

According to one legend, it appears the steep buttes of the Santa Claras are home to the site of the "lost mission" of Santa Clara, where a fabulous treasure is supposed to be buried. Early Jesuit records mention a proposed mission of Santa María Magdalena, to be founded near the Pacific coast west of San Ignacio. Apparently the Indians who once occupied this area were instead moved to San Ignacio. Some old maps allegedly show a mission in the general direction of the Santa Claras, and it was called San Juan Bautista. If the Jesuits did establish a mission in the area, it has been hidden for about 250 years.

Other legends say that the "Lost Mission of Santa Clara" is just a southern version of the Jesuit's more infamous northern "Lost Mission of Santa Isabel." *¿Quien sabe?* (Who knows?)

Nakedness Bothered Junípero Serra

Serra Notes "No Shame"

Immense difficulties were encountered by Padre Junípero Serra on his historic trek with Portolá through Baja to Alta California. He nursed his badly infected leg, he endured chest pains, and his party fought off Indian attacks. However, in his diary Serra noted that he felt that one of the most horrendous encounters was the nakedness of the savage people.

In the virgin territory north of the last Jesuit mission, Serra established Mission San Fernando. There, for the first time, Serra personally encountered truly primitive Indians untouched by civilization.

In his diary, he noted, "He [the Lord] now permitted me to be among the pagans in their own country. I came out at once, and found myself in front of twelve of them, all men and grown up, except two who were boys, one about ten years old and the other about fifteen. I saw something I could not believe when I had read of it. Or had been told about it. It was this: they were entirely naked, as Adam in the garden before sin."

Serra went on to say that even though the Indians obviously noticed that the padres were well clothed, he could not notice the least sign of shame in the Indians. He could not get over the fact that not only were they naked but "they had no shame over their nakedness." (One may speculate that shame is in the eyes of the beholder.) The local culture didn't value clothes, and the Indians didn't understand the fuss made by the padres over them.

By the time the Portolá/Serra party reached as far north as San Quintín, Serra still had not seen any female Indians. In his diary, Serra confessed that he had not been anxious to see any because he feared that they too would be naked.

Later Serra did encounter some women and he wrote: "But when, in the midst of all this entertainment, two women appeared. Talking as rapidly and as efficiently as that sex is accustomed to do, and when I saw them so decently covered that we would feel happy if no greater display of indecency were ever seen among the Christian women among the missions, I no longer regretted their arrival."

Chapter 3: Writers/Adventurers Become Baja Lore

The Early Explorers

It started with a writer.

Garcí Ordóñez de Montalvo, in his early 16th century book *Las Sergas* (The Exploits of) *de Esplandián*, applied the name "California" to a fictional island at the end of the world.

Then another writer, Francisco Preciado, who traveled with Francisco de Ulloa in the Sea of Cortez and along the Pacific Coast, applied the name "California" to that mysterious "land" across the sea from New Spain.

Of course Hernán Cortés wrote about the new land, keeping the King of Spain abreast of his doings. Then in 1602, Sebastián Vizcaíno's records forever changed the nomenclature and existing cartography of the peninsula.

The Writings of the Padres

Some of the padres who established missions and settlements in Baja for Spain did a good job of documenting their affairs. The writings of other padres helped catapult them into legendary renown.

Johann Jakob Baegert, S.J.

The negativism in a book by German Padre Johann Jakob Baegert helped it become one of the most-mentioned Baja books of the missionary era. A Jesuit in Baja from 1751 to 1768, Baegert returned to Germany and released a powerful and detailed book in 1771. His *Observations in Lower California* records the Baja he experienced, the dry harsh land, and the indigenous people who occupied it.

Often repeated has been Baegert's negative opening, quoted earlier in this book.

Historian Pablo Martínez refers to Baegert's book as "The Black Book of Lower California" and lambastes him for such negative reporting and making "such odious comparison between the savage Indian and cultured European society, Germany in particular." He also chastises him for using the experience at one mission to represent the entire peninsula.

Baegert became one of the first Baja legends in the process.

Jesuit historians

The Padres Miguel Venegas, S.J., Andrés Marcos Burriel, S.J., and Padre Francisco Javier Clavigero, S.J. never set foot in California, but painstakingly and scientifically researched and collected letters and memoirs of the early Jesuit pioneers. Padre Miguel del Barco, S.J. served 30 years among the California missions, and as an inspector, traveled to all the missions. Later, in Italy, he recalled his experiences and those of some colleagues, which resulted in *Natural and Civil History of California*. The works of those four authors have become the basis for historians and researchers to follow.

Jesuit Father Peter Masten Dunne, S.J. was an American professor of history at University of California whose epic book *Black Robes in Lower California* was published by the University of San Francisco Press in 1952. It is the first attempt to chronicle the entire 70 years of efforts put in by the Jesuits in Baja California.

Other padres

The Dominicans, who occupied Baja California for over 70 years, left almost nothing in writing. An exception is Dominican Padre Luis Sales whose *Three Letters of a Preacher* somewhat chronicles the era. The Franciscan Father Zephyrin Engelhardt, OFM wrote *The Missions and Missionaries of California* in 1929. The first volume of that work has factual information of all Baja California missionary history and is often used for research.

Legendary Adventurers/Historians

William Walker

There's one American that Baja schoolchildren read about in their third grade primer — and he's not known for his benevolence. One of the largest legends of an American in Baja is attributed to a five-foot, four-inch renegade, William Walker, who tried to take over the place and establish his own country.

In 1853, Walker, who was born in Tennessee, sailed from San Francisco with 45 men to take over what was then called Lower California. His original plan was to go to the mainland, form the Republic of Sonora, and protect the locals from the Indians. He changed his plans, deciding to take Lower California first before advancing on Sonora.

He and his army, mostly young Southerners like himself, stopped in La Paz, where they captured the governor, hoisted their own flag, and proclaimed their land the Republic of Lower California. Mexican forces gathered, and after one skirmish, Walker fled to Ensenada, where he proclaimed himself president of his new republic. Even though his army was bolstered with 230 more volunteers, he was attacked by Mexican forces. There were a few fatalities, but Walker and his men were able to repel the attempts.

After a U.S. government ship came to Ensenada to persuade him to leave, he marched his army south and relocated his "capital" in the old mission town of San Vicente.

In March 1854, he lost most of his troops to suffering, thirst, and abandonment as he tried to cross the desert to realize his original dream, that of capturing the mainland state of Sonora. He returned to San Vicente to learn that most of the small force he left there had deserted, and those who did not were killed by the Mexican army. In May, he and the remainder of his troops fought their way back to the United States.

He was captured crossing the border, tried by an American jury, fined, and imprisoned for violating neutrality laws.

William Walker had not reformed, however, as he formed a new army and took over the Central American country of Nicaragua. The little man became a big shot in Central America, but he lived by the gun and died by the gun. In September 1860, at the age of only 36, Walker was executed by a Honduran firing squad, ending a chapter of piracy by an American citizen.

William Walker

J. Ross Browne

In December 1866, J. Ross Browne, a 45-year-old Dublin-born traveler, author, cartoonist, and diplomat, was commissioned by wealthy New York capitalists to lead a scientific expedition into Baja California. They had obtained land grants and mining privileges from the Mexican government, but aside from the mines at El Triunfo and San Antonio, knew little about Baja California.

Browne and his party took a ship from San Francisco to Cape San Lucas and traveled over much of the southern part of the peninsula. His resulting records, including some outstanding pen and ink caricatures, were published in three 1868 installments in *Harper's New Monthly Magazine*. It was later released as a booklet, *Explorations in Lower California*. It has become an excellent record of activity in Baja California during the middle years of the 18th century.

Arthur Walbridge North

Arthur Walbridge North could be considered the first tourist who traveled the length of the Baja California peninsula. He grew up in northern California, where his father had earlier turned down an attempt to be recruited by the filibustering William Walker. North went on to become a member of the California State Legislature and the California Bar. However, loving the outdoors and intrigued by Walker's earlier ill-fated attempt to take over Baja, North went to see for himself.

In early 1905, he spent time in the area around Mexicali. He returned to explore the entire peninsula between December 1905 and September 1906. His hunting and camping explorations over all of Baja by burro and horseback resulted in eight *Sunset* magazine articles, the book *The Mother of California* in 1908, and more reminiscences of the trip itself in the book *Camp and Camino in Lower California*, published in 1910.

In his preface to *The Mother of California*, North reveals that Walker had earlier allowed his soldiers to destroy documents in La Paz. He said he hoped his "romantic narrative of 'poor lower California' might make some reparation to the elder California for the misdoings of Walker."

The Chroniclers

Hubert Howe Bancroft put together the massive six-volume *History of California* between 1884 and 1890. He also authored the two-volume *History of Texas and the Northern Mexican States*, which was released in 1890.

George Butler Griffin, one of the vast army of writers and researchers Bancroft employed during 1886, referred to his boss as the "managing editor" of the work.

Bascom A. Stephens, writing in the 1888–89 publication of the Los Angeles Historical Society, notes favorably about how Bancroft had interviewed early Pacific Coast pioneers: "H.H. Bancroft, more than any other man, has gone systematically to work, and, by throwing an army of canvassers into the field, has saved a great many of these personal sketches." Between the two impressive Bancroft works, there are nine whole chapters on Baja California.

Pablo L. Martínez is best known for *A History of Lower California* (1956); the English version was translated by Ethel Duffy Turner in 1960. Martínez spent more than 20 years researching the book, and the result is an important history of Baja California, especially the political history.

Dr. W. Michael Mathes

Dr. W. Michael Mathes, a professor emeritus of history at the University of San Francisco, is a native Californian who lived in Baja California. Between 1948 and the present, he traveled the dirt road and highway from Tijuana to Cabo San Lucas some 80 times. He was director of the Archivo Histórico de Baja California Sur and commissioner of the Commission of the Californias for the State of Baja California Sur.

Mathes' *Las Misiones de Baja California* (1977) contains historic capsules of each Baja mission, with outstanding color photos. It is a thorough work by a respected master of Baja California mission history. He is also the translator and author of such works as *Pearl Hunters in the Gulf of California, 1668, A Brief History in the Land of Calafia, 1533–1795*, and works by Miguel Venegas.

Harry W. Crosby

Harry W. Crosby could easily be covered under the heading "Adventurer" rather than "Chronicler," but his completed books of Baja California are of such importance to Baja California historians, Jesuit historians, and the study of early peoples, that he is one of the few Baja California writers still active today whose life's work has become legendary.

During the 1960s, Crosby, a La Jolla–based writer, photographer, and historian, rode muleback over 600 miles to the most remote regions of Baja California to photograph a book celebrating the U.S. state of California's Bicentennial.

In his 1974 book, *The King's Highway in Baja California*, he tells how traveling by muleback, he uncovered many lost sections of the original roads used by the padres.

Crosby's 1994 huge, well-researched and -organized book *Antigua California* has become the standard of Spanish California's first 70 years. The history of the Jesuit occupation is a comprehensive account and includes many charts, maps, and easy-to-read lists.

Crosby's *The Cave Paintings of Baja California*, complete with many of the author's

Harry Crosby

wondrous photographs, documents the searches that resulted in over 200 previously unknown rock art sites. The first edition was printed in 1975 and his current edition with all new reproductions of the photos was released in 1997.

Having written such definitive works, the 75-year-old is not slowing down, as he is currently working on another book about early California.

Famed Beyond Baja

Hundreds of contemporary writers have written about Baja California over the past half century or so. Some of the books have been excellent, but only a handful of those writers or their books have become legendary in that short time. Those I have singled out are, in my opinion, significant for various reasons and have or will become "Legends of Baja Lore."

It is difficult not to highlight such classic books as Gerhard & Gulick's *Lower California Guidebook* and the wonderful guides and maps put out by the Automobile Club of Southern California since 1927.

Likewise, others might consider the outstanding contributions of Cliff Cross, Joe Cummings, Fred Hoctor, Fred and Gloria Jones, Fernando Jordán, Joseph Wood Krutch, Max Miller, Shirley Miller, Choral Pepper, and Walt Wheelock, to name a few.

Walter Nordhoff

The Journey of the Flame, by a certain Antonio de Fierro Blanco, is an historical novel about the red-headed Juan Colorado (The Flame) who was born in the south of Lower

California in 1798, traveled throughout California and died near Rosario, Mexico in 1902.

The book was presented to the publisher Houghton Mifflin in 1933 through an intermediary, with an understanding that if any attempts were made to learn the true identity of the author, the book would be withdrawn and the manuscript destroyed. The publishers consented, but some people tried to learn the identity of the author of this fine historical tale, among them Harrison Leussler, a Houghton Mifflin western sales representative who did some detective work on his own.

The book's title page reads: "Written down by Antonio de Fierro Blanco" and below that "Englished by Walter de Steiguer." Leussler located de Steiguer in Glendale, California, but learned nothing.

Finally, while taking a book order in Santa Barbara, he overheard someone's guess as to the author's identity. He dismissed the suggestion as preposterous. It wasn't until many months later, when the mysterious Fierro Blanco published his second novel under the same shroud of secrecy, that he heard the name again. The name was Nordhoff. It couldn't be! Charles Nordhoff, the author of the best-selling *Mutiny on the Bounty*, was too young a man to have penned *The Flame*.

Could he have been a relative? Leussler searched *Who's Who*, looking at past issues and comparing biographies. In Charles Nordhoff's biography, he found a line had been omitted from later editions. The line read: "brought up on his father's ranch in Lower California."

Aha! He knew that the person who penned *The Journey of the Flame* must have lived in Baja California to be that familiar with it, and it looked like someone was trying to cover his tracks. Charles Nordhoff's father, Walter Nordhoff, must indeed be Fierro Blanco. Braced with a name this time, de Steiguer relented and agreed.

Walter Nordhoff was found living in Santa Barbara and admitted to being the author. Apparently Nordhoff did not want to capitalize on the name of his father, who was a well-known editor of *Harper*'s, nor of his son, who had written a series of very successful books, including *Mutiny on the Bounty*. Baja bibliophiles recognize *The Journey of the Flame* for what it is, an outstanding book in a very realistic setting.

John Steinbeck

The famous writer John Steinbeck, who studied marine biology at Stanford University but failed to graduate, had an opportunity to study his interest firsthand when he was invited by his friend, marine biologist Edward F. Ricketts, to collect marine invertebrates from the beaches of the Sea of Cortez. In 1940 they sailed in a sardine boat on the expedition. The resulting 1941 book *The Sea of Cortez: A Leisurely Journal of Travel and Research* was coauthored with Ricketts. The reminiscences, musings, and philosophy throughout are pure Steinbeck at his best. He followed it up with *Log from the Sea of Cortez*, a day-to-day adventure of the trip. The *Log* itself is exciting, thoughtful, and revealing. For example, Steinbeck wrote, "We said, 'Let's go wide open. Let's see what we see, record what we find, and not fool ourselves with conventional scientific strictures. We could not observe a completely objective Sea of Cortez anyway, for in that lonely and uninhabited Gulf our boat and ourselves would change it the moment we entered.'"

The journey also provided the setting and background for Steinbeck's best-selling book *The Pearl*, which was about La Paz.

Erle Stanley Gardner

Beginning in the 1930s, Erle Stanley Gardner wrote the popular Perry Mason mystery series. By the 1950s and '60s, Gardner was extremely successful with radio and television shows. But he came to love Baja California and wrote the *Land of Shorter Shadows* about Baja in 1948.

His appetite for the remoteness of Baja not whetted, he organized numerous trips into the interior of the peninsula, traveling by airplane, helicopter, experimental motorcycles, and even by horses and mules. During the height of his popularity, he still penned six other Baja-related books, *Hunting the Desert Whale* (1960), *Hovering over Baja* (1961), *The Hidden Heart of Baja* (1964), *Off the Beaten Track in Baja* (1967), *Mexico's Magic Square* (1968) and *Host with the Big Hat* (1969).

He was one of the the first outsiders to view numerous cave paintings; one, the Gardner Cave, was even named after him. That cave is also referred to as Cueva Pintada. On some trips, Gardner brought in archeologists to validate the significance of his finds.

Due to his own popularity, Gardner's romps through Baja California brought enormous attention to a previously neglected region. After he died in 1970, his ashes were scattered over his beloved Baja countryside. When one thinks of a legendary Baja writer, Gardner's name usually is at the top of the list.

Jack Smith

Jack Smith was one of the most popular columnists in the long and successful history of the *Los Angeles Times*. Writing classes at UCLA studied his colorful, yet succinct style. During the late 1960s and early 1970s Smith wrote regularly in his column about the trials and tribulations of building a house in Baja.

Baja California, that part of Mexico to the south, suddenly became a real place to the thousands of readers who followed Jack Smith's daily column. The Baja stories later became the 1974 book *God and Mr. Gómez*, referring to Mr. Romulo Gómez of La Bocana at Puerto Santo Tomás, who built the Smith home. The book is warm, funny, and philosophical. It became a legend, as it served as an inspiration to many who followed and built their own dream homes in Baja in the decades to follow.

They Introduced Baja to Many

Ray Cannon

Ray Cannon was probably more responsible for increasing tourism in Baja than any other person during his prolific years as a writer for *Western Outdoor News*. Originally invited to Baja in 1947 to write about its fishing potential by former Baja California governor and Mexican President Abelardo L. Rodríguez, Cannon fell in love with the land and spent most of his remaining years there.

His regular fishing column inspired new generations of aficionados and led to his landmark book, *The Sea of Cortez*, published by Sunset Books in 1966. The former Hollywood actor/director/writer had also written *How to Fish the Pacific Coast* and did not even discover Baja until he was 55 years old. He was big in Hollywood, but it was during his twilight years that he truly became a legend.

Gerhard and Gulick

Peter Gerhard was an historian and former resident of La Paz who teamed with an engineer from Glendale, California named Howard Gulick (1910–1983) to create the definitive Baja California guidebook. Widely known simply as "Gerhard and Gulick" or "the bible," their *Lower California Guidebook* became the most important piece of baggage to those traveling the peninsula for two decades. Published in 1956, new editions were released in 1958, 1964, and 1967.

Tom Miller

Tom Miller used modern technology in the form of space maps to highlight the Baja peninsula, one of the world's few holdout areas from such technology. In fact, Miller used the NASA satellite photos for the first time *ever* in a commercial product, paving the way for NASA to explore new uses for their products.

Miller, who held numerous saltwater fishing records, had a trailer home near Ensenada before building a palm-thatched hideaway south of La Paz. For three decades he covered all of Baja, which resulted in over 1,000 articles for outdoor publications and his weekly column in *Western Outdoor News*.

His original book, prominent because of the maps overlaid on NASA space photos, was *The Baja Book*, cowritten with Elmar Baxter and released in 1973. *The Baja Book II* came out in 1982 and *The Baja Book III* in 1989. The Baja Books updated the old Gerhard and Gulick book as the indispensable guides over the next two decades.

My personal favorite Tom Miller book is his 1982 *Anglers Guide to Baja California*, a practical, easy-to-follow guide highlighting where the fish are, what kind of fish, and how to catch 'em. I referred to it often on my trips into the remote regions of the peninsula.

Known as "Mr. Baja" to hundreds of thousands through his books, articles, radio, and television work, Miller also wrote *Eating Your Way through Baja* in 1986. As its name implies, it covers everything from upscale restaurants to fish taco stands.

Mike McMahan

There's a wall map of Baja California you see everywhere. It's huge, has a yellow peninsula set against a powder blue ocean, and has the effect of being printed on old parchment paper. It's even detailed with the curling edges and antiqued compass and lettering. They've reproduced it, and now copies hang on the walls of a successful California fish taco restaurant chain. Except it says "Rubio's" where it should say "Mike McMahan."

Mike McMahan and his brother owned the large office furniture company, McMahan

Brothers Desk Company in Los Angeles, but he preferred to be in Baja. He served on the Board of Directors of the Mexican Hunting Association, and along with fellow Baja buffs Ray Haller, Ralph Hancock and Frank Alvarado, made an adventure all the way down Baja that resulted in the 1950 book *Baja California*. In addition to the map, McMahan also wrote *There It Is: Baja*. McMahan had a daughter, Ginger Potter, whose husband Chuck Potter continues to this day to distribute Baja books through the company *Baja Source*.

Gene S. Kira/Neil Kelly

When it comes to fishing books, *The Baja Catch* by Gene Kira and Neil Kelly (1988) is a must. This large-format book is well organized and includes maps of all the hot spots, outstanding in their detail. From my campsite I could look out over a reef, read about what kind of fish are there, wade out, and catch them. A very impressive fishing guide.

Beyond the one book that itself could qualify for legend status, Kira's novel *King of the Moon*, about a small Baja fishing village coping with difficult times, is a classic that should endure. It is a work of art.

Following his novel, Kira sequestered himself to research, emerging with the epic book about Ray Cannon in 1999. Titled *The Unforgettable Sea of Cortez*, it is subtitled *Baja California's Golden Age 1947–1977, The Life and Writings of Ray Cannon*. The year 2000 winner of the Outdoor Writers Association of California (OWAC) Book of the Year honors, it is massive in size and scope. In addition to all you want to know about Cannon, it does a great job of providing a written history of that era.

Graham Mackintosh

In an age when all of the world's continents have been explored, some would-be adventurers might decry that it's all been done. Not Graham Mackintosh, the modern version of "The Flame." Born in London of an Irish mother and Scottish father, Mackintosh, with his flaming bright red hair, was a teacher looking for adventure. So he decided to walk around the rugged and inhospitable coastline of Baja California.

As Mackintosh even said, "I had never done anything adventurous in my life. I wasn't fit. I knew nothing about the desert. I couldn't speak Spanish. I had no money. With my red hair and fair skin, I was probably the last person in the world to go traipsing around a sun-baked wilderness."

But he did it anyway, and two years, 3,000 miles, seven pairs of boots, two scorpion bites, and numerous rattlesnake dinners later, he survived to write *Into a Desert Place* (1988). The book won several awards in England and a legion of fans among Baja buffs.

Mackintosh has since walked down the old mission trail from Tecate to Loreto, and that introspective book *Journey with a Baja Burro* is filled with tales of his journey, interspersed with Baja history, and was published in November 2000. His adventures have made him one of the most popular modern Baja legends.

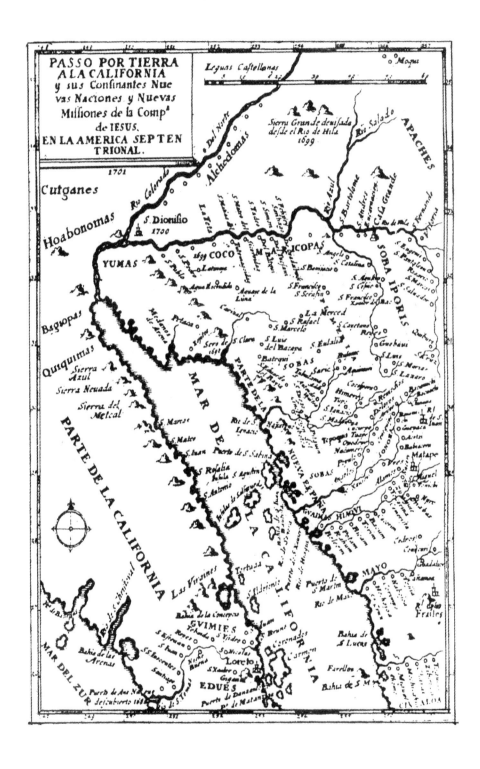

Chapter 4:
Bajacalifornios *Who Made a Difference*

Mexican Leaders Shaped the Frontier

There is no question that many Anglos had a hand in shaping the tourist destiny of the Mexican states of Baja California and Baja California Sur. That is one of the primary thrusts of this book.

But we would be more than remiss if we did not include some of the Mexican leaders and politicians who have advanced the progress of all the people of Baja California. While most Americans who read this are tourists and have an interest in the gringo involvement in the development of the peninsula, numerous *bajacalifornios* are rightly proud of some of their forefathers who put the interests of the people first.

I have selected a handful of movers and shakers, looking for those Mexican and Baja California leaders who made a difference in Baja's struggle from missionary days, through independence and into statehood. These are some of the true Baja legends.

Lt. Col. José María de Echeandía

Following its independence from Spain in 1822, Mexico initially established an empire with Agustín de Iturbide as emperor, but Mexicans didn't like that form of government. Less than a year later, the new constitution created democratic representation with a federal republic. Iturbide abdicated in March 1823.

The new centrist government then had the problem of administrating its far-flung regions, including all of California. The first Jefe Político sent to Baja California was Lt. Col. José María de Echeandía. He set about dividing the peninsula into municipalities and established rules for distribution of former missionary land and property.

Echeandía was impartial in his administration and decreed that the Indians and *mestizos* had equal rights with the European settlers. In essence, he removed the barriers of racial concepts and determined that legislation should include all the citizens from all of the classes.

By so enforcing, he turned around the enslaving missionary concept that had been in effect for about 150 years. While strict administration of the Indians might have been necessary early on, it had regressed to an oppressive society.

Echeandía was also responsible for separating Upper California from Lower California, a decision which would have a major impact later on as to which would become the U.S. territory and which would remain as part of Mexico.

It seems that while Echeandía began to administer the Californias from San Diego, other politicians had ensconced a Captain José María Mata in Loreto, where he was intervening in local politics. Echeandía complained to Mexico City about the intrusion, so the matter was solved in 1828 by separating Lower California from Upper California. And then there were two.

Luís del Castillo Negrete and Francisco del Castillo Negrete

The Jefe Político of Lower California from 1837–1842 was *licencio* Luís del Castillo Negrete, of Spanish origin. He had spent the previous two years as a judge in the District of Upper California and took over at a difficult time, when political jealousies and spitefulness were just part of the problems.

Captain José María Mata was being vengeful; there were several Indian uprisings against missionaries, and the missionaries themselves still wanted to reap the profits from land that had been divided up.

Castillo Negrete also created and had to enforce an act in 1841 that spelled out the distribution of the missions. For example, parts of the act read: "1. — That where there is no community of neophytes, there is no mission. 2. — That the rooted possessions of the terminated community of neophytes, through the rights of reversion, belong to the Republic." The act goes on to spell out that the products and benefits of the lands no longer automatically belonged to the clergy.

The president of the Dominicans, Padre Gabriel González, who was stationed in Todos Santos, fought the act and Castillo Negrete with fury. This is the same padre who fathered much of the town. Unfortunately for the new civil leaders, the missions possessed the only lands capable of being cultivated. Retaining them by custom, without their original purpose, would make it impossible to increase the population and improve the economy.

The verbal fights escalated into armed conflict with a rebellion provoked by Padre González. Castillo Negrete and his brother, Captain Francisco Javier del Castillo Negrete, principal commandant in Lower California, were captured by a group of insurgents and destined to be shipped to the mainland when they were rescued by the people of La Paz.

The 25 armed rebels of Padre González realized public opinion was against them and left. The brothers hastily formed an army and took off after the rebels. With 40 men, brother Francisco Javier fought a battle in Todos Santos. The rebel leaders including Padre González were tried and sent to Mazatlán. A new government allowed the rebels to return under amnesty, but they had forever lost the lands.

A paradox, but a testament to history's timing, is that Padre González later created fear in the hearts of the American aggressors in the Mexican-American War. After the *bajacalifornio* leader Captain Pineda was captured in 1848, Padre González took over the Mexican political and military command, wielded great influence over his people, and even had two of his sons as officers.

Lieutenant Colonel Francisco Javier del Castillo Negrete become Chief of the Army from 1840–1842 and later fought the opportunist William Walker in 1853–1854.

Captain Manuel Pineda

The war hero recognized for keeping the Baja California peninsula in the hands of the Mexicans during the Mexican-American War was Captain Manuel Pineda, who repelled the Americans at Mulegé.

When war broke out, Baja's military leader, Colonel Francisco Palacio Miranda, declared himself neutral. This act got him fired for treason. The new principal commander appointed by Mexico City was Captain Manuel Pineda, who since 1833 had been part of the Loreto Presidio. Brave and loyal at all costs to his country, he had extensive knowledge of the terrain and the people of Baja.

Captain Manuel Pineda

Under threat of an attack in Mulegé, Pineda, with just a few officers and arms, crossed the gulf from Guaymas to Mulegé. An American ship flying English colors entered the Mulegé River under false pretenses, hoisted the American flag once in port, and seized the ship that had earlier brought Pineda and his men.

The Americans tried to get Pineda to lay down his arms and plead neutrality. His scathing response on Oct. 1, 1847 is classic. Part of it reads, "If the ex-jefe politico Francisco Palacio Miranda, who through cowardice declared himself to be neutral to your government, now on today's date they will be joined to the forces that are in La Paz. This Headquarters of the Command will do just the opposite; it will preserve every communication with the Mexican Government, even if the whole fleet of the United States wants to stop it. This Commandery with the valiant soldiery that it has at its orders will defend and protect itself until the last drop of blood is shed."

Pineda got many loyal Mulegé residents to help the soldiers of the town's small garrison to repel the invaders. Pineda organized his people, dispatching some to cover the town entrances, and commissioned others to lead the guerrillas. They engaged in battle near El Somberito at the mouth of the river; the Americans, despite their larger force, retreated.

The Battle of Mulegé on October 2 helped galvanize the Mexican army and civilians in Baja. They learned the enemy was not invincible. As a direct result, in San José del Cabo the people, without the support of a garrison, tore down the foreign flag and kicked out the American civilians.

The Mexicans then went on the attack, and Pineda led a growing army of conscripts south. Pineda led a surprise attack on La Paz on Nov. 16, 1847. After 10 days of difficult

53

battle, several times almost taking the town, Pineda realized a scarcity of ammunition. American sloops arrived in La Paz and San José del Cabo to help quash the attack, and Pineda was forced to lay low.

After the ships left, Pineda and his troops continued to harass the Americans, successfully cutting off their supply lines. Pineda was finally captured by the enemy on Mar. 23, 1848. Captain Pineda was a heroic *bajacalifornio* who helped turn the tide of public opinion during a difficult war.

His gilded bust, replete with goatee, now dominates the small square at the entrance to Mulegé. The accompanying plaque mentions that the hero had repelled the Americans but somehow omits his name. I asked a local if the bust was indeed of *Capitán* Pineda. He said, "Sí Señor," but just shrugged when neither of us could find the name "Pineda" anywhere. I guess they all know who their local hero is. Why bother naming the obvious?

General Agustín Olachea Avilés

By the early 20th century, several native-born *bajacalifornios* had achieved positions of prominence. One of these, General Agustín Olachea Avilés, was born in the small Baja California village of Todos Santos. As a member of the "reform" movement on the mainland, he earned the rank of Brigadier General. He became governor of the Southern District of Baja California (BCS) from 1929 to 1931.

His countrymen loved him, and he was noted for his aid to workers and farmers. He imposed labor laws limiting workday hours and emphasizing fair pay.

On Feb. 7, 1931, the division between Baja's two districts was legally formed, and Olachea became governor of the Northern District (BC) later that year. You would think that serving as governor of what are now two Mexican states would be enough, but Olachea was just getting started. He became President of the national PRI party and also Secretary of National Defense.

Then in 1946, Olachea returned to Baja California Sur to become governor again, a job he performed until 1956, the longest governorship in the independent era. His accomplishments during that long tenure are many and legendary. He saw to it that many areas were cultivated, with new irrigation projects, mills, and agricultural plants.

He tried to resurrect old mining projects, including pumping water out of inundated mines at San Antonio. When the El Boleo mine suspended operations at Santa Rosalía, he intervened to help the town survive. He encouraged tourism, worked at improving health and welfare, and helped develop the infrastructure.

According to Pablo L. Martínez in *A History of Lower California*, "...we can or others can be in disagreement with some aspects of the policies of General Olachea; but no one can fail to recognize the valuable achievements of his administration."

Colonel Esteban Cantú

The winding mountain grade that drops from the tree-covered forests atop the Sierra Juárez down onto the desert floor between Tecate and Mexicali is called the Cantú Grade. It may seem an inglorious attribute to a real pioneer in the development of Baja California.

Major Esteban Cantú is known for single-handedly keeping all of Baja California out of the Mexican Revolution. He was Chief of the Line in Mexicali in 1911. In August 1912, he had his own cavalry regiment. During the Mexican Revolution, federalist Major Cantú and his men fought off revolutionists in several skirmishes along the Colorado River and its confluence with the Gila.

He also turned back a handful of revolutionary soldiers at Las Islitas on Nov. 14, 1913, effectively ending military action against the Federals in the northern area. Not many civilians supported the Federal government during this war and at war's

Colonel Esteban Cantú, with his father, José Antonio Cantú
(Photo: San Diego Historial Society Collection)

end Francisco "Pancho" Villa was recognized as leader. In recognition of his military prowess, Esteban Cantú, now a Colonel, kept the military command.

By Jan. 1, 1915, Cantú had successfully become the political leader as well, a fact confirmed by General Villa in a Jan. 20, 1915 telegram which appointed Cantú as the political and military chief, a position he would hold for 5 and a half years. His first act was to transfer the capital of the district to Mexicali.

He took over a land devastated by war and left bankrupt by his predecessors. To begin the reconstruction, he levied trade duties and imposed personal taxes. He began the long process of economic development of the Mexicali valley. He opened schools even in the smallest villages; encouraged industry, agriculture, and commerce; and started important infrastructure, including drainage, roads, streets, electricity, and bridges.

He put down a U.S. conspiracy, apparently led by Harry Chandler of the *Los Angeles Times*, who had considerable holdings in the Mexicali Valley. It was another futile attempt to wrest the peninsula away from Mexico. (There have been numerous attempts since the days of William Walker in 1853). Two of the conspirators were found guilty, but Chandler was acquitted.

By May 1, 1917, Cantú was named governor and military commander of the Northern District.

Cantú even entertained the idea of having Baja California break away from Mexico, except instead of the U.S. getting the peninsula, it would be its own country with — you guessed it — Cantú as president. He even had American allies, most notably the *San Diego Sun*, but Mexican President Carranza got wind of this brainstorm, set up an investigation, and squelched the idea.

Baldomero Almada was appointed governor, but Cantú refused him entrance. They had to get former hero Cantú out by force, sending troops under the command of General Abelardo L. Rodríguez. In July 1920, Colonel Cantú abandoned his post and retreated.

President Abelardo L. Rodríguez
(Photo: San Diego Historial Society Collection)

While he was considered despotic and difficult, his legacy is voluminous: He kept peace and order and began unprecedented constructive activity. He developed the Valley of Mexicali for the benefit of Mexicans and the city of Mexicali. He built the road that bears his name, a link between coastal Tijuana and Mexicali, as well as a road to San Felipe. He extended education. He helped void contracts the Mexican government had made with colonization companies that thwarted economic and social development. In spite of the black clouds and monumental ego, Colonel Esteban Cantú brought unprecedented prosperity to Baja California.

President Abelardo L. Rodríguez

You've probably seen it many times — that palatial ranch house sitting back from the highway amid olive groves, six miles north of Ensenada at El Sauzal. It's now a school, Tecnológico de Baja California, but in 1932 and 1934, it was owned by Mexican President Abelardo L. Rodríguez.

He was General Abelardo L. Rodríguez when he was called upon to help oust Governor Cantú in 1920. In October 1923, Rodríguez became governor of the Baja California northern territory. His tenure was aided by prohibition in the United States, which brought great economic growth.

While vice began operating under Governor Cantú, the creation of so many saloons and restaurants near the border made it even more evident in the early 1920s. Tijuana became a boomtown and was established as a municipality in 1925. Rodríguez was able to capitalize on the good economic times and get much done.

He constructed numerous public buildings, including hospitals and schools; he encouraged teachers and paid them well; he promoted colonization with Mexican nationals; he encouraged cattle raising and farming; he promoted industry and founded an agricultural bank, the first in Mexico; he started work on the dam near Tijuana that bears his name. Along with infrastructure, he paved streets in Mexicali and Tijuana. He built libraries and theaters and the paved road from Tijuana to Ensenada.

At the end of Rodríguez' term in 1929, not only was there a worldwide economic crisis, but the U.S. had repealed prohibition, and progress in Baja California slowed.

Rodríguez became president of Mexico (1932 to 1934), and one of the things he did for Baja California was to declare the peninsula a duty-free port, an action that helped spur economic development.

Across the road from the Rodríguez estate north of Ensenada is the large Pesquera del Pacífico fish cannery, which Rodríguez established and owned. It is reputed that workers at the odoriferous fish cannery received annual dividends.

While according to writer Enrique Krauze in *Mexico: Biography of Power*, Rodríguez made a fortune during prohibition days, his legacy was a long list of improvements for the people of Baja California. He died in La Jolla, California in 1967.

Rodríguez's son Abelardo (Rod) Rodríguez was also instrumental in the development of Baja California Sur, establishing several resort hotels in the La Paz and Cabo San Lucas areas.

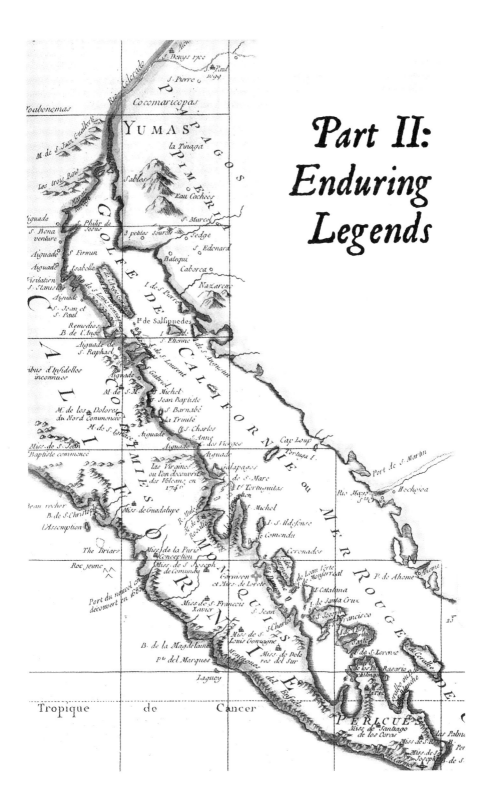

Part II: Enduring Legends

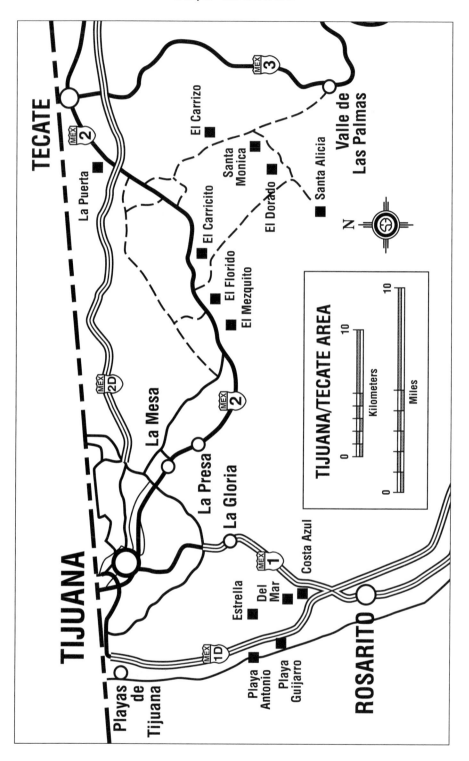

Chapter 5: Tijuana/Tecate Area

Tijuana — Who Was Aunt Jane?

A literal translation of Tía Juana means "Aunt Jane." If the second largest city on the coast of western North America wasn't named for an Aunt Jane, what was it named for? And how come it's spelled Tijuana, one word and without the "a"?

Several versions of the name's origin are extant. One legend has it that a Cochimí Indian chief who inhabited the Baja peninsula was named Tehuana and that's where the name came from. Along the same vein, another version states that Tehuanaque or Teguanaque means "inhospitable place" in Cochimí and that's where the name came from.

Years after the Spanish padres first crossed into the San Diego area in 1769, it is said that there was a very poor inn near what was then called the Corpus Christi River south of San Diego, where travelers could rest and dine. It was managed by a very dynamic lady who prepared wonderful dishes and served them with grace and charm. The travelers started calling her Aunt Jane (Tía Juana).

After the Mexican Independence in 1822, many land grants were made by Mexico's first *Californio* governor, Don José M. Echeandía. The property known as Rancho Tía Juana was granted to Don José Dario Arguello in 1825. In a later publication by attorney Alfonso Salazar Reynosa, "Chronology of Baja California" it states that on May 4, 1846, "It has been confirmed the rights of Santiago Arguello, a descendant of José Dario Arguello over the place known as Rancho Tía Juana."

Santiago Arguello, who obtained that first concession of the Rancho of Tía Juana, was himself born in what is now the U.S. city of Santa Barbara in 1792, became a U.S. citizen in 1848 following the war, died in Tijuana in 1862, and is buried in the U.S. city of San Diego.

Another reference to the Tía Juana ranch is in the Pablo Martínez book *History of Baja California* where he states, "The first border was created in Tía Juana, on August 6, 1878."

It is on record that the Rancho Tía Juana was baptized as a settlement in 1889, the date which marks the city's founding year.

General Don Abelardo L. Rodríguez, who was governor of Baja California's Northern Territory from 1923–1929, mentions "Tía Juana" several times in correspondence. During that time, written accounts somehow dropped the "a" from Tía Juana. There was no more "Aunt Jane," except for the Tía Juana River which most often is still spelled as two words. In 1925 the municipality was created there under the township name of "Zaragoza."

Somehow in the next few years the name "Zaragoza" lost favor to the more historic name of "Tijuana." Thus the official name was changed to the Municipality of Tijuana on Nov. 15, 1929 by the then Mexican President Emilio Portes Gil.

In 1921 the population of Tijuana was listed as 1,028. By 1969 it had reached 350,000 and by 1999, over a million and a half, or two thirds of the state's population of approximately 2.3 million.

In 1998 eight million tourists visited Baja California, generating an estimated $1.25 billion for the local economy. Tijuana is now the world's largest international border crossing and accounts for over 84 percent of all Baja California visitors. That's a whole lot of travelers visiting the rancho of Aunt Jane.

AGUA CALIENTE RACETRACK

The Legendary Glitter of Caliente

It seemed the racing gods didn't want Tijuana to have a racetrack. The first track, the Tijuana Jockey Club, was destroyed twice in its first year before Adolph Spreckels, who owned the Hotel del Coronado in San Diego, stepped in to save it.

Originally financed by San Francisco boxing promoter James W. Coffroth, the Tijuana Jockey Club opened with a lot of publicity in January 1916, following Mexico's 1915 decision to legalize gambling. Joining Coffroth was Baron Long, the owner of San Diego Hotel U.S. Grant. The track location was near the U.S./Mexico border, and opening day's six races drew 10,000 Californians, who were legally denied betting on horse racing at home at the time.

The *San Diego Union* reported, "Surrounded by the mauve hills of old Mexico, as though nature intended the spot for the site, lies the magnificent new Tijuana race course, a few miles from the thriving little village."

Its border location was also its downfall, as it was built on the low ground of the Tijuana riverbed. The sparkling new facility was only one week old when the nature that "intended the spot" included heavy rains and the worst flooding in 25 years, which destroyed the track. To keep the momentum, they hastily rebuilt and reopened in April. But fortune smiled not upon them, and that same season fire ravaged the track. That's when Spreckels stepped in to help; they reopened the following year.

Prohibition in the U.S. had fun-seeking Americans flocking south to newly opened Baja resorts and casinos. In 1928 American entrepreneurs built a beautiful casino at Agua Caliente (hot water) on higher ground on the outskirts of Tijuana. The following year, they added the Hipódromo Agua Caliente (Caliente Race Track) on the location. The horsemen from the Tijuana Jockey Club had moved up the hill.

Hollywood celebrities flocked to Caliente

From the very beginning, Caliente attracted celebrities. Western cowboy Tom Mix was once an honorary field judge at the racetrack. Jack Dempsey, who became one of the principals of the Riviera Resort and Casino in Ensenada, was also an honorary starter at Caliente. Charlie Chaplin, John Barrymore, Babe Ruth, Wallace Beery, Buster Keaton, Al Jolson, Constance Collier, and Jean Harlow all visited Caliente during its heyday.

Guests were entertained in the lounge by the song and dance team of Rita Hayworth (Margarita Cansino) and her father, who were billed as "The Cansinos." The daughter of Spanish dancer Eduardo Cansino and his Irish wife Volga Haworth, young Rita was eventually "discovered" in Baja by a Fox Studios executive. By the early 1940s she was a Hollywood star, featured in movies with the likes of Tyrone Power and James Cagney.

The publicity surrounding the Caliente Race Track and its predecessor, the Tijuana Jockey Club, helped attract top horses from the very beginning. In 1917, the Spreckels Handicap, which offered a $4,000 purse to the winner, honored the man who helped resurrect the track. It grew in value and prestige until 1930, when its name was changed and it became the Agua Caliente Handicap, the first in North America to offer a $100,000 purse.

Horses were attracted from all over, including the eastern U.S. and abroad. Even the great Australian horse Phar Lap raced in the Caliente Handicap in 1932. Seabiscuit ran at Caliente in 1938, and Round Table did 20 years later.

Caliente's famous 5-10 was the forerunner to the pick-six wagers now found at most racetracks and from the start had big payoffs. Caliente was the first place I'd ever seen greyhound racing.

One Baja legend concerns Kentucky Derby day at Caliente in 1974. It was long a tradition at Caliente to keep the betting windows open as long as possible to accommodate every possible bet. Well, that day one over-zealous clerk was still selling tickets on the Derby long after the winner, Cannonade, had crossed the finish line. A handful of lucky touts who appeared to have had a crystal ball have been telling their winning story for years.

In more recent decades, Caliente was important to the California thoroughbred racing community, as lower training costs and lower purses made it economically feasible to test young horses in competition. It was a wonderful training ground for horses preparing to race elsewhere. Then the grooms decided to strike and while shut down, the track owners found Sports Book wagering to be extremely profitable, especially without the overhead of live thoroughbred racing.

By the early 1990s, active horse racing had closed down. The greyhound racing has continued, however, and many dogs break in at Caliente, where there are 13 races every night and matinee races on weekends.

In addition to the greyhounds, the venerable Caliente Race Track is open to the Caliente Foreign Book wagering, where closed circuit TV monitors offered a sports medley that should provide a fix for the most discriminating sports betting junkie. Caliente Sports Books can now be found in almost every town of any size in Baja California. There's one in San Felipe, one in Rosarito Beach, and one in the San Nicolás Hotel in Ensenada.

But the original, Agua Caliente itself, has turned from an international gathering place into a shadow of its former self. Even part of the grounds have been put to a more practical and beneficial use than the glitter of yesteryear. There's now a school at Caliente to help educate the children of Tijuana.

BEER HALLS AND NIGHT CLUBS

Border Boom Town

During the Roaring Twenties, Tijuana became the town for nonstop action. Even later, after prohibition in the United States was repealed, Americans crossed the border in droves to drink and gamble.

One such destination was the Mexicali Beer Hall. Until it was demolished to make way for Woolworth's department store in downtown Tijuana, the Mexicali Beer Hall boasted the "World's Longest Bar." The polished wood bar, which became affectionately known as the "Long Bar," ran the entire length of the block-long building. That held a lot of *cervezas*!

Then there were the floor shows. In post-WWII Tijuana, the town had a lot to attract young servicemen from booming southern California. Cheap beer and go-go joints where strippers would shed their clothing became part of Tijuana folklore. The town earned a wide reputation and spawned many wild stories. While most of the reputation was deserved, some of it was gross exaggeration or, in some cases, never did occur.

Strip joints in much of suburban America have often been much more risqué than what was offered on the small stages in Tijuana. It seems the tenor of the shows in T.J. has throughout the years fluctuated with changing laws and enforcement of same.

By the 1950s, however, the strip clubs nevertheless rendered Tijuana a sin-city image, and to many that image has lingered for over half a century. Back in the early 1950s there were the Sans Souci, the Club Unicorn, the Club Aloha, and the Bambi Club, among others. Those four, along with a few others, are still operating today.

But Tijuana has come a long way and is now a vibrant city of well over a million people; the influence of a handful of strip bars is negligible to the economy or attitude of the city. Unfortunately, or fortunately (depending on how one looks at it), they're all on the one main street traversed by most visiting Americans.

CAESAR'S HOTEL/RESTAURANT

A Salad Is Born

The Caesar Salad wasn't named for Julius Caesar, nor was it invented in some gastronomically inventive country known for rich and varied adaptations of traditional foods, like France or Italy. The Caesar Salad was first concocted in 1930 in Mexico, in Tijuana's Hotel Caesar.

The Hotel Caesar, S.A. had opened for business earlier that year at the corner of Avenida Revolución and 5th Street downtown. On the ground floor of the hotel was a bar and restaurant. That's where the innovative chef Señor Caesar Cardini applied his culinary imagination and created the tableside masterpiece that bears his name.

The original two-story 72-room hotel has been renovated and is still in existence. The restaurant in the rear was undergoing some restoration on my last visit, but people comfortably ensconced in thick leather booths in the sports bar and grill were still

Hotel Caesar, Tijuana

ordering the famous salad prepared as it first was almost 70 years ago.

Whipped up tableside by attentive chefs amid "oohs" and "ahs," the original Caesar Salad with garlic bread is the closest thing a diner can come to being pampered for only about $3.95. Even those who are not fans of Caesar Salad are usually impressed with and delighted by the tableside ceremony.

The cool, restful restaurant is a welcome relief to the frenzy on the sidewalks outside, where throngs of American tourists gawk awkwardly at foreign wares while hustling shopkeepers do their best to lure them inside.

Caesar's diners start out with the customary tortilla chips and salsa, fixtures in Mexican restaurants. Shortly the ingredients for the salad are wheeled up in a two-tiered cart. With gustatory flair, the waiter will unveil a large wooden bowl, and salad tongs, dispatching the eggs, lettuce leaves, sauces, and oils like a painter creating a masterpiece. After almost 10 minutes of careful blending and folding, rather than haphazard mixing, the work of art is presented on chilled plates.

The "Original Caesar's Salad" as presented by the Hotel Caesar is as follows:

Original Caesar Salad (For 4 persons):

3 Medium Heads Romaine Lettuce, Chilled, Dry, Crisp
Dash Worcestershire Sauce
Grated Parmesan Cheese, 5 or 6 Tablespoons
Croutons, about 1 Cup
Salt
Garlic Flavored Olive Oil, about 1/3 Cup
Wine Vinegar, 1 to 2 Tablespoons
Juice of 1 and a half Lemon
1-Minute Coddled Egg
Freshly Ground Pepper

To add to the confusion of those seeking the original salad, another place also hawks Caesar's Salads, and it's only a few doors from the original. At the corner of 4th and Revolution is Caesar's Palace, an upstairs restaurant that looks like a dance hall, which one enters by an elevator. Caesar's Palace also consists of a streetside corner patio where Caesar's Salads are enjoyed by those dining alfresco.

Dining behind glass and brass railings, patio patrons can watch the street scene under umbrellas that clearly state "Caesar's Palace," although one of them actually says "Little Caesar's," causing one to wonder if they serve pizza, too.

There are notices and old photos on the walls stating that the Caesar Salad was first served at Caesar's Palace in 1932. What they don't tell you is that they were two years behind their neighbors, who invented it in 1930!

Jai Alai Palace, Tijuana

They, too, offer the public their recipe, and there are only a couple of minor discrepancies between the recipes. Instead of "Olive Oil," Caesar's Palace merely says "Salad Oil" and instead of "Coddled Egg," theirs says "Raw Egg."

Both restaurants charge about the same, and they're both on the same block in Tijuana, so who really cares, anyhow? Maybe it's another legend rooted in fantasy and the first guy to mess around with lettuce and eggs was really that Roman emperor. Somehow I doubt it. I mean, after all, he's not only got a month named after him, but a pizza place as well. So let's accept the fact that Tijuana was the birthplace of the famous Caesar Salad. Croutons, anyone?

JAI ALAI PALACE
The Fastest Game in the World

One of the Tijuana landmarks is the Frontón Palacio (Jai Alai building), an ornate 1920s structure right in the heart of the tourist district on Avenida Revolución. Thousands walk past the building each day unaware of the exciting sport inside.

Jai Alai, considered the fastest game in the world, is played every Thursday, Friday, and Saturday at the Frontón Palacio. The original Basque sport that means "Merry Fiesta" comes from the ancient sport of handball. Seven centuries ago they started playing it with sticks, a forerunner to today's racquetball. For over 300 years, the Basques have been playing it with a *cesta*, a long, curving basket affixed to the player's hand. It catches the *pelota* (ball) and whips it back against the wall.

The game is fast, exciting, and mesmerizing, but the biggest attraction for most fans is that the action might just be profitable. With betting windows just off-court, the involvement of having a few dollars wagered on the player of one's choice can transform a mildly interested spectator into a enthusiastic and fanatical participant.

THE OLD WORLD CHIKI JAI
The Taste of Spain

There is a nondescript little Spanish restaurant across the street from the Jai Alai palace in Tijuana that seems to have been there forever. Well, not forever, just since 1947.

It's called the Chiki Jai; we used to go there during the 1980s occasionally for what some friends referred to as the best *bolillos* in the world, smothered with melting Roquefort cheese. Now, a *bolillo* is a Mexican roll to die for when it is piping hot and fresh, soft and doughy with a crisp exterior. But adding Roquefort cheese was an acquired taste sensation on an epicurean level, a unique blend of old world and new, Spain and Mexico. The taste of Spain is decidedly from north central Spain, the Basque region that also gave the world the game of Jai Alai.

To this day, the place has hardly changed, while in the 53 years it has been there a major city grew up around it.

Chiki Jai was established by a Señora Aviña in 1947 at Avenida Revolución #1388, at the corner of 7th Street downtown. It was owned in turn by Pedro Garante and then Juan Olasolo before its current owners, Paquita and Manuel Monje, bought it in 1998. The earlier owners all are deceased, but left their mark on the place, and the exotic menu still attracts those who get tired of typical Mexican food.

The appetizer menu (Tapas y Pinchos) would do a Spaniard proud. Along with the Roquefort, one can order Spanish Chorizo, Cantimpalo Chorizo, Tuna Croquette, Baby Eels, Sea Mussels in Ribeiro Sauce, Calamari Rings, Spanish Tortilla, and Galician Octopus. All appetizers are reasonably priced and each could be a meal in itself.

The meal menu features *bolillos*, cheese, soup or salad, and dessert. It features authentic Spanish paella and various fish, calamari, shrimp, and steak dishes.

Chiki Jai is a downtown Tijuana legend. Called Chiki Jai, Sol y Sombra (sun and shade), it is a continent and a mood away from the Mexican tourist area boulevard out front.

TOWN OF TECATE
Which Came First, the Town or the Beer?

Was Tecate beer named after the town in which it is brewed or was the town named for the beer? Or was the town named for a type of ceramic tile (Tecate Tile) made there?

Problem is, no one's sure exactly where the word "Tecate" came from. One reference says it's a Kiliwa Indian word that is said to signify "where the sun shines." Another says it came from the Spanish *tecats*, a type of gourd. Others say it's either an old Spanish or Indian word that means "the water in which a baker moistens her hands while making tortillas."

It was called the Cañada de Tecate (Canyon of Tecate) when 1,600 hectares were granted to the original owner, Juan Bandini, in 1830. By 1876 the area became the Colonia Agrícola Tecate, with a population of over 100. By 1917, under the leadership of Governor Esteban Cantú, the municipality of Tecate was created.

When the brewery came into existence, the name Tecate was fully entrenched, its meaning obscured.

The Brewery in the Hills
Cerveza Tecate — The Pride of Baja

The most ubiquitous symbol in Baja California is undoubtedly that of Tecate Beer, the *cerveza* that is a source of pride to *bajacalifornios*. The familiar red and gold symbol with a stylized eagle is seemingly everywhere; huge signs hang above every bar, restaurant, and market where the product is sold.

Card tables, umbrellas, and white plastic chairs are emblazoned with the logo and provide a sometimes-obtrusive backdrop for many functions, even weddings, graduations, and *quinceañeras* (a girl's 15th-birthday coming-out celebration). Unless you use tablecloths, when you rent party equipment, the Tecate logo is almost always visible.

But most party attendees could care less; in fact, many love it. They grew up with Baja California's most popular product and consider Tecate to be Mexico's best beer, if not the world's.

It started in 1944 when Alberto Aldrete took over an old brick building that had been producing vegetable oil since it was built in 1929. Aldrete was operating a small malt factory in Tecate and had been brewing beer as a sideline for over a year. He named his new brew after the town, and it became the first *maquiladora* in Baja California.

In 1954 the brewery was sold to Cervecería Cuauhtémoc, a major brewer in Monterrey, Mexico, that had been producing Bohemia and Carta Blanca beers. Today, the Cuahutémoc brewery also produces Superior, Sol, and Dos Equis along with the others, in several different locations.

Today only Tecate and Carta Blanca are produced in the Tecate Brewery. Carta Blanca is a lighter pilsner beer, and most Baja beer drinkers feel it doesn't have the full rich flavor of Tecate. The Tecate beer that is exported is of a slightly lesser alcohol content, but that doesn't make it any less popular north of the border. Tecate has the highest canned beverage sales of any import to the U.S.

Tecate's international acceptance goes beyond North America. It has garnered prizes in competitions in Madrid, Rome, and Paris. The mother brewery, Cuahutémoc, is the only Mexican company to earn the distinguished ISO 9002 international designation based on the consistent high quality at its seven production plants.

Tecate Beer is one of the major sponsors of the Tecate SCORE Baja 1,000 off-road race, the Rosarito-Ensenada 50-Mile Bike Ride, and many other promotions throughout Baja California. It's also sold at Padre games in San Diego's Qualcomm Stadium and has become a tradition at many other southern California sporting events.

Tours are offered

The brewery, only seven blocks from the international border crossing in Tecate, offers 30-minute guided tours in groups of 30–40 people. Most tours are on Saturdays, but special groups can make arrangements for tours during the week. One combination attraction is a 15-mile train ride from Campo, California, which crosses mountains and winds through numerous tunnels. Included in the train ride package is a brewery tour.

The brewery tours feature 24 large 900,000-liter tanks that produce 20 million liters of beer each month. The product takes 25 days from start to final packaging. Once in the canning facility, 4,000 cans per minute can be processed. The cans themselves are manufactured by a subsidiary company, Ensenada's Fábrica Famosa, and shipped the 70 miles to Tecate. Every effort is made to recycle (cardboard boxes, etc.) or reuse (bottles are sterilized and reprocessed) all materials generated by the company.

In 1994, to celebrate its 50th anniversary, Tecate Brewery opened a beer garden at the side of the brewery. On a recent visit, I stopped by. I quit drinking about 20 years ago, so was unable to indulge in their offered product. Numerous chairs and tables (guess what logo is on them?) are scattered in a pleasant garden setting where a bartender pours samples. Locals on their way home from work stop by, as do those who took the tour. In one corner of the garden is a shop where you can purchase caps, shirts, and anything else you might want with the Tecate logo.

I chuckled, reflecting how whenever you drive Baja's Transpeninsular highway and come across a stalled truck, an accident, or construction, the shiny bright red and glimmering gold Tecate can is so often used as a highway flare. Even the residual effects of the product have a value to the enterprising *bajacalifornio*.

RANCHO LA PUERTA SPA

First Fitness Spa a Baja Legend

Sitting snugly among the oak-dappled Baja hills about three miles from Tecate, the legendary Rancho La Puerta emerged as the first fitness spa in North America.

La Puerta means "door" or "gate" in Spanish, and beautiful ornate bronze gates provide privacy to the spa's 300 serene acres off the Tijuana-Tecate highway near the international border. A large parking lot and an employee checklist at the adjacent gatehouse give testimony that this gringo fitness resort provides employment to over 100 local residents.

While the fitness trainers are North Americans, all the other employees, from grounds-keepers to cooks to gift shop workers, are local Mexicans. Many of the workers, as well as the 160 spa guests each week, are transported to the remote site by shuttle bus. Rancho La Puerta fills up 52 weeks a year.

What a setting! The buildings are all but lost among the mature oaks and shrubs and boulders. Wandering on the roads and paths, one can quickly and willingly become lost in the enchanting grounds.

On the slopes of Tecate Peak, called Mount Kuchumaa by the indigenous tribes, the 75 guest *casitas* in several different villages are well interspersed with nature. The *casitas* are little Mexican Colonial homes, each with fireplace, private patio, and garden sheltered by foliage. Small pools and hot tubs are strategically placed. The guest rooms themselves are accented with local arts and crafts.

The scent of herbs and flowers

Wandering the well-maintained paths of La Puerta, a visitor is quickly impressed with the olfactory ambience. The overwhelming scent of sage, herbs, and flowers becomes even more welcome than the visually pleasant and beautiful harmony of the hillside setting.

Looking into gyms and common buildings, a visitor can spot small groups here and there with trainers, practicing yoga or deep breathing, stretching, or engaged in more vigorous aerobics.

The ornate dining room reminds one of a Spanish castle. Behind a large swimming pool is an oval track bordered with rose bushes and grapevines rather than turf, as well as ponds, marshes, statuary, and trails. The entire feeling of beauty and serenity at La Puerta leaves a lingering impression.

But to the guests who arrive at La Puerta each week, the idyllic grounds are secondary to a regimen that will rejuvenate them and help them in their personal fitness attempts.

Rancho La Puerta was established in 1940 by the Hungarian-born Professor Edmond Szekely and his 17-year-old Brooklyn-born bride Deborah. For $10 a month, they rented an old one-room stable building in the middle of a vineyard called Rancho La Puerta and began to preach the philosophy of healthful living.

They originally called the enterprise "The Essene Science of Life" and charged $17.50 a week for their followers to pitch their tents on the site and share in the West Coast's first organic vegetable garden and the bounty of goat cheese and milk. Added to this was whole grain bread from wheat the Szekelys grew and germinated, and wild-sage honey.

The guests helped milk goats

In the early years all the guests pitched in with chores, gathering firewood and tending the goats. By 1950 the initial rate had escalated to $25, but the 35 or so guests no longer had to milk the goats. Even though it would be decades before Szekely's fitness concept would achieve popularity in the United States, postwar affluence helped it prosper. By 1955 the Essene had retaken the name of the original rancho, La Puerta, and had added a pool, library, and dining room.

In the early years, many people looked at the concept as a "fat farm" where weight reduction was the sole objective and women were the only guests. Since more Americans have gotten health and fitness conscious, the Rancho La Puerta attracts both men and women. Overall health, good diet, and fitness are stressed, rather than a one-time weight reduction program.

By 1958, the Szekelys had been approached by many of their graduates, who were prominent directors, producers, and actors in Hollywood and wanted a little more privacy and intimacy than was possible in Tecate. They found a location in Escondido, California, and opened The Golden Door, a sister fitness resort that is regarded as one of the world's finest.

From the early days, La Puerta offered stimulating seminars and presentations. The noted author Aldous Huxley was one of many luminaries who attended. Huxley, author of *Brave New World*, gave a symposium in 1960 on the "Human Potential."

Guest list is a Who's Who

The guest list at both spas over the years could resemble a "Who's Who," but the management does not like to invade their privacy by mentioning it. That's the attraction. Often people at Rancho La Puerta will find Hollywood celebrities in their midst, but others would not be aware of it. It is known that when *Titanic* was being filmed a little over an hour away in Rosarito Beach, actress Kate Winslett spent a lot of time at Rancho La Puerta.

The weekly rates, from Saturday to Saturday, pretty much preclude all but more affluent people from partaking in the hedonistic week. The rates include a comprehensive hiking program on 3,000 acres of natural terrain, the skilled training staff, 70 different fitness classes, all gourmet meals plus snacks, cooking demonstrations, evening lectures and movies, four tennis courts, volleyball and basketball courts, a library, 10 gyms, three swimming pools, and separate men's and women's health centers with steam rooms, whirlpools, and saunas. Extras would include massages, facials, body wraps, manicures, and more.

The rancho menu is mostly home grown from the organic vegetable garden and is considered to be a modified lacto-ovo-vegetarian diet (fish twice weekly). The menus of Rancho La Puerta and its sister spa, The Golden Door (now sold), anticipated Jean Troisgros's concoction of la nouvelle cuisine and inspired Seppi Renggli to coin the term "spa cuisine."

The founding philosopher Edmond Szekely passed away, but the philosophy lives on. Deborah and the two Szekely children, Alex and Livia, continue to own the resort, and Alex is the general manager.

On an October 1999 visit, I noted that the 160 guests came from 27 different U.S. states, Canada, and the District of Columbia. Who would have thought that a fitness farm would put the bucolic border village of Tecate on the map? But it did, and to many Americans Rancho La Puerta *is* Tecate and Tecate *is* Rancho La Puerta.

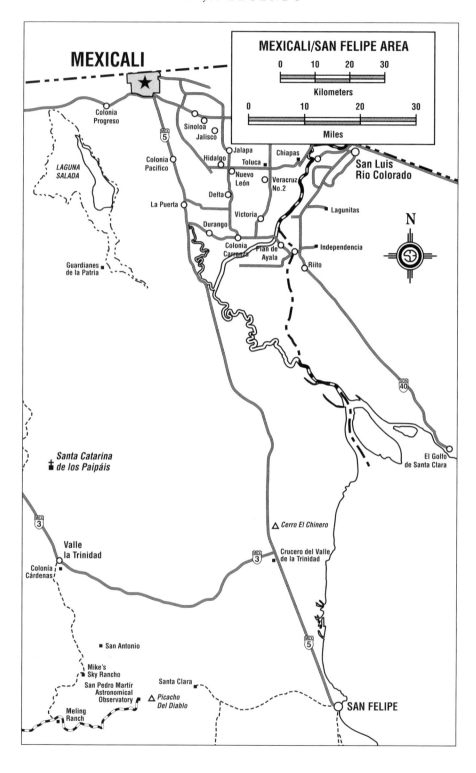

MEXICALI

MEXICALI/SAN FELIPE AREA

Kilometers

0   10   20   30

Miles

0   10   20   30

Colonia Progreso

LAGUNA SALADA

Sinoloa
Jalisco

Jalapa
Colonia Pacifico
Hidalgo
Toluca
Chiapas
Nuevo León
Veracruz No.2
Delta
Victoria
La Puerta
Durango
Colonia Carranza
Plan de Ayala
Independencia
Riito
Lagunitas
San Luis Rio Colorado

Guardianes de la Patria

N

El Golfo de Santa Clara

Santa Catarina de los Paipáis

Cerro El Chinero

Valle la Trinidad
Colonia Cárdenas
Crucero del Valle de la Trinidad

San Antonio
Mike's Sky Rancho
San Pedro Martír Astronomical Observatory
Santa Clara
Picacho Del Diablo
Meling Ranch
SAN FELIPE

Chapter 6: Mexicali/San Felipe Area

Taming the Desert

All a desert needs is water, but then it's no longer a desert, right? The area that became Mexicali was a hot (exceeding 115°F in the daytime) barren desert with dust storms and desolation. But not far away was the Colorado River, and about 100 years ago Americans began building canals to divert the water to their vast Imperial Valley.

Mexicali had been barren desert since before it was first explored by Europeans. It is known that Juan Bautista de Anza camped near the site back in December 1775. But the desert was forbidding, and for the next 100 years the area was claimed by no one. Then some former miners from the El Alamo area near Ensenada settled in 1898 and called the place La Laguna del Alamo.

North of the border, agriculture began to boom. One of the American agricultural pioneers, C.M. "Limpy" Holt, was the first to coin the "Imperial Valley" name, thinking the word "Imperial" projected a more positive image for a difficult and desolate area. But Holt did not stop there. He tinkered with the words California/Mexico, switched some syllables around and came up with names for the towns on opposite sides of the border (Calexico and Mexicali), and the names stuck. La Laguna del Alamo would forever be called Mexicali.

After the Imperial Canal was finished in 1902, Mexicali began to grow as water became available for irrigation. Many of the earliest settlers came to work on the irrigation projects for the Colorado River Land Company, an American company that owned practically all of the land in the valley. The company then leased land for cotton, and the workers stayed to cultivate their ensuing crops.

The founding date of Mexicali was Mar. 14, 1903, and Manuel Vizcarra was elected the town's first Civil Authority. In 1904, Mexican President Porfirio Díaz authorized Mexican canals to divert water to the Mexican side of the border.

A big flood occurred in 1906 as the waters of the Colorado River went over their banks. Levees and dikes were reinforced, and the planting of cotton, cantaloupes, alfalfa, and corn continued.

The Intercalifornia Railroad, a branch of the Southern Pacific, was built and went south from Calexico through Mexicali, continued east through Baja California farmland, and reentered the United States at Yuma. Not only was it a shorter route from the Imperial Valley to eastern markets, but it was able to tap the rich cotton and agricultural areas south of the border.

During the Revolution of 1910–1911, soldiers of fortune came into Mexicali. Under the banner of an American labor movement, the International Workers of the World, better known as the Wobblies, tried to make Mexicali a socialist enclave. They were driven off by the Mexican army, but not before lives were lost and numerous wounded. Once the Wobbly leader was shot, the rest finally gave up.

Stability was restored in 1915 by Colonel Esteban Cantú, who served as the Baja California Norte Governor in 1915–1920. He moved the Baja California territorial capital to Mexicali.

During the early years of Mexicali's history, the town was a paragon of diversity, with one report listing among the laborers approximately 5,000 Mexicans, 3,500 Chinese, 300 Japanese and 200 Hindus. But it doesn't mean they got along. For example, many Mexicans blamed the Chinese for taking "their" jobs. Where have we heard this refrain?

In 1936, the Colorado River Land Company was ordered by the Mexican government to sell most of its holdings to Mexican farmers and farm communities known as *ejidos*.

Today Mexicali, the capital of the state of Baja California, covers 5,254 acres and is home to about 850,000 people. In 1986 Mexicali achieved international recognition with a meeting between Mexican President Miguel de le Madrid and U.S. President Ronald Reagan.

The desert has been tamed.

Flores Magón and the Magonistas

Socialists Invade Baja

To many of the peons, it *was* the Revolution. The year was 1911, and Francisco I. Madero had been leading revolutionaries against Mexican President Porfirio Díaz for almost a year.

While the uprising in Baja California took the appearance of being part of the overall Mexican Revolution, it was actually a socialist revolution engineered by a longtime enemy of the Díaz dictatorship, Ricardo Flores Magón.

Ricardo Flores Magón, born in Oaxaca in 1873, had fought the Porfirian dictatorship in every way, going back to 1892 when he was a Mexico City law student. His street demonstrations and dissident writings landed him in prison, but did not deter him. President Díaz controlled the media, so Ricardo and his brother Enrique Flores Magón went to the United States in 1904 and continued their diatribe, running the operation from Los Angeles.

After Díaz placed a price on their heads, they even fled to Canada for a while. Later in Los Angeles, they were able to control their revolutionary activities under the auspices of the Mexican Liberal Party.

In 1908 all the leaders were arrested while crossing into Mexico to begin an insurrection and jailed again. When they were released from this incarceration, they were able to join the cause of the 1910 to 1911 revolutionaries.

But the *Magonistas*, as the liberal movement became known, wanted not only to topple the men in power, but the entire economic structure. They were true socialists and wanted total distribution of land and wealth.

With Baja California so physically close to the Los Angeles base of *Magonista* activity, it became the focus of their activities. They were well financed with money from liberal American sympathizers. They attracted the support of liberal workers and U.S. labor groups, including the most radical and militant of all, the IWW (Wobblies).

When the Mexican Revolution broke out in 1910, the Mexican Liberal Party was prepared and carried out its own, more economic revolution. There were no Maderists fighting in Baja California, so it was up to the *Magonistas.*

In the early morning hours of Jan. 28, 1911, a handful of men were sent by the Magónistas to Mexicali, then a village of about 400 people. They killed the

Ricardo Flores Magón

jailer and released the prisoners, including two liberals. The town's leaders either surrendered, paid cash for their liberty, or fled.

Soon the Mexican Federalist army took off after the by-then-reinforced rebels. There were a few skirmishes, a few deaths on both sides, and two bridges near Mexicali were destroyed. The Americans watched with interest and by March 7 had 30,000 troops lined up along the border, standing by for possible intervention in another country's civil matters.

On March 12, the border town of Tecate fell to a handful of socialists, led by a member of the Wobblies.

The rebel forces were soon composed principally of foreigners either sympathetic to the cause, like the Wobblies, or soldiers of fortune like the Welshman Caryl Ap Rhys Pryce, who led an attack on Tijuana. His week-long march culminated in a hard-fought battle on the morning of May 9, 1911, during which the town fell to the liberals. Much looting followed.

Pryce began collecting taxes, licenses, and customs fees, generating revenue for the *Magonistas*. He even had the audacity to open the city of Tijuana to tourism, charging 25 cents per visitor, further enhancing the coffers.

Ricardo Flores Magón had Pryce begin planning to also attack the town of Ensenada, but it never happened.

After the Madero government toppled Díaz and requested the *Magonistas* to disband, Pryce had a falling out with Ricardo and Enrique Flores Magón, who wanted to continue the struggle. Pryce quit and disappeared, taking with him those funds collected. That left a fellow named John R. (Jack) Mosby in charge, but the socialist revolution of the brothers Flores Magón and their supporters was at a standstill.

In the confusion, a Los Angeles self-promoter named Dick Ferris stepped in. A promoter, publicity man, dreamer, and a bit of a clown, Ferris was responsible for the publicity of the Panama-California Exposition to commemorate the canal's opening. He had previously tried to blackmail President Díaz into selling the Baja California peninsula.

After he stormed into Tijuana with reporters in tow, he tried to establish Baja California as an independent republic, in the manner of William Walker and numerous other filibusterers in the late 1800s.

Mosby, who was now in charge of Flores Magón's socialist forces, denounced Ferris as one who had absolutely nothing to do with the revolutionary movement.

Meanwhile, Mexico's new President Madero wanted to make peace with the *junta* of the Liberal Party (meaning Flores Magón) and tried to convince Ricardo and Enrique to join him. He even sent their oldest brother, *licencio* Jesús Flores Magón, as part of the peace emissary. They emphatically rejected all offers.

While peace talks were going on, Federal forces attacked Tijuana, taking control of the town and throwing the rebels out. Out of about 500 insurgents in town at the time, 31 were killed and many wounded. Mosby crossed the border, but was arrested.

While the taking of Tijuana signaled the end of the *Magonista* movement, the zealot Ricardo Flores Magón refused to recognize it and continued to fight for social upheaval.

On June 14, he and his small band of core followers were arrested in Los Angeles and sentenced to the maximum 23 months in prison. Upon appeal, U.S. President Woodrow Wilson himself wrote to California Congressman John P. Nolan, "I took up and examined very thoroughly the case of Ricardo Flores Magón..., and I am sorry to say that, after looking into the case as fully as possible, I am convinced that it would not be wise or right to grant a pardon."

Never relinquishing his beliefs, Ricardo Flores Magón spent a total of 10 years in prison during the time from when he fled to the U.S. shortly after the turn of the century until he died in his prison cell in November 1922.

Baja California survived another attempt by those whose ideals dictated their actions. The legacy of the idealist lives on, with photos of Magón often encountered in books and stores. There is even a community south of Tijuana called the *Ejido Flores Magón.*

50 Million Fish Tacos
Rubio's Born in San Felipe

The now ubiquitous fish taco, which first appeared in seaside Baja towns, long remained primarily a south-of-the-border delicacy with many of us having a hard time getting friends to try them. Once they did, they were usually as hooked as the fish they were munching once were.

It took an enterprising young man named Ralph Rubio to bring the fish taco to the U.S. and create a following that has since wolfed down over 50 million fish tacos. Rubio and his buddies used to camp on the beach at San Felipe every spring and he was intrigued by the deliciously simple fish tacos served at one of the first stands there. Rubio befriended one taco stand owner, Carlos, who showed him the proper method of creating a fish taco masterpiece.

Back home, Rubio made fish tacos for his friends, perfecting his recipe. Several years passed while Ralph completed college, and he took a variety of jobs in the restaurant business. Finally, his father Ray suggested Ralph get off his surfboard and "make something of himself." Recalling those Baja-style fish tacos, Ralph Rubio decided to specialize in them, and in 1983 he opened a restaurant with his father as his partner. That first restaurant in San Diego's Mission Bay district was a walk-up stand with a sign that read, "Rubio's, The Home of the Fish Taco."

The stand's immediate success got the whole family involved and they never looked back. Rubio's is now Rubio's Fresh Mexican Grill, and serves a variety of authentic Mexican favorites. All are freshly prepared and made to order using Baja-inspired recipes. That little fish taco chain is now a publicly traded company with revenues exceeding $120 million from over 140 restaurants in six states.

Rubio's still recognizes the source of its inspiration with restaurant décor depicting Baja scenes. And while today's menu has expanded, Rubio's fish tacos would still make a San Felipe vendor named Carlos proud.

VILLAGE OF SAN FELIPE GROWS UP

The Rock of Consag

At times heat waves across the gulf create such an illusion that the rock out across the water appears to get larger with the afternoon sun and then actually lift off the water, looking like a dazzling UFO about to take off. At other times, the haze from San Felipe renders Consag Rock totally invisible.

The 2.2-acre rock, 22 miles from shore, was named for the explorer Jesuit Padre Fernando Consag, who first landed at San Felipe in 1746. Following approval from Spain's King Fernando VI, Jesuit explorers were to seek a route around the gulf. Consag left his base mission of San Ignacio for Loreto and was outfitted with four small boats with crews of Yaqui Indians from the gulf and docile Mission Indians.

After strong resistance by fierce Indians to their attempted landings, they made landfall at San Felipe, which Consag named San Felipe de Jesús. On Jul. 14, 1746, they arrived at the mouth of the Colorado River, where they nearly drowned, losing one boat in the tidal bore. Consag's map from the expedition was published in Madrid and widely used.

Later on, another padre from Mission San Pedro Mártir tried to establish a mission and supply port at San Felipe, but the enterprise failed. However, the Dominican padres used the small protected anchorage under the 940-foot hill of San Felipe Point to supply their two northern missions of San Pedro Mártir and Santa Catarina in the mountains to the west.

No permanent settlement was attempted until a road was put in to a radar station south of town by Abelardo L. Rodríguez, Governor of Baja California from 1923–1929 and later President of Mexico. The paved highway came in 1951 and hastened the development of San Felipe, as fishing and tourist activities have attracted many to the little village between the mountains and the Sea of Cortez. The population of San Felipe increases from about 20,000 to 25,000 during peak season.

The shimmering 286-foot-high rock offshore is a microcosm of life, with fish, sea lions, seals, and thousands of sea birds. Being named for the daring Consag (sometimes spelled Konsag), who explored the area with just a handful of natives, is a fitting tribute.

Where Did the Water Go?

The tides of the upper reaches of the narrow Sea of Cortez are among the world's largest (third in fluctuating the most between high and low each day). Water comes rushing through the gulf, rising higher and higher as it travels north. At La Paz in the south it is only about 4.5 feet. The tidal fluctuation increases to 11 feet by the time it reaches Bahía de los Angeles, and about 14 feet at Gonzaga Bay. But at San Felipe, Baja's northernmost gulf town, fluctuations of 20–22 feet are experienced, and at the Colorado River, the tides are over 30 feet, creating a tidal bore (or wave) as the sea water displaces the river's own water.

The shallow beach at San Felipe makes the low tide even more pronounced; distances of up to a half mile from high tide mark to the water's edge are common.

Unaware visitors are often startled by the extreme tides at San Felipe. They arrive and swim in the tepid waters of the Sea of Cortez that lap lazily on the sandy shore just 30 feet or so away. Later, they are amazed to see small wind-driven waves in the distance, way out across about a quarter-mile of wet, sandy ocean bottom.

At low tide you can walk out over the littoral, passing shells, trails of critters, and crabs that call the ocean bottom home. We've walked out so far we could actually look *back* to the rocky promontory with the shrine on top, even seeing the camps on its northern side.

If San Felipe is number three for tides, where are the bigger ones?

Cook Inlet outside Anchorage, Alaska, boasts the world's second largest tides. At low tide the entire Turnagain Arm of Cook Inlet is just a pile of mud that looks like chocolate pudding.

Number one is Canada's Bay of Fundy, where an inlet that begins in Maine rushes up between the Canadian provinces of New Brunswick and Nova Scotia, and the tides regularly reach 45 feet. That place is awesome; tidal bores can fill broad river valleys in minutes.

Alaska and Canada hardly qualify for "fun in the sun" though. Visitors to the fishing and tourist village of San Felipe, those who delight in the shallow beach and experience the phenomenon firsthand, know that San Felipe is really number one.

The Legend of El Chinero

About 33 miles north of San Felipe is a desert peak rising 200 meters above the desert floor just north of where Highway 3 from Ensenada joins Highway 5 from Mexicali. It's called El Chinero, and every time I drive past it I'm reminded of a grim episode in the history of Baja California.

El Chinero Peak

It was named for 160 Chinese laborers who died trying to cross the San Felipe desert. Indeed, at one time the entire desert was called the "Desert of the Chinese," honoring their demise.

In the early 20th century, many Chinese laborers came to Baja to work on the railroad or in the booming agriculture and irrigation systems around Mexicali. Some traveled overland and others came by ship.

Deserted in the San Felipe area, the 160 unfortunate and ill-advised Chinese laborers decided to walk across the hot, forbidding desert to Mexicali, about 125 miles away. Many never got past the hill in the desert; none made it to Mexicali.

First European in Northern Baja
The Grave of Melchior Díaz

In 1540, just after Francisco Coronado determined that Cíbola, the fabled Seven Cities of Gold, was nothing more than Zuni Indian pueblos whose pale-yellow adobe walls glistened deceptively in the southwest sun, the Spaniard explorer launched a small offshoot expedition, to be headed by Captain Melchior Díaz.

Díaz was sent west with 40 men to search for Hernando de Alarcón, who went by sea up the Colorado River a ways and was not heard from again. Díaz established the land route across the Sonora desert and became the first European ever to set foot in the northern reaches of Baja California and the present U.S. state of California.

He and his men stumbled into an area of hot springs and mud volcanoes near the Cócopa Mountains north of San Felipe. Díaz was accidentally impaled on his own lance while chasing his dog. His men tried to take care of him, while fending off Indian attacks, but he died 20 days later, on Jan. 18, 1541. His journals and diaries were never found.

A writer traveling with Coronado, Pedro de Casteñada, wrote a manuscript based on hearsay from the survivors of Díaz' party. A passage reads, "On a height of land overlooking a narrow valley, under a pile of rocks, Melchior Díaz lies buried."

In the early 1930s, the illustrious southwest desert explorer Walter Henderson came across such a pile of rocks while hiking in an area south of La Ventana. He noted the tops of the rocks had been darkened with "desert varnish," signifying they had been in that position for at least scores, if not hundreds, of years. Not realizing the significance, he left the obvious gravesite and hurried to reach his car before dark.

Years later, Henderson read about the Díaz gravesite and felt sure that is what he had stumbled across. He tried to enlist the aid of the Mexican government to help him go back and search, but found the bureaucracy daunting and never again located the pile of stones.

San Felipe writer Bruce Barber has searched the San Felipe desert, particularly around the Sierra Pinta area, for years, looking for the site without success. Without much reliable material from which to draw information, Barber has become so familiar with the story that he drew his own conclusions.

Based on the time it took the Díaz party to report his death and the personal dynamics of the people involved, Barber feels that Díaz was murdered by his own men. Even though soldiers of the time were periodically impaled by their own lances, which protruded awkwardly from the saddle, there were other clues and inconsistencies which led Barber to his conclusion.

Seems fitting, if true. The first European in southern Baja California, Fortún Jiménez and his men had mutinied and killed their leader before landing at La Paz. Another mutiny among the first people in the northern reaches of the California peninsula looms prophetic.

A San Felipe Character

Pasqual the Clam Man

As sure as the ubiquitous camp dogs, the spectacular sunrise and the awesome tidal fluctuation, campers along the San Felipe beaches during the 1970s and 1980s were inevitably greeted each day by the Clam Man. Some bought his clams, others just listened to his litany.

"Clam Man here. I'm the Clam Man. Wanna buy some clams? My clams make you horny," the bearded old man used to chant, always implying that eating clams did wonders for the sex drive. San Felipe's resident eccentric used to drag an old gunnysack full of small butter clams through the campgrounds. While selling clams was his business, the camaraderie and banter with visiting gringos were what the Clam Man really enjoyed.

Pasqual "Cruz" Guerrero (the Clam Man) operated out of his home/restaurant, a unique ramshackle structure adorned with whalebones and signs extolling the virility of clams. It's still on the right-hand side, between the famous San Felipe arches and the traffic circle, as you enter town.

Years after those regular visits in the 1980s, I wrote an article about the Clam Man, who had passed away in 1988. The story was published with a photo in a 1997 *Discover Baja* newsletter. On my next visit to San Felipe I stopped by the restaurant and presented a copy to his widow, Marcelina Abúndez. Even though she could not read English, she appeared to cherish the reminder.

The next day at the El Cortez restaurant I was approached by a young woman who said, "Señor, I understand you wrote that article about the Clam Man. Do you have another copy?"

I did, and when I gave it to her she identified herself as Margarita, a daughter of the Clam Man. She is one of the Clam Man's five daughters and three sons.

The Clam Man

Only two of the Guerrero children have left the area; Francesca moved to the United States and María Elena relocated to Mexicali. The sons, Miguel and the twins Smith and Hector, work in San Felipe. They operate a trucking concern, and Hector delivers water to the various camps. Apolonia (Pola) works for a camp in town, Margarita works at the El Cortez Hotel, and Theresa helps her mother run the Clam Man Restaurant.

The restaurant is not much, just a few rickety tables on freshly swept hard-packed dirt, and no menu. Why do they need a menu when all they have is clams? Family members regularly venture to some broad flat beaches north of town where they gather the staple that made their family famous. The small butter clams are inexpensive and can be ordered by the dozen. "We can steam them or barbecue them, and fix them up with *limón* and *salsa*," explained Theresa.

I stopped by recently to give them a photo I had taken of the Clam Man's widow and a grandson, Miguel Angel "Miguelito." "My father was a beautiful man," said Theresa, her eyes damp with reflection. "Everybody knew him and he knew everybody. We were a lucky family." He is a Baja character who is missed.

Hotel Riviera/Hotel Las Palmas
San Felipe's Original Inn?

In front of San Felipe's Hotel Las Palmas is a sign that reads, "Hotel Las Palmas, San Felipe's Original Inn." But was it the "original?" Or does that honor belong to the Hotel Riviera across the road?

The *malecón* at San Felipe

There appeared to be a lot of confusion as to which was San Felipe's "original inn." The hotel managers and/or owners of both the Las Palmas and the Riviera weren't positive. The files at the tourism office downtown were inconsistent. Phone calls to senior residents and present and past officials around town shed light on the subject and changed the legend, if not the sign at the Las Palmas.

Even with the original dirt road to San Felipe completed in 1925, by the end of that decade there were only about 100 people in the village. By the 1940s, a census still listed only 287 permanent residents of San Felipe.

In 1947, the Industrial Company of the Gulf of Cortez acquired much of the San Felipe land with the intention of developing it.

In 1948, pavement had begun linking San Felipe to Mexicali and the rest of the world. The paved road was completed in 1951. The year the paving started, 1948, also marked the opening of three guest rooms for visitors to San Felipe, the village's first inn.

They were built on the hill just to the south of town and called Augie's Riviera. By 1951, when the highway was finished, owner Armando Vásquez had added 12 more rooms, and the 15-room Augie's Riviera Hotel was *the* place for sportsmen visiting town. Guests could even fly in, landing at the small airstrip near the hotel.

Today, the Hotel Riviera (having dropped the name "Augie's") still rests on the hill overlooking the Sea of Cortez south of town. It is now owned and managed by the government, along with a sister hotel in Mexicali, the San Juan Capistrano Hotel. The Riviera, which bills itself as "El Mas Agradable de San Felipe" (The Most Friendly) now has 42 moderately priced, air-conditioned rooms, a swimming pool, Jacuzzi, and a *palapa* bar.

While Augie's Riviera grew in smaller increments, most townspeople noted that the

Hotel Villa Del Mar across the street on the same bluff was a legend from the start. Even the town's written history was confused, merging Augie's Riviera with the Villa del Mar.

The Hotel Villa Del Mar opened in 1956, was later named the *Trucha Vagabunda* (Vagabond Trout) and finally, the Las Palmas Hotel. While not quite the town's oldest, it has a long and colorful history, even welcoming celebrities like Dolores Del Río.

The current owners, the Alfredo Bellinghieri family, have had the place for 13 years. There are 48 spacious air-conditioned rooms in a hacienda atmosphere with bougainvillea-covered patios, fountains, and statuary.

The family has expanded their innkeeping interests and one son, Joseph Bellinghieri, owns and runs the successful St. James Bar and Restaurant in La Jolla, California.

While the townspeople seem to remember the old Villa Del Mar Hotel the best, it was not the town's first. But it really doesn't make much difference, as both have survived through the years on the same bluff, just south of the little fishing village of San Felipe.

El Cortez Hotel
The Hotel on the Gulf

Former President of Mexico Abelardo Rodríguez, who had been Governor of the Baja California territory in the 1920s, wanted to develop San Felipe. With partners he acquired land, hoping to establish casinos there. Unfortunately for him, a subsequent Mexican president decided reform was in order and was able to get casino gambling outlawed in Mexico. So before anything got started, San Felipe languished for a couple of decades.

By the 1940s, Rodríguez still wanted to attract American tourists, this time fishermen instead of gamblers. He was instrumental in grading and paving the road into San Felipe. In 1947 he even hired outdoor writer Ray Cannon to come to the region and write about the area's fishery.

That same year the brother of President Rodríguez, José María Rodríguez Luján, had formed the *Compañía Industrial del Golfo de Cortez* and owned some 10,000 hectares (over 4,000 acres), a major chunk of San Felipe. The company established the Port of San Felipe and other ventures.

José María Rodríguez finally started work on the El Cortez Hotel, which was right on the sand a half mile south of downtown. The hotel opened in 1959 with about 25 one-story bungalows.

By 1966 there were 60 rooms, all with shower baths and 20 with air conditioning and heating. Six of the rooms had kitchens, and there was even a larger family unit. In 1966 there were a large *palapa* on the beach, a concrete boat ramp, and boats for rent.

José María Rodríguez's son Nepo took over the El Cortez, and today it is run by Nepo's five children, Alejandro Rodríguez Romero, Jorge Rodríguez Romero, María Esthela Rodríguez Romero, Nepo Rodríguez, and Victor Rodríguez, all grandchildren of the founder.

While not the town's first inn, it was most certainly the first one on the drawing boards and it has been in the same family for almost half a century.

One frigid winter day in the late 1970s, I was alone in San Felipe. I knew of the Hotel El Cortez on the gulf from previous visits when I had camped nearby. It was too cold to camp that day, especially for a wimp like me, so I checked in.

There was no central heating, especially in a town where the summer sun is relentless and the desert heat is legendary. I called the management for a heater, but it appears I was not alone. They said there were no more heaters available but they would try to find one. They must have scoured the town, because they arrived at my room with a space heater at just about the time I was considering chopping up the dresser for firewood.

I chuckle thinking about that trip, which was ill-fated in more ways than one. The extreme cold and heavy rains were not the relaxing antidotes I sought while I was trying to make some of life's heavy decisions. But the decisions turned out well, and I have always remembered the El Cortez and often stay there.

Today there are 109 rooms and 45 employees, a class restaurant, the Barefoot Bar (where the *palapa* used to be), swimming pool, boat ramp, trailer park, boutique, laundry, gift shop, and beauty shop, all hugging the sand on the shore of the Sea of Cortez.

The walls of the popular Barefoot Bar are adorned with signed photos of famous off-road racers and pictures of people holding big fish. It's a place where you can eat peanuts and throw darts and tell tall tales. One wall boasts a beautiful stained-glass window with a colorful map of Baja outlined in lead — I'd love to steal it. But, hey, if I didn't chop up their furniture, I doubt if I could cut out the window. Besides, I like the place.

TONY REYES SPORTFISHING

Mothership to the Midriff

To many Baja sportsmen, fishing means a week-long adventure aboard a "mothership" that dispatches *pangas* (fishing skiffs) daily to work the productive "midriff" waters of the Sea of Cortez.

An example is the 86-foot *José Andrés*, one such mothership that leaves San Felipe (some 250 miles to the north of the midrift) each week with 18 fishermen, a crew of 12, and a half dozen *pangas* on board. Three anglers and a guide are assigned to each *panga*.

The mothership concept was started by San Felipe fishermen exactly a half-century ago, in the early 1950s when the town's tourism was in its infancy. Midriff sportfishing legend Tony Reyes, who owns the *José Andrés*, has been involved all those years.

Born in Mexico City in 1923, Tony went to the U.S. as a farm laborer at age 19. He followed the crops, working in Minnesota, North Dakota, and Wyoming. In San Jose, California he was apprehended by the Immigration Department with an expired permit and deported to Tijuana, Mexico. "I really felt alone there," he said. "I had no relations, no friends, no money, nothing. At first I slept in a pool hall, then a small hotel gave me a room and meals for working there, but no money."

Then something happened that would change Reyes' life. A San Diego tuna boat fisherman rented a room at the hotel in 1950. He advised Reyes to go to San Felipe to try to get a job on one of the commercial shrimp boats there. "Looking back, I'm glad they caught me and sent me to Baja California, because otherwise I might have been picking fruit all my life," he told me.

So Reyes went to San Felipe and worked as a shrimp boat deckhand to learn the business. Other crewmen told him that Ensenada sportfishing boats needed good crew members for their summer seasons. So Reyes became an apprentice guide in Ensenada aboard the 30-foot *Gaviota #1*, where Captain Eddie Celaya helped him hone his skills each summer.

He and Celaya met many American sportsmen, and Reyes learned diplomacy and better English along with fishing. He still has many photos from the Ensenada summers of the early 1950s. In one, he's posing with a huge white sea bass with outdoors writer Lupe Saldana of the *Los Angeles Times*.

At the end of that first summer he returned to San Felipe with a second-hand *panga*. With no engine, he began rowing guests out to the local points, where they caught *corvina*, *cabrilla*, and the large *totuava*.

An American named Ralph said Reyes needed a motor and advanced him his first $50 outboard motor. "Ralph just liked to go fishing, and every time I took him we deducted from the $50 until it was all paid off," recalls a grinning Tony Reyes. Shortly thereafter, he began acquiring other *pangas* and motors and hiring other guides.

When the paved road brought the anticipated fishermen in 1951, Tony Reyes was ready. He knew how to fish, he had the boats, and he had developed the contacts.

He had access to 50-foot shrimp boats and began taking anglers out for extended trips, expanding the trips to two and three days. The local fishing was great, but more species could be found in the waters to the south.

The Sea of Cortez narrows in an area called the "midriff," a term popularized by the fishing/writing legend Ray Cannon. It refers to an area about 250 miles south of San Felipe where rich nutrients in deep channels are upwelled to the surface by the rushing tides. Fishing in the midriff is legendary, but in the 1950s there were no roads to the area.

Pangas aboard a mothership

Even today, the small village of Bahía de los Angeles is a 400-mile drive from the border. So several San Felipe fishermen including Charlie Rucker and Tony Reyes developed the "*pangas* aboard a mothership" concept. Reyes is quick to admit that Rucker was actually the first one to do it and that he had copied him. Regardless, Rucker didn't stay involved long, and the Tony Reyes fleet has endured for a half century.

The Tony Reyes trips expanded to five- and six-day jaunts into the midriff. Fishermen traveled, ate, and slept aboard the mothership, which launched the *pangas*. Early on, Tony rented the boats before purchasing his own. His first boat was the *Santa Mónica*.

The *José Andrés* has been the flagship since 1987 and features three heads, two showers, a full galley, and inside staterooms, although most anglers prefer to sleep in the open-air bunks. There are bait tanks, a walk-in refrigerator, a walk-in freezer, and other amenities dedicated to a week's fishing (Sunday through Friday, each week).

I'd seen fishermen from the *José Andrés* in action, but was too busy catching fish to pay much attention. Yellowtail were all over the channel between Punta La Gringa and Smith Island that day. It was hot stand-up fishing action, the feisty yellowtail chasing the largest concentration of boiling baitfish I'd ever seen.

My fishing buddy Don Lund and I each picked up several nice yellowtail, trolling Rapalas north along the island shore, having hired a local guy out of nearby Bahía de los Angeles.

Then the fish went deep and we had to work to get them. By the time we'd arrived at the rocks north of the island, several *pangas* were already there working a deep hole. There were three fishermen and a skipper in each of the small boats.

The *pangas* were landing beautiful "yellows" right and left, with their sunburned occupants doing a lot of whooping and hand-slapping. That's when I noticed most of them were in *pangas*, all from the same larger vessel we'd seen anchored at Punta la Gringa. It was the *José Andrés*.

Americans have long played a hand in the Tony Reyes success story. David Fink of Davey's Locker in Newport Beach suggested that Reyes rent out those shrimp boats for the extended trips. Davey's Locker then helped supply anglers. For awhile Tom Payne of Redondo Beach supplied the booking. Today, it's Tom Ward of Longfin Fishing Suppliers in Orange who helps Reyes book the trips.

75 years of experience

While Tony Reyes still coordinates the trips, he turned the captain's chair over to his son Tony Reyes Jr. in 1990. Between them, they have over 75 years of experience fishing the bountiful waters of the Sea of Cortez. Tony Reyes Sr., who knows about all there is to know about fishing the Sea of Cortez, modestly says that his son is the better captain.

Others now fish the midriff from long-range ships leaving San Felipe. The other son of Tony Reyes, Heriberto, works the midriff boats for Captain Villegas charters. Captain Villegas trips can be booked through the Jig Stop in Dana Point.

Bob and Celia Castellón run Sea of Cortez Sportfishing and feature three-, four-, and six-day trips aboard the 87-foot *Celia Angelina*.

Baja Sportfishing features the 105-foot steel hull *Erik*, which offers six-day trips from San Felipe. Poseidon's Sea of Cortez, Inc., based in Torrance, has also been offering six-day trips aboard the 90-foot *Poseidon*.

In the tiled dining room of his trim home in San Felipe, Tony Reyes reminisced about fishing, San Felipe, and his life. He has an attractive wife and numerous friends and associates who extend way beyond San Felipe. His local friends regularly drop by for favors and advice, and the spry Tony Reyes seemingly has time for everyone. He does not look or act 77 years old.

This "living legend" developed a small resort south of San Felipe called Okie's Landing, and has since sold it. In 1967 he joined other world-class fishermen for a kingfish adventure in New Zealand. "They call them kingfish, but they're really yellowtail, much bigger, however, than anything in Baja California. We caught some up to 120 pounds," he recalled.

Tony Reyes has caught *totuava* up to 300 pounds and currently advocates their protection. He's caught a 500-pound black sea bass, his largest fish, he said.

The old photos showed bigger fish and a younger Tony Reyes and a sleepy San Felipe that is no more. One photo shows a small wooden Tony Reyes fishing shack on a dirt road in "downtown" San Felipe. It was right where the El Marinero liquor store is at the stoplight. But the photo he saved to show last was of Tony Reyes and his mother (who lived to be well over 100), with their heads both facing the same way. Obviously, it was his favorite. "Tom Miller took this photo," he said, referring to a longtime Baja buff, the author of several Baja-related books.

These are nostalgic times for Tony Reyes. He says his sons are better fishermen than he ever was. "Smarter, always looking," he explained. Tony Reyes doesn't fear the Immigration these days when he goes north to work the trade shows. He's well known and well liked. "You know, people keep coming back. I think this year we'll get the fourth generation of one family," Reyes beamed. A restaurant owner from Long Beach has already brought his son and grandson on the Tony Reyes trips. This year the great-grandson should be ready.

The "*pangas* aboard a mothership" concept is popular, effective, and practical for long-range Sea of Cortez fishing adventures. It took farsighted, hardworking people like Charlie Rucker, Tony Reyes, and others to make it work. When many sportsmen think of fishing the midriff region of the Sea of Cortez, they think of Tony Reyes.

Bar Miramar

The San Felipe Watering Hole

San Felipe has one business that's known far and wide. The Bar Miramar is more than a bar; it's an institution where party animals drink, people meet, friends rendezvous, and strangers get together. Visitors to San Felipe are often asked by their friends to meet at the downtown bar called the Miramar.

The place is not much, entered through a front door high above an elevated sidewalk. Fortunately, there's a railing to steady those leaving. Falling off that curb could hurt. On the right of the entrance is the bar, with about 15 to 18 stools where serious drinkers hold court and tell tall tales about the "San Felipe way back when..."

There're some naugahyde booths against the wall surrounding a tile dance floor. An often-busy pool table rests on a corner of the dance floor. A humongous jukebox graces the wall across from the bar. Straight ahead is a larger room with another pool table and more tables. That room goes right out to a deck and the seafront. Old photographs and posters and stickers are everywhere, lending the Miramar a funky ambience.

The bar's logo says, "Bar Miramar, 1948," which I understand marks the year the owner arrived in San Felipe.

Beating out the Miramar for oldest bar honors (if one can call it that) is the El Puerto Bar, whose proprietor Alfredo García Martínez arrived in San Felipe in 1927. The bar is still in existence down a side street, and is now owned by García's son, Alejandro García Arvizu.

But the Miramar crowd could care less about other places. The owner of the popular Miramar is Francisco Aróstegui, and as long as most people can remember, his place has been the one where the action is. Just remember not to fall off that curb.

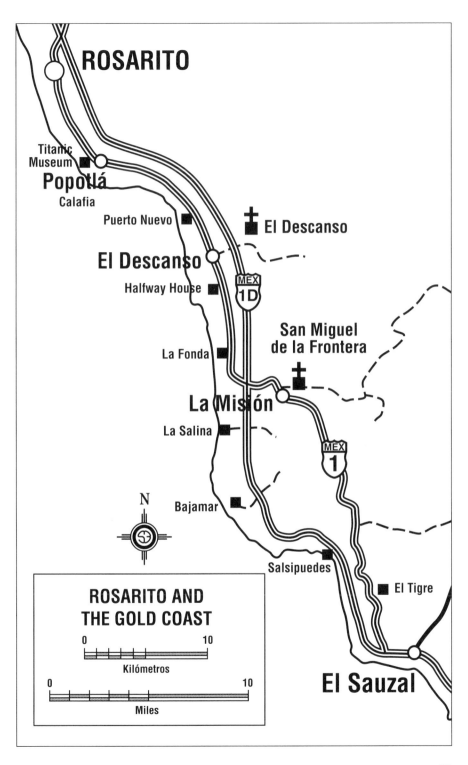

ROSARITO

Titanic
Museum ■
Popotlá
Calafia
Puerto Nuevo ■
✝ El Descanso
El Descanso
Halfway House ■
MEX 1D
San Miguel
de la Frontera
La Fonda ■
✝
La Misión
La Salina ■
MEX 1
N
Bajamar ■
Salsipuedes ■
■ El Tigre

**ROSARITO AND
THE GOLD COAST**

0   10
Kilómetros

0   10
Miles

El Sauzal

Chapter 7: Rosarito and the Gold Coast

THE HALFWAY HOUSE
First Bar between Tijuana and Ensenada

The Halfway House (*Medio Camino*), a small restaurant on a bluff over the pounding ocean, is not only one of Baja's legends — it was already a legend well over half a century ago.

There is evidence from the *San Diego Union* that in 1894 Mexican authorities reported that a place called "halfway" had the only fresh water between La Misión Valley on the south and El Descanso on the north.

When a small cantina opened at the site "halfway" between Tijuana and Ensenada in 1922, it became the first and only bar between those two cities. The rustic bar featured the classic western-style swinging doors and catered to the occasional travelers. It would be several years before the venerable Rosarito Beach Hotel (1926) and nearby René's (1924) would open in Rosarito Beach, creating several other places where those seeking a beer or a tequila could "wet their whistles."

Two years later, in 1924, the Halfway House expanded to accommodate clientele brought in on the new paved road to Ensenada. A dining room with a stone chimney was attached to the north side and still stands today. The restaurant originally offered Chinese food.

By the 1930s the Halfway House had become a regular stop for most travelers. One of them, Alejandro Villalvazo, who was married the year before, had wanted to find a place where he could establish some roots. He bought the Halfway House in 1937. Alejandro and his brother Carlos were partners in a gas station enterprise that included stations in both Tijuana and Ensenada. Back then it took a full day to get from one city to the other, longer if it rained. It seemed natural, then, that Alejandro would offer gasoline along with food and drink. So cars were originally serviced out of a small pump that dispensed about 200 gallons a week out of four 50-gallon drums.

By the '40s and '50s, the Villalvazo family had quit selling gasoline, and the cuisine had turned to more traditional Mexican fare. But the wood frame structure with swinging doors and stone chimney still looked much the same as it had for years.

The Halfway House

By the '70s there still were few restaurants along the Gold Coast, and the Halfway House was known for good value meals. The patio on the cliff overlooked the surf crashing upon rocks and a small beach. Visitors often wandered around the shoreline exploring the diverse sea life at low tide, where tide pools revealed the creatures of the littoral: sea urchins, crabs, starfish, mussels, and sea cucumbers.

During the mid-1970s hang gliders used the Halfway House as a destination, shuttling to the steep inland cliffs and soaring birdlike out toward the ocean. They circled out over the ocean, then turned back to that small beach where their colleagues had laid out a small cloth target that seemed about the size of a washcloth.

The gliders dropped down, attempting to land with both feet touching the cloth. Many scored a perfect touchdown. Others were extremely close. Then, pumped up and rejuvenated, they'd gather their gliders, load them up on trucks, and head off to the mountain rim to do it all over again. It made for fascinating spectator sport for those sitting on the patio.

The Halfway House has almost completed its eighth decade of existence. Alejandro Villalvazo Jr. has been running the place, and another generation of the family is now learning the ins and outs of management. Beautiful new beachfront homes now cover the blufftop in the family's development to the immediate south.

For a few years in the mid-1990s, the old place appeared to be caught in a time warp as more modern developments and restaurants and bars opened to the north and south along the coast.

A new restaurant manager was hired in 1998 and changes were made. Johnny Villegas, the original chef at the Newport Beach Hotel up the coast, was brought in to head up the Halfway House restaurant staff. While the decor and hardwood floors still remind you that you're in one of the older Baja establishments, elaborate table settings and real tablecloths create a different impression, and there is nothing halfway about the food. The menu, a blend of Mexican and French cuisine, is broader and more versatile.

When you pull off the old road onto the broad gravel parking lot about 15 miles south of Rosarito Beach and enter the Halfway House through the swinging doors, you're not only halfway between Tijuana and Ensenada on the old road, but in an historic establishment as well.

RENÉ'S, ROSARITO BEACH

Catch a Ball Game at René's

Back in the early 1970s, few people along the Gold Coast had television sets in their modest trailers and cottages. Indeed, many didn't even have electricity. But when the Rose Bowl game was on — or the Super Bowl game or any other can't-miss "big game" or "big fight" — everyone knew where to head.

The parking lot at René's Sports Bar and Restaurant, on the southern fringes of Rosarito Beach, was always crowded. The bar/dance hall/restaurant known simply as René's became one of Baja's first true sports bars. With the new phenomenon called "cable" and several large TV sets, almost any weekend afternoon you could hear the whooping and hollering of addicted fans from the crowded bar.

Americans instinctively turn right upon entering René's and find themselves in the bar with small round tables, upholstered naugahyde swivel chairs, waiters adroitly running around with trays of margaritas and *cervezas*, and lots of companionship.

Many long afternoons turned into long evenings, and there's always been a cadre of regulars who have been known to hug the bar until they needed help crawling off the bar stool. Personable bar manager Lupe Angel, who has long known his charges, has helped many exit, while preserving as much of their dignity as possible.

On weekend evenings, another mood prevails: the place is invaded by locals who turn left upon entering, heading for the dance floor where live music of top Mexican groups packs 'em in. So on the left, you have tables and booths full of fun-loving *rosaritenses* oom-pa-pahing to the strains of *Norteña* or *Ranchera musica,* and on the right, separated by a divided wall, is the bar where a primarily American clientele watches TV during the day and tells tall tales at night. When the band stops playing, a mariachi group serenades folks on both sides of the divider.

The restaurant is to the left, through the bar, and creates another mood altogether. Bright, with lots of windows and a view of gardens and the ocean, René's restaurant has a long history of serving fine meals to Baja travelers — three quarters of a century, in fact.

Back in 1923, under the direction of then-territorial Governor Abelardo Rodríguez, the road south of Tijuana was paved all the way to Ensenada. Just months later, in May 1924, Sr. Juan Ortiz opened what was originally called the Rosarito Beach Resort, becoming only the second bar between Tijuana and Ensenada. The resort also included rental cottages on the ocean bluff behind the Bar/Restaurant. Today that business is still operating, now known as the Motel Paraíso Ortiz.

Juan turned the business over to his children, and for a while around 1940, the enterprise was called Ortiz Brothers Bar and Café.

Juan's son René Ortiz took over what became widely known as René's Bar and Café, and over the decades, he made friends with a growing number of American tourists.

L.A. County issues proclamation

In fact, when René Ortiz passed away in 1988, the County of Los Angeles issued a proclamation that reads in part: "When the sun sets on the Pacific Ocean and the warm red glow reaches through the windows of this cantina, the fading light will fall upon the vacant chair where so often René sat. The chair may be vacant but the warm glow will last forever, for René was that in life as he is in death, a warm glow of friendship and kindness to all who met him. ...Seldom has one man meant so much to so many. February 16, 1988."

The proclamation, which hangs on a wall in the restaurant, was signed by all five L.A. County Supervisors.

But as a sports bar, there are many athletic souvenirs adorning the old place as well. There are NFL team caps and other photos and mementos, including a photo of actor Phil Harris and a riding jersey worn and signed by the champion jockey Laffit Pincay Jr.

Also in evidence are trophies from the numerous seafood competitions, a reminder that the restaurant does not play second fiddle to the sports bar.

Today René's is run by René Ortiz Jr. and family. Norma Ortiz, who helps manage René's, is the daughter of René Jr., the granddaughter of the original René Ortiz, and the great-granddaughter of the founder, Juan Ortiz. While the Los Angeles Board of Supervisors singled out the legendary René Ortiz Sr., they could just as easily have recognized the entire family, who made their imprint along the Gold Coast.

While most folks along the Gold Coast now have television, there's something about the camaraderie of a bar full of enthusiasts for that "big game." René's, anyone?

Rosarito Beach Hotel
The Legendary Queen of the Coast

There's a graceful old dowager down in Baja that wears her age well. She's the legendary Rosarito Beach Hotel, the first and still the greatest attraction of the seaside community of Rosarito Beach, now the newest municipality (incorporated city) in the state of Baja California.

For over three quarters of a century, the venerable Rosarito Beach Hotel has welcomed over 4,000,000 guests, from celebrities to newlyweds to Americans on their first visit to Mexico. And still they come, lined up in the spacious lobby every weekend to register and enjoy all the amenities the hotel has to offer.

The four million guests since 1926 have entered under the curved portal above which is inscribed in Spanish, "Through These Doors Pass the Most Beautiful Women in the World" alluding to the in-crowd that's romped through the place for years.

The "party" attitude has long been a part of the attraction at the Rosarito Beach Hotel. Prohibition in the U.S. forced developers to look south across the border for a more tolerant atmosphere. In just 80 years a major Baja California city has come into being.

Following the occupancy of local Indians and the passage of Spanish soldiers and missionaries, the area around Rosarito Beach was not developed until the territorial governor granted 407,000 acres to Juan Machado. Machado took over Baja California's northernmost mission, Descanso (in the valley just south of Cantamar) and developed a large ranch.

In 1920 a Los Angeles investment group acquired 14,000 of those acres and began to develop what was originally named El Rosario Resort and Country Club. That first hotel, which opened in 1926, had only 10 rooms and one bathroom. A small ad in the *San Diego Union* heralded the opening. Soon a larger hotel and beautiful casino were constructed. Adorned with ornate tile, relief sculpture work, wondrous paintings, and bold Matias Santoyo murals, it immediately began to attract an international crowd.

Enter Manuel Barbachano

Three years later, in 1929, an enterprising man named Manuel P. Barbachano bought the property and continued to expand it. Barbachano's nephew Hugo Torres Chabert runs the place today.

Torres says that if there ever was a "Baja Legend" it should be Barbachano. "He was a real Baja pioneer," says Torres. "He was progressive and had a vision for Baja California. He was responsible for bringing in the electricity for the Tijuana and Rosarito area. He also established the first telephone company for all of northern Baja California."

Barbachano, however, was forced to close the casino when the Mexican government banned casino gambling in the mid-1930s, but by this time the Hollywood crowd had already made it the "in" place for romantic interludes.

Movie stars Joan Bennett, Rita Hayworth, Gregory Peck, Vincent Price, Lana Turner, Debbie Reynolds, Mickey Rooney, and Spencer Tracy were guests. So were Marilyn Monroe, Jack Palance, Clark Gable, Victor Mature, Orson Welles, and Peter Lorre. Also spending time at the hotel have been the singing group *Temptations*, director James Cameron, Tiny Tim, Dolores Del Río, and Larry Hagman.

Paulette Goddard and Burgess Meredith married there. Race driver Barney Oldfield and author Damon Runyon spent time at the Rosarito Beach Hotel. The king of Egypt was also a guest, along with his sister and mother.

The international playboy Ali Kahn and actress Gene Tierney took over the entire hotel with Kahn's entourage for two weeks in 1954. "He brought his own cook, because he didn't trust anyone," said Torres. "And then when they started to leave, his manager didn't want to pay the several thousand dollar bill, saying that the publicity should be worth something. So my uncle told them that if they didn't pay, they'd never get back across the border. He told them he'd have the police arrest them there. That scared them into paying."

A lifetime at the hotel

Torres, born in Mexico City in 1936, was a young boy in 1943 when he came to his uncle's hotel. While he was later educated in Mexico City, Monterrey, and San Diego, Torres has spent most of his life involved with the grand old hotel.

He remembers a number of the famous guests and still greets newer generations of them today. "That Kim Novak was a beauty," he recalls. "I also remember meeting Mickey Rooney and Vincent Price. Vincent Price, of course, was on vacation and seemed so much more friendly than those roles he used to play."

After the death of Barbachano, his widow leased the hotel operation out to a Mexican/American partnership, Chávez and Greenburg, who ran the hotel from 1964 to 1974. Hugo Torres took over his uncle's venerable hotel in 1974 and has run it ever since. There were only 51 rooms in 1974; it has 280 rooms today.

"It was like a white elephant at the time," recalls Torres. It was spacious, with big gardens that required a lot of maintenance, and large rooms. It was just not very cost-effective, so we've made a lot of changes."

The large hotel is continually remodeling, adding, and retraining their people. For example, they hired a biochemist to constantly check the quality of the food and drinking water served. Upon his recommendation, they bought a new reverse osmosis water purification machine.

Also, rather than dumping raw sewage in the ocean, they installed an artificial ecosystem sewage treatment plant that is checked regularly and approved by the appropriate state agencies. Those are the kinds of changes, not noticed by the public, which illustrate the attention to detail.

Torres himself has become somewhat of a Baja legend. For years he spearheaded the movement to incorporate the City of Rosarito Beach, creating the state's fifth municipality. It finally happened in 1995, and Torres served as Rosarito Beach's first mayor, a three-year term.

In recent years the Rosarito Beach Hotel has been the setting for several U.S., Mexican, and Japanese movies. The movie *Baja Run* was filmed there. A popular episode of the TV show *Simon and Simon* was filmed there with the usual cast and guest star Morgan Fairchild. If you know what he looks like, you would notice that the counter clerk welcoming the actors is Hugo Torres himself.

Big times and visions of Hollywood returned to the old hotel when the Fox Baja Studio opened. Many of the people working on the studio about four miles south of town stay at the Rosarito Beach Hotel. During the filming of the blockbuster movie *Titanic* the hotel was a home away from home for many of the movie's cast.

The Rosarito Beach Hotel never has a shortage of events. The hotel is constantly hosting meetings, shows, and special events. The amenities are endless. The sedate Chabert's Restaurant is by far Rosarito Beach's most upscale restaurant. Tennis courts, swimming pools, horse rentals, and much more make the old dowager a true resort.

The Rosarito Beach Hotel's Casa Playa Spa is a full service spa and salon, offering therapeutic massages, seaweed facials, herbal body wraps, and much more.

The natural attractions of pounding surf and a broad sandy beach have recently been enhanced with an 1800-foot pier that extends from the Beachcomber Bar. On April 15, 2000 the first daily gambling cruise ship from San Diego arrived, heralding yet another chapter in Rosarito Beach.

The children of Hugo Torres (Hugo, Daniel, Gustavo, Laura, and Rose), are now active in the management of the hotel, serving in various functions.

The Rosarito Beach Hotel is over three quarters of a century old, and the graceful old dowager has seen it all.

Fox Studios Baja
Studio's First Movie an Instant Legend

When *Titanic* Director James Cameron accepted the Motion Picture Academy's Oscar for best picture of the year he threw out his arms and proudly said, "I'm King of the World." A lot of people in Baja shared his excitement. After all, *Titanic*, the top-grossing movie of all time, was filmed in Baja at a place called Popotla, just south of Rosarito Beach.

People along Baja's Gold Coast were quite surprised to hear that a major movie studio was to be built nearby, but it happened. *Titanic* began filming right away, even before the new 20th Century Fox studio was completed. Little did any of the locals realize that the new studio's first movie was to become an instant legend, a classic film for all time.

Residents were excited as work began on the studio at Popotla. Before June 1, 1996, the 33-acre Fox site was a wind-blown dusty plateau sandwiched between the Old Road (Libre) and the ocean cliffs, adjacent to the Popotla arch, just a few miles south of Rosarito Beach.

Like an army of ants, workers from both sides of the border were abuzz with activity on this Baja bluff, pouring tons of concrete, framing buildings and stages, painting sets, and beginning the construction of a detailed life-size replica of the historic ship *Titanic*.

The *Titanic*, renowned for its ill-fated maiden voyage from Southampton, England to New York in 1912, cost $10 million to build at the time. The movie *Titanic* cost over 20 times that, over $200 million, making it the most expensive movie ever made. The combined Mexican-American effort was originally planned to be 20th Century Fox's next summer's box office draw, but the overall quality of the movie dictated it be saved for a late-in-the-year Oscar bid. A sound decision, it seems.

The studio was originally planned for only one production, but once underway, it was decided to construct a studio that will long endure.

World search ends in Baja

The Baja site was not selected lightly. The search literally took them all over the world, from Malta to the Czech Republic, Australia, the United Kingdom, Italy, and California. When they saw Popotla, Fox executives said, they stopped looking. Chief Financial Officer Simon Bax said, "It had everything we needed. And the great thing is, it's so close to California. It's an easy drive from Los Angeles."

Filming on the movie started on Sept. 16, 1996, using finished parts of the studio while the remainder was still being constructed.

Fox sent down its top facility executive, Fernando Carrillo, Director of Studio Operations, to get the studio job done while keeping the production team on schedule. No stranger to Baja, he and his wife Lilia had owned a vacation home at nearby La Paloma for nine years previous.

"It would have been ideal to have the studio completed before production took over," said Carrillo, "but we're making the best of it and we're staying ahead of them."

The studio contracted out about 700 workers, most of them Mexican citizens, to build the tanks and pumps and roads and buildings. More than half were bussed in from Rosarito, Ensenada, and Tijuana.

According to contractor Howard Hargrove, the benefits of building the studio and making the movie in Mexico were great. "If this was being done in the States, it would cost five times more and take 10 times longer. At this point, we'd probably still be getting permits in the States," he said.

Production had about 500 people building, preparing, and painting sets, producing scenic art, filming, and making sure the *Titanic* got finished.

The bow of the *Titanic* had been constructed on a large hinge above a pit. The bow would raise, dropping stunt people into the airbag-filled pit. I noticed stunt people, secured by rock-climbing straps, going through the choreography of who would bounce off of which boom or obstacle, which side they would carom off, and the sequence of who would land in the air bag first. The average moviegoer could hardly suspect the depth of the planning, only seeing in the final film a few seconds that appear spontaneous and tragic.

The world's largest water tank

One of the main things the Popotla site offered was the unobstructed ocean view.

The world's largest water tank, covering eight total acres, was dug and concreted. In it, the *Titanic* was reconstructed. Called Stage 1 or Tank 1, the entire irregular-shaped eight-acre tank can be flooded to its 3'8" depth. The ship was built in two deeper pools in the center of the more shallow one.

A weir, or waterfall, on the ocean side of the eight acres can render the visual effect of a ship at sea as the cameras look out over the tank to the open ocean.

The entire tank holds 17 million gallons of water. They scraped a channel out of the rocks below the bluff to pump seawater into the tanks.

Stage 2 is the world's largest *covered* tank at 100 × 200 feet. Elaborate sets were constructed in the bowels of this tank and flooded as needed during filming. Entire rooms of the *Titanic* were duplicated in all their original splendor, with gilt-trimmed ornate ceiling designs, and beautiful thick, flowered carpets. Stately curved wooden banisters and fully-furnished staterooms were all built to be destroyed. It seemed wasteful to those not in the entertainment business, but a more discerning moviegoing audience demands such attention to detail.

Fox Studios Baja during the filming of *Titanic*.

The number one movie of all time!

The attention to detail and enormous cost paid off for all involved with *Titanic*. Released in December 1997, the hit movie became the number-one grossing movie of all time. It was the first film ever to gross over $1 billion worldwide.

The 3-hour, 15-minute epic drama also quickly smashed records in video form, becoming the most rented movie ever and the most purchased video ever. The soundtrack from *Titanic* became the Number 1 Album of the Year.

The public was not alone in heaping praise upon the movie made in Baja. The 11 Oscars *Titanic* picked up at the 70th annual Academy Awards in 1998 tied a record for most wins. Its 14 Academy Award nominations also tied a record.

Along with Director/Writer/Co-producer James Cameron picking up the year's top two awards with Best Picture and Best Director, *Titanic* also won Oscars for Cinematography, Film Editing, Art Direction, Costume Design (Costumes by Deborah Lynn Scott), Original Dramatic Score (Music by James Horner), Original Song ("My Heart Will Go On"), Visual Effects, Sound, and Sound Effects Editing.

Other nominations were for Make-up, Best Actress (Kate Winslett, who played Rose), and Best Supporting Actress (Gloria Stuart, who played the older Rose). The movie also starred Leonardo DiCaprio, Billy Zane, and Kathy Bates. The success of the movie helped catapult DiCaprio into a teenage idol.

The ship was dismantled

The *Titanic* sets, including the ship, were built to be dismantled, and just as the huge ship suddenly appeared on the bluff, so too did it vanish. The buildings of what has become the Fox Studios Baja remain, along with the world's largest water tanks. Anyone who saw the old pirate movies of the 1950s, where miniature tall ships bobbed in bathtub-sized tanks, will appreciate the difference.

The *Titanic* experiment made the movie industry sit up and take notice. Other movies have now been filmed at the new studio in Baja.

The James Bond thriller *Tomorrow Never Dies*, portions of the movie *In Dreams*, and the 1998 Warner Brothers movie *Deep Blue Sea* were all filmed at Fox Baja Studio.

At the studio's inauguration in 1996, Baja Norte Tourism Director Juan Tintos Funcke said, "Hopefully, this will put Baja California on the map as a major location for filmmaking." It appears he's already correct, and that the enterprise is a big boon to the entire Baja area and to the movie industry.

The success of the instant-legend movie *Titanic* and the Fox Baja Studio has also spawned a curious public. So many people stopped by to ask if they could "take a look," that the studio opened up a *Titanic* exhibit on the lot. The original *Titanic* Museum exhibit, only opened on weekends, featured a one-hour tour and an 8-minute video-documentary about the *Titanic*'s construction and shooting of the movie. Between 500 and 1,000 visitors had been visiting each Sunday during the summer.

All the interest prompted Fox to capitalize by building an adjoining theme park called *Foxploration*, which opened on the lot to the north in March 2001. In addition to a Main Street, other movie exhibits and tours, a small park, gift shop, and restaurant, the entire *Titanic* exhibit has been moved to the new park.

A representation of about 30 percent of the sets and props are now in the *Titanic* exhibit, which are duplications of some of the rooms and halls where scenes were filmed.

At the end of the guided tour, visitors can wander among props and some remaining parts of the ship, such as the communications room and the bridge. Most popular is the bow, reached by a short stairwell and strategically positioned in front of a large sunset photograph. Sometimes there's a line of people going up to the bow to lean forward and raise their arms up in a swan dive simulation while loved ones below click away to record the scene for photo albums.

The city of Rosarito Beach, which has already doubled in only five years to 110,000 in 2000, expects the park will help attract a half-million more tourists each year. The town already swells by about 15,000 each weekend, and double that for holidays.

The studio has certainly been alluring to the residents along Baja's Gold Coast. Many of the approximate 10,000 Americans living in the area joined the *Titanic* excitement and went back to work for a few long days. Fellow Baja writer Graham Mackintosh, with his flaming red hair, is easily spotted spilling beer in the steerage party scene.

But all of us in the Rosarito Beach area, whether or not we were directly involved in the movie, feel a sense of pride in the first movie filmed in our area. We know that in one of the movie's most memorable scenes, where the lovers stood on the bow with that magnificent sunset in the background that "we" were in the movie. That was "our sunset" and no movie magic could have improved upon it.

Calafia Restaurant on Punta Descanso.

CALAFIA RESORT

Historic Calafia Straddles Early Border

Baja's northernmost missions were San Miguel, near the present La Fonda Restaurant, and its sister mission El Descanso, just south of the Cantamar sand dunes. How is it then that the Calafia Resort, a few miles to the north, claims that it too was an historic mission site and besides that, also the boundary between the United States and Mexico?

Their historic claims are true, but there was never actually a mission building on the site. Punta Descanso, upon which now rests the delightful and dramatic Calafia Resort, was the northern parish limit of El Descanso/San Miguel missions and also served as the official boundary separating the Dominican Order to the south and the Franciscans to the north.

This Dominican-Franciscan boundary was also designated in 1777 to separate the New Spain provinces of Alta and Baja California.

The current international border between Baja California and the U.S. state of California was moved farther north as a result of the 1848 Treaty of Guadalupe Hidalgo, which ceded Alta California to the U.S.

A link between the Californias

Franciscan Padre Francisco Palóu, who succeeded Padre Junípero Serra in Baja, had by the early 1770s delivered the northern missions to the Dominican Order, but over the next decade they had not established many new missions. The King of Spain wanted a link between the two Californias and had given orders to the Dominicans to proceed immediately and create whatever was necessary to forge that link.

So in 1787 Dominican Padre Luis Sales established Mission San Miguel Arcangel de la Frontera (St. Michael Archangel of the Border). The area about 14 miles south of Calafia is now called La Misión.

The mesa upon which the San Miguel Mission was built was an old Indian site and currently houses a school. (A cyclone fence in the center of the schoolyard now protects the mission ruins from the children).

The school is just inland on the old road south of La Fonda Restaurant. It is just past the estuary at the base of the steep hill, on the left side. Behind the school a huge cross has been erected to commemorate the site.

In 1817, floods in the San Miguel Valley forced the mission to move five leagues north to El Descanso, where Padre Tomás de Ahumada then established El Descanso Mission (about 12 miles south of Rosarito Beach). El Descanso was so interlinked with San Miguel that for a while it was called Nueva [New] Misión de San Miguel; the same padres administered both congregations, changing the base of operation from one to another.

The El Descanso missionaries used the Punta Descanso (Descanso Point, which now houses Calafia) as their northern boundary, and that's what created its historical significance.

In 1938 the Acevedo family moved to Punta Descanso. In 1959 they constructed the Calafia Villa, a private residence, on the historic barren point, and in 1964 opened an adjoining tourist camp. In 1974, they opened their restaurant by expanding part of their residence.

In 1984, partners Gordon West and Francisco Araujo, who developed Las Gaviotas, began to develop Club Calafia, a community of timeshares and condos, on the site.

The Calafia owners have been adding on and making improvements ever since and have welcomed more than a million visitors through the years.

A marketing genius

The marketing genius of the owners of Calafia, now run by Conrado Acevedo Cárdenas, is impressive. They have capitalized on the significance of their point, and by reconstructing replicas of several missions and sprinkling the area with artifacts, they suggest that the Punta Descanso is of more significance than it really is.

They even built an old ship into the rocks below the point, causing some wags to wonder about its significance. Maybe people might believe that Columbus actually made landfall along the Baja coast.

Regardless, the ship, named the *Corona Aurora Galleon*, has become part of an alfresco dance floor called Club 1773, reflecting the year when Padre Palóu helped establish the border. With terraced tables overlooking the crowded dance floor and the crashing surf, it is one of Baja's most romantic settings.

The Calafia Hotel and Suites has become an Historical and Cultural Center and is the official headquarters of the Historical Society of Rosarito Beach, as well as the Association of Writers of Tijuana and other Baja California organizations. It also houses an extension campus of the university, and features a conference center with an Oriental meditation pavilion in a garden overlooking the ocean.

Calafia has replicas and artifacts from the mission days and copies of mesoamerican anthropological art, including drawings of original cave paintings found in Baja.

There is a wedding chapel called *Cristo del Mar* (Christ of the Sea) at Calafia, along with a reception area in a dramatic setting on the Punta Descanso bluff.

Smashing views from everywhere

There are smashing views from everywhere at Calafia. You can sit out on the quiet deck at night and watching frothy white waves erupting from the dark ocean and crashing onto the rocks below. Several of the hotel rooms and suites share the view, where from your bed you look out over the horizon.

Most popular is the Sea Gull Restaurant, a terraced restaurant right on the edge of the rocks. It's one of those few places with righteously awesome ambience and atmosphere that also boast very good food. If it's a night out you want, by dining at Calafia you can save the moderate cover charge at the dance floor, which is reached by a separate entrance. Hotel rooms include the cover charge, as well as free breakfasts and welcome margaritas.

When you look out at the ocean from anywhere at Calafia, it's easy to think back over 220 years and realize that Descanso Point is not only beautiful, but also historic. Plus, during the season you'll probably see gray whales heading south.

PUERTO NUEVO RESTAURANTS

Lobster, Baja Style

Locals in the area have watched it grow into a real tourist destination for those seeking what has become the "signature" Baja meal. It's not the place for steak, chicken, ribs, or quiche. It's a lobster (*langosta*) village, and lobster is king. Virtually unknown to outsiders just two decades ago, Baja's Puerto Nuevo (Newport) is now more popular than the surrounding communities.

The busy village boasts approximately 35 restaurants lining four block-long streets on an ocean bluff about 11 miles south of Rosarito Beach (one mile north of Cantamar). Puerto Nuevo seems to grow a little bit each summer, a new restaurant here, a large curio shop there, another road paved. Tourists these days are bussed in from hotels in Rosarito Beach and as far away as San Diego. Charter busses bring in squeaky-clean groups of tourists for the "Baja culinary experience." Parking on summer weekends is at a premium.

The town got its start in a tiny cove where a trail drops down from modest fishermen's dwellings between the restaurants and the sparkling sea. This cove allows fishermen to penetrate the surf with shallow *pangas* and fish the area. About 50 years ago several families of fishermen from Lake Chapala in Jalisco relocated there and began a modest fishing enterprise.

The plentiful succulent California spiny lobster in the area lured the fishermen to set traps. Aside from supplying local restaurants and markets with their catch, the fishermen would sell lobster and fish directly to tourists and locals alike.

In the mid-1950s the first modest restaurant opened. By 1970 several of the families had set up tables in their living rooms and the term "Puerto Nuevo style" was born. "Papa" passed the freshly severed lobster halves through the kitchen window to be cooked while guests gathered round to watch.

Grab your own sodas

In those early days, the customers actually felt like members of an extended family and just went in the kitchen and grabbed sodas or beers out of the family refrigerator. Before the guests left, the owners would simply tally up the number of empty bottles on the table, a practice many restaurants still employ.

Even today the basic meal is almost the same in each restaurant: two halves of *Langosta* fried in lard (now also boiled or grilled), mouth-watering hot, home-made flour tortillas, beans, rice, butter, salsa, chips, and limes, all served family style. Some restaurants include a tortilla soup or salad, others a guacamole dip, and others a margarita included in the package lobster dinner price.

Mariachi music wafts through the now-cobbled and paved streets as musicians stroll from restaurant to restaurant along with purveyors of freshly cut flowers and trinkets made of seashells.

For decades Puerto Nuevo was hard to find. Even giving directions was cryptic. We used to tell people, "About a quarter mile south of El Pescador restaurant, you'll see an old white building with a 7-Up bottle painted on it; turn down the dirt road next to that building. Stop at the first house on the left and knock on the door; it's really a restaurant. If they're out of lobster or too busy, go to the second house."

Interestingly, the place was named for a cigarette. Back in the early days, there was also a huge sign advertising Newport cigarettes near the village entrance. So people began calling the place "Newport." The name stuck and soon, the Spanish version "Puerto Nuevo" began to replace its English equivalent.

A big demand for lobster

By the late '70s, demand outpaced the supply. Long lines formed at restaurants not "sold out." Many people were turned away, no lobster to be had. Now the village imports most of its lobster.

Today the restaurants run the gamut from a few tables in a modest house to beautiful marble and tile three-story extravaganzas. The meals are fairly consistent, with many places also offering mixed drinks in addition to beer and sodas. The broader menus now even include steak.

Most people in the village are related. Brothers, sisters, cousins, and in-laws may all own restaurants on the same street. The Ortega family (Juan and Petra and their 10 children) was one of the first to offer home serving in the mid-1950s and now boasts five Puerto Nuevo restaurants and two in Rosarito Beach, further spreading the "Puerto Nuevo style" fame. Prices have risen at all of the restaurants over the years, but still remain about half of most stateside prices. Smaller places on the side streets usually have the best buys, and the quality is the same or better.

The busloads and carloads of tourists that make for busy weekends at Puerto Nuevo now call for a different strategy. Do like a lot of the Mexicans and eat your main meal earlier in the day. Go during the week. Go only before Memorial Day and after Labor Day. Today Puerto Nuevo is a far cry from the days when we used to give directions based on a well-placed 7-Up sign.

Take the free (*libre*) road 11 miles south from Rosarito Beach. From the toll road, there is a marked "Puerto Nuevo" turnoff in about 10 miles. Or you can take the *Cantamar* turnoff and go north on the old road one mile. Puerto Nuevo is now well identified, with a welcoming arch; highway bus stop; neon signs; modern buildings; throngs of cars, busses, and tourists; and numerous curio shops.

Puerto Nuevo is more than eating a dinner out. It can be a complete Baja experience: the succulent food, strolling mariachis, vendors and purveyors of trinkets and curios, a bustling village, and killer sunsets over the sparkling blue Pacific.

La Fonda

Romantic Getaway on Baja Bluff

La Fonda, which bills itself as "The Most Beautiful Place on the Coast," certainly can boast one of the most memorable and romantic settings. It's an old Mexican inn perched on a verdant brush-covered cliff overlooking a broad, sandy beach where dolphins frolic offshore and whales can be seen in winter. It's an old tile patio where tables half-hidden behind dense potted palms, thick banana trees, and flowering magenta bougainvillea are shaded with thatch umbrellas, providing a frame for dynamite views of dramatic sunsets.

That outside patio on the beachfront bluff 37 miles south of the border (19 miles south of Rosarito) is the crowning glory of La Fonda, which is why it fills up quickly for breakfast. They have a wide variety of choices, including *huevos rancheros* and an excellent *machaca* (dried beef or chicken) *con huevos* (with eggs).

The restaurant inside is perfect for cooler evenings. A rip-roaring fire in the fireplace and dancing to live music make it a fun place to be.

Originally the land on the bluff near the mouth of the La Misión Valley was part of the Mission San Miguel Arcangel de la Frontera. After the mission lands were secularized in the early 19th century, an American of Irish descent, one Felipe Crosswaithe (whose progeny is found throughout the Rosarito Beach area) purchased the land. He married a Mexican woman and ranched in the fertile valley.

Many years later, John Stocker bought a lot of the beachfront property in La Misión from the Crosswaithe descendants. Stocker was well known to many Hollywood

La Fonda Restaurant

celebrities. According to his daughter Druanne, she even remembers Clark Gable coming down to go duck hunting with him.

Stocker married several times, but it was his wife Eve, a New York socialite, who would eventually establish La Fonda. After Eve and John divorced, Eve Stocker continued to live in the La Misión area in her beautiful little hideaway known as Eve's Garden.

Wanting to bring a little class to the area, Eve built and developed La Fonda in 1962. It is said that she was a demanding proprietor, insisting that the waiters wear white gloves and constantly checking and rechecking the kitchen and dining room.

Current owners Sara and Orest Dmytriw bought the place in 1975 and made many improvements to the popular retreat. It was a small, intimate restaurant with a few hotel rooms and 16 employees when the Dmytriws took over. Today La Fonda provides employment to 100 local people and features 26 guest rooms.

No two hotel rooms are alike. There are suites and rooms with private balconies and kitchens and/or sunken fireplaces and big tubs. The rooms all peek out of the foliage for dramatic views of the ocean.

The Old Mexico feeling is everywhere, from the cobblestone parking out front, to the tile throughout to the broad, sweeping window views, to the tropical plants and thatched patio.

People from southern California who like to spend hideaway weekends at La Fonda usually reserve the treat for a special occasion. Many from Hollywood have discovered the charm of Old Mexico just down the coast from the border. Eva Gabor spent her honeymoon at La Fonda, in #14, the Gold Room. Frank Sinatra, Phil Harris, and Bob Crosby have also reputedly been among the legions of customers of the romantic inn on the bluff.

Local expatriates along the Gold Coast are very loyal La Fonda customers. And with reason. The host Orest Dmytriw, whom everyone knows only as "Dimitri," has a knack for making his customers feel special. He has a warm, "Hey, good to see you again. How have you been?" greeting to friends old and new. He makes your first-time guests think that the two of you go way back, even if he can't quite recall your name.

Dimitri's personal charm and his and Sara's dedication to preserving the charm and vision begun by Eve Stocker are integral to the success of La Fonda. Not only have the customers been loyal, so has the staff. Some of the waiters have worked there for decades and are in the habit of warmly greeting the customers they have come to know.

GUADALUPE ISLAND

Chinese and Russians Hunt Fur Seals

Mexico's Guadalupe Island, 80 lava-capped square miles rising out of the ocean about 240 miles south of San Diego, has attracted its share of adventurers throughout the years. The island's visitors have included Russian and native Alaskan seal hunters, Chinese oyster fishermen, American whalers, and others. While these days long-range sportfishing draws primarily Americans to Guadalupe, early 19th-century visitors had different agendas, almost destroying the native habitat.

The Russians, after decimating vast populations of sea otters from northern waters, sent Aleut hunters south from Alaska seeking California fur seals. They virtually wiped out the fur seal population along the way, eventually ending up at Guadalupe Island.

They were not alone. It is on record that shortly after the turn of the 19th century, American vessels were harvesting fur seals at Guadalupe Island. In fact, Captain Charles Scammon, who was known for decimating much of the California gray whale population, also got into the act and wiped out many elephant seals, even writing about it in *Overland Monthly* in 1870. The Americans were soon joined by seamen from other countries. Unhampered for years, the slaughter of fur seals went on and on without any regard toward the annihilation of the species.

Chinese divers also went to Guadalupe, harvesting oysters out of their junks. They also got into the act of taking many fur seals, not only at Guadalupe, but also at the Los Coronados islands closer to shore.

The many caves and nooks and crannies around Baja's rocky Guadalupe Island saved the fur seals from total extinction. A small colony was finally spotted there in 1926–27 and two bulls were taken for the San Diego Zoo.

Guadalupe Island was also one of the last holdouts for the elephant seals. They too were being slaughtered until in 1922, following a joint U.S.-Mexican expedition, Mexico's President Alvaro Obregón declared the island a reservation and banned the killing and molesting of elephant seals. A small colony of elephant seals also endured, suggesting that in Baja, even on the islands, the hardy have somehow learned to survive.

Los Coronados

Smugglers Hid on Offshore Islands

The Coronados, being only 18 miles from San Diego, are about the most accessible islands on Baja's Pacific side. The word "legend" could have been coined to define them. From the toll road between the border and Rosarito Beach they loom just a few miles offshore, glistening in the morning sun and beckoning imaginations to reveal their mysterious past.

History indicates that because of the lack of fresh water, no Indians ever lived permanently there. Only one Indian shell midden has been discovered, probably left by visitors seeking fish or lobster.

When the Portolá-Serra land expedition saw them in 1769, they recognized them from earlier records by Cabrillo and Vizcaíno and figured correctly that they were just eight leagues from their destination of San Diego.

Pirates did stop by, and one old legend has it that a pirate named José Arváez used Pirates Cove (also called Smugglers Cove) as a base of operations. He allegedly killed the crew of a British ship, the *Chelsea*, but he and his men were caught when they returned to their cove and hung from the yardarm of their own schooner.

In 1911, a group of 10 Chinese were stranded there by two San Diego smugglers, who never returned to pick them up. They were starving and delirious when spotted by some fishermen. Food and water were thrown to them, but due to political implications they were not picked up for some time. After the ordeal, they returned to Ensenada where they started.

Various people tried to make a go of living on the Coronados. A robust woman called "Crawfish Jake" ran a small eating house at Smugglers Cove, catching, cooking, and serving lobster to boaters who went ashore.

One Manuel Aguilar lived alone on the North Coronado catching lobsters. A small boat from Ensenada picked up his lobsters and brought him water and other supplies. Then one time they didn't show for two weeks, so he had to row his small boat all the way to San Diego. The dependency that almost cost him his life was not for him. He never went back.

Gambling brought speculators to South Coronado Island. With prohibition in the U.S., Mexico's casinos were flourishing in Rosarito Beach and Ensenada, so an elaborate two-story gambling casino and hotel was constructed on the rocky cliffs. Their timing couldn't have been worse, however, because before it got up and running, Mexico clamped down on casino-style gambling.

Abandoned and forlorn, it later housed soldiers based on the rocky island. Their water and provisions were shipped out to them.

Today, the islands are visited regularly by divers and snorkelers, along with fishermen. "Pukey Point" on the north end of North Coronado has rough currents and is for more experienced divers. Easier are the "Lobster Shack," a cove on the east side, and "McDonalds," an arch at the south end of North Coronado.

Rosarito Beach officials have in recent years been speculating on ways to somehow use the island as a tourist attraction. That would be nice, as long as they remember to take drinking water out for visitors.

Steve McQueen Sought Cancer Cure

On the bluff a mile or so north of La Fonda Restaurant are what appear to be pre-Columbian statues and a pyramid resembling a Mayan temple. The replicas, on a slight hill next to the Plaza Del Mar resort, were constructed not a millennium ago, but in 1975.

The place was originally a clinic, more specifically a laetrile clinic, where cancer patients could make one final attempt to find a cure after all other avenues had been exhausted. Not legal in the United States, the controversial treatment still attracted those with but a few strands of hope remaining.

One early patient was the popular actor Steve McQueen. Born in Indiana in 1930, McQueen starred in *Great Escape*, *The Sand Pebbles* (for which he received an Academy Award nomination), *Bullitt* (in which he met his wife Ali McGraw), *Papillon*, and others.

From a troubled youth, McQueen served in the U.S. Marines and always enjoyed living life to the fullest, riding motorcycles and racing cars. He became the highest paid and most popular movie star of the '60s and '70s.

By 1980, McQueen had contracted mesothelioma, a rare and painful form of lung cancer. One of the main causes is asbestos, a substance the actor had been around much of his life.

In fact, while in the Aleutian Islands with the Marine Corps, McQueen had been sentenced to six weeks in the brig, where he was assigned a work detail in the engine room of a ship. He had to rip out and replace the asbestos linings on the pipes. He later complained that the air was so thick with asbestos particles that the men could hardly breathe.

By the time the cancer is detectable, the patient usually has just months to live.

After being told his condition was inoperable, he went to Baja and underwent a three-month crash program at what was then called the American Biologics-Mexico SA Medical Center. At Plaza Del Mar, McQueen was housed in a doublewide trailer near the bluff top. Some of the old-timers there can show visitors the exact trailer.

His treatment included the powerful B-17, or laetrile, animal cell injections, over 100 vitamin pills a day, diet, and exercise. Unfortunately, it did him little good. While laetrile clinics have had some anecdotal successes reported, there has been little documented evidence to those claims.

McQueen's condition deteriorated, and he left the Plaza Del Mar for a clinic in another part of Mexico. There he died on Nov. 7, 1980 at age 50 after undergoing surgery to remove a tumor. He was cremated, and his ashes were scattered in the Pacific Ocean.

The Plaza Del Mar has been a hotel with tennis courts, swimming pool, restaurant, and bar. Twice it has been a clinic. The statues out front look hundreds of years old, and the temple, which has been recently repainted, looks like the Mayan Chichén Itzá.

The Plaza Del Mar doesn't contain the history the artifacts suggest it might. But it is the place where actor Steve McQueen tried to save his life.

Chapter 8: The Ensenada Bay Area

THE RUSSIANS OF GUADALUPE VALLEY

Milk Drinkers in Wine Country

Various groups of foreigners have attempted to settle in Baja California, but perhaps none has piqued more interest than the colony of Russians who relocated to the Guadalupe Valley north of Ensenada.

The curious settlement started a century ago in Kars, Russia (now Turkey) where a religious group which called themselves Molokans (milk drinkers) split from the official church of Russia at the time, the Eastern or Greek Orthodox Christians. The Molokans followed strictly their interpretation of the laws of Moses, abstaining from pork, tobacco, and alcohol. They interpreted the term "spiritual milk" noted in the Bible to mean they should receive much of their nourishment from milk and dairy products.

Not their diet, but their conviction as conscientious objectors, got them into trouble with Czar Nicholas II. The pacifist Molokans refused to serve in the military, and with a war going on, they found it prudent to seek a more mellow climate.

So they moved to California, some to the northern part of the state, but most settling around Los Angeles. This rural group, however, found a big-city environment unsuitable for farming and had to look elsewhere.

Their prayers were answered in 1905, as Mexican President Porfirio Díaz agreed to sell the sect 13,000 acres of lush, productive land in Baja California's Guadalupe Valley. Signing on behalf of the approximate 500 settlers in 105 families were Simón Babichoff, Basilio Pivovaroff, and Basilio Tolmasoff. Leadership of the sect fell into the hands of Moisés Samaduroff.

The Russian settlers laid out their town the way they had at home, equally partitioned lots along a broad tree-covered avenue. The front doors of their whitewashed adobe and wood homes, with steep-pitched wooden (some thatched) roofs, faced away from the street.

They set out to plant grains, vegetables, olives, and grapes and raised geese and honeybees. Their homes had basements for storing their jams and preserves and honey. They baked an excellent Russian bread and drank tea or "chai" made in the samovar. The main dish was borscht, which they made with meat and vegetables and stirred with wooden spoons.

Russian gravestone in Guadalupe Valley.

The Molokans worked hard and prayed hard. They dressed simply; the women covered their heads with homemade *kosinkas* or shawls, and the bearded men wore high-collared shirts called *rubajas* which had drawstrings around the waist.

They became splendid citizens of Mexico, and while they spoke Russian in church and at home, were ever loyal to their adopted country. It is said that Russian-born Mary Rogoff, while she had only a third-grade education, delivered over 1,000 babies in the valley.

It wasn't long before non-Russians began arriving in the valley and the fledgling viniculture of the area, along with cattle ranching and other farming, had begun.

In 1938 the populist Mexican President Cárdenas designated lands for the peasants of Mexico. Guadalupe was engulfed by 3,000 Mexicans and the town was renamed Francisco Zarco. Many Russians left at that time. Others stayed and over time have assimilated into the culture.

Plentiful water in an attractive valley

The beautiful and fertile Guadalupe Valley has long been an attraction for settlers. The Kumeyaay Indians, who had been in the area for thousands of years, found the plentiful water and the flora and fauna to their liking. They called the place Oja Cuñurr, or Painted Caves, alluding to some crude rock art found in nearby rock outcroppings. The paintings have since been destroyed, but the rich, lush rolling hills dappled by mountain oaks made the valley attractive to all who came through it.

Baja's last mission was established in Guadalupe Valley in 1834. In fact, the mission was referred to as the peninsula's most prosperous and powerful, with over 400 Indians, 4,915 head of cattle, and fertile fields fed by an intricate irrigation system. But it had the shortest life of all the missions, as in 1840, the leader of the Nesi Indians, Jatñil, didn't like the forced conversion of his people and led a successful revolt against the mission, chasing the padres out of the valley. It is said that Padre Félix Caballero fled, leaving most of the mission's livestock.

On a trip to Guadalupe a couple of years ago, meeting some Russian descendants was a bonus. The wineries of Baja California drew me there. While I no longer drink wine, I'd written an article about the wineries of Baja California and needed photos.

Most of Baja's wineries, including Santo Tomás, L.A. Cetto, Domecq, Mogor-Baden, and Monte Xanic, are in the Guadalupe Valley some 20 miles or so northeast of Ensenada on Highway 3.

Coming from the north, rather than backtracking from Ensenada, it's easier to take the graded road off the old (libre) Highway 1, about 12 miles south of La Misión.

I'd driven that dirt road several times before, continually delighting in the trim ranches; fertile farms; numerous orchards with straight rows of peach, apricot, and olive trees; the gnarled stumps of the vineyards; and the bright multihued flower fields along the way.

While I'd heard of the Russians who had settled there, I was usually searching for something else, like this trip's wineries. Other times it was to follow the route of the gold miners who went through Guadalupe in the 1870s and 1880s, or to visit the remains of the old mission.

This time we saw the sign "Museo Comunitario 'Valle de Guadalupe' Tel: (615) 5-20-30" nailed to a huge eucalyptus tree in front of a white block house with a steep roof that looked incongruous in the Baja sunshine. [*Museo Comunitario del Valle de Guadalupe is about one and one half miles west of Highway #3 off the main road in Guadalupe, on the road to Francisco Zarco. Open Wed.–Sun., 9–4, Donations accepted.*]

The museum consists of a couple of rooms; we entered to discover an old world heritage proudly displayed in a new world setting. We were enthralled by the old photos and Russian artifacts, including a photo of Molokan leader Moisés Samaduroff with the Mexican President. We were enraptured by the charm of our hostess, Francisca Samarin, herself a Molokan Russian descendant.

According to her, "Today there are only 20 pure Russians left in the Guadalupe Valley, but," she added with a grin, "there are about 240 of us with mixed blood." While Señora Samarin showed us around, a couple of light-haired, light-eyed children played at her feet.

Around back was a special room, the sauna. Like many others in the community, it was a small room with heated stones in a platform in one corner. Pouring water on the red-hot stones causes their bodies to perspire like they'd entered the gates of hell.

Construction was going on in one room. "This we hope to turn into a restaurant," she said. "We want to serve traditional Russian food like our ancestors used to make."

Later, we drove over to the old Russian cemetery, where headstones inscribed in Cyrillic script attest to the legend of the Russian colony of milk drinkers, who found their peace so far away from home.

That the area is surrounded by Mexico's top wineries is further proof that Baja has something for everyone.

An early view of the Hotel Riviera

LEGEND OF THE RIVIERA

Jack Dempsey's Ensenada Casino

The large white castle on the Ensenada beach, a hybrid of Spanish- and Moorish-style architecture, has long been a focal point for visitors. For years the dominant Riviera Hotel has dwarfed the other buildings in Baja's picturesque fishing village, and like most imposing structures, it is filled with history and intrigue.

Known today simply as the Riviera, the Hotel Playa Ensenada, as it was known then, opened on Oct. 31, 1930, an elegant hotel with a gambling casino said to rival that of Monte Carlo. To help attract the Hollywood and international set to Ensenada, world famous heavyweight boxer Jack Dempsey, one of the most recognizable names on the planet at the time, became part of the developing corporation. A huge villa was even built for Dempsey just to the south of the main building. It was rumored that gangster Al Capone was one of the corporation's silent partners.

Work had begun on the Riviera in 1928, two years before the opening, by James L. Miller, contractor. The elaborate building's architect was Gordon E. Mayer. And, with its tile roof and wondrous gardens, the inspiration was purely Hearst Castle, a similar-looking structure built earlier about 400 or so miles up the coast.

Big names in Ensenada

During the early 1930s, the hotel flourished, attracting not only the Hollywood crowd but royalty as well. The opening act in the hotel ballroom was Bing Crosby, accompanied by the Xavier Cugat Orchestra.

A local Latin singer named Margarita Cansino, who would later find fame in Hollywood as Rita Hayworth, sang and danced at the Hotel Playa Ensenada. She and her father also entertained the tourists at the Agua Caliente Casino in Tijuana.

When prohibition was finally repealed in the United States in 1933, attendance started waning as fun-seekers no longer had to leave the country. But the final death knell came five years after that, when Mexico outlawed casino gambling in 1938. The place closed down.

The beautiful building sat vacant until 1941 when it was used by the military. In 1942 a newly renamed Riviera del Pacífico reopened under the management of Jerome Hutley and Margarita Plant. The hotel fell victim to the times, a white elephant that had lost its major attractions and never really took off, closing its doors in 1948.

While there were several openings and closings under the name Riviera del Pacífico, the huge building eventually fell into disrepair. By the 1960s squatters had occupied the formerly opulent Dempsey Villa, by then windowless, doorless, and stripped of furnishings.

During the 1960s it floundered, and by the '70s a group that wanted to destroy the building had organized and if nothing else, caught people's attention. The Mexican federal government stepped in and began restoration in 1978. A couple of years later the state of Baja California took over and completed the restoration.

The Riviera Cultural Center of Ensenada

For the past 22 years the Riviera has been known as the Centro Cultural Riviera de Ensenada, or the Riviera Cultural Center of Ensenada. And it is used by the people of Ensenada, dispensing knowledge and art and pride to a degree much more beneficial to a society than one-armed bandits fleecing tourists from another country.

The people use the Riviera Cultural Center. Once while attending a seafood competition among the area's restaurants, I wandered the ornate hallways, replete with inlaid tile, gorgeous chandeliers, painted ceilings, and beautiful murals. The three courtyards, with potted geraniums and bright billowing bougainvilleas, are refreshing and restful. The compact, timeless Bar Andaluz off one courtyard is a hideaway respite.

Nowadays the cruise ships that make Ensenada a port of call offer excursions to the Riviera, and freshly-scrubbed tourists wander the courtyards looking for bargains among the displays of local artists and vendors.

One wing of the Riviera has a library with textbooks, history books, and novels. People studying or poring over old books are seemingly always in evidence, and late one evening I noted a chess club had commandeered the library for some head-to-head matches.

Above the library is the museum, el Museo de Historia de Ensenada, which features the history of Baja California and some of the finest photographs of the Baja missions I've ever seen. Open from 9 a.m. to 5 p.m. Tuesday through Sunday, the museum takes viewers from the indigenous peoples through the conquest and colonization of Baja

California. It's a small but wonderful exhibit and is well worth the minimal fee.

A Convention Center by the Sea

The greater part of the building is reserved for weddings, parties, and conventions. The Riviera has been home to both national and international conventions, bringing added importance to the former fishing village.

There's always some type of event happening at the Riviera. A recent visit showed posters for upcoming events: Fiesta Viva from Oct. 13 to 17, a concert featuring the Mexican soprano Ivette Pérez Mazón, the Festival de Atún (Tuna Festival) on October 17 (benefiting the Cancer Association of Baja California), a poets' conference, and a song festival.

Much of the building is used for various classes. There are classes for kids, as well as classes for adults on how to raise kids. Budding ballet stars and artists and folkloric dancers come and go all afternoon. Cars pull up to the side entrance to drop off their children in tutus and regional dance costumes. There's an ongoing cultural tapestry being painted these days at the Riviera.

My family used to camp down the beach from the Riviera during the 1940s, and I used to look at the building in awe, knowing it had to be for rich people. It turned out those childhood dreams were accurate. But the richness is far more substantial than the surface glitter for which it was originally intended. It took a while, but the Riviera has realized its dreams of wealth with its vast richness of culture and art and history.

HUSSONG'S BAR, ENSENADA

The Bar From 1892

Ensenada's famous Hussong's Bar, founded in 1892, has changed little over the years, still ensconced mid-block in an old yellowing clapboard building on Avenida Ruiz.

This landmark attraction, which became Baja's most famous watering hole, was established by German immigrant Johan Hussong back when Ensenada's non-Mexican population of gold miners, settlers, and adventurers was in the majority. Johan's son Juan Hussong ran the place for many years, and now yet another generation is in charge, with Ricardo Hussong the current owner and manager.

On busy weekends for many decades you'd see a crowd outside the old tavern as soon as you turned the corner from Ensenada's main drag onto Avenida Ruiz. It was usually so crowded that a continuous line formed. Police at the door not only had to "card" drinkers, but only allowed a few people in at a time, when a like number decided to leave.

You often heard the noise and revelry from Hussong's before you actually spotted the old place. Inside it was loud and raucous, with boisterous conversation and laughter often punctuated by enthusiastic whooping and chanting, energetic yelling, and plain old, unruly, alcohol-induced clamor.

Margaritas were not only rock-bottom cheap but extremely potent. Beer was

Hussong's in the 1930s.

inexpensive, and they served "Sol" brand in the clear bottle. Of course, that was before they came out with their own brand of "Hussong's" beer.

In fact, Hussong's seems to have its name on everything. An official outlet store for their merchandise is now next door. There are other Hussong's stores as well, in the mini-mall on the corner where the gas station used to be, and one farther down on the main street. You can buy the Hussong's name on everything from caps and T-shirts to ashtrays and swizzle sticks.

There used to be a roving artist in Hussong's who painted charcoal sketches of customers. During my single years in the mid-1970s, I had one done and donated it to grace Hussong's wall with a few others. They hung my portrait right by the front entrance. It was fun taking unwary dates and guests in there and having them spot my likeness on the wall.

For drinkers, I would have to rate Hussong's right up there with the Holy Grail. It's loud and raucous; there is more beer spilled in the place in one day than many bars sell all weekend.

These days nearby competition has quieted Hussong's down just a bit. For one thing, the two-story Papas and Beer restaurant across the street is so much larger and has much more to offer. While it's not for everybody, Hussong's is still the classic bar and most definitely a true Baja Legend with a capital "L" — and has been for well over 100 years.

The Legend of Treasure Island

One Baja legend that endures is that Robert Louis Stevenson was inspired by the Todos Santos Islands and wrote much of his famous book *Treasure Island* in Ensenada. Unfortunately, it too is another Baja myth.

Indeed, there is no evidence that the famous Scottish author ever visited Baja California. He did live in northern California for a while before going to Samoa, where he died on Dec. 3, 1894. The sickly Stevenson lived for a time in Monterey, California and even got married in foggy San Francisco, but moved to the sunnier Napa Valley for his health.

The inspiration for Stevenson to write *Treasure Island* came from seeing a child's map, drawn from imagination, in a Scottish cottage. His fertile mind was also admittedly inspired somewhat by Daniel Defoe and Washington Irving. The speculation as to the supposed model of the island itself runs from islands off Puerto Rico and Cuba to the Shetland Islands. It is even said that the wild coastline around Monterey definitely had an influence, but that's a long way from Baja.

The Baja connection came about when Stevenson's widow, Fanny Stevenson, moved to La Jolla, California in 1904. Finding it too cold for her there, she, her maid, and others joined mining engineer George Brown on Baja's Cedros Island and lived there for three restful months. On her return trip she leased a small ranch house in El Sauzal, six miles north of Ensenada, where she and others lived for almost two years.

Over 25 years later an East Coast journalist was in Ensenada and came across old lease papers signed by Mrs. Robert Louis Stevenson and assorted papers written by members of Mrs. Stevenson's party. Thinking she had a real scoop, the reporter thought she had unpublished works by the famous author and also incorrectly assumed that the islands poking up across the bay were Stevenson's inspiration.

It seems like people everywhere want their islands to be the model for *Treasure Island*. Unfortunately, they weren't Baja islands.

A Culinary Legend

The El Rey Sol appears to be an anomaly, a fine, serene, and sedate French restaurant with a menu that includes duck aux "Beaux Arts" and grilled salmon with champagne sauce, just steps from fish taco stands and vendors of blankets and trinkets and tacky T-shirts.

Ensenada's El Rey Sol restaurant is now a culinary institution, having celebrated its 50th Anniversary a couple of years ago. Spanish for "The Sun King" (*Le Roi Soleil* in French), it was a popular title given to France's King Louis XIV. El Rey Sol opened its doors on May 23, 1947 as a modest 10-table restaurant on Ocean Blvd. at Calle

Primera y Blancarte.

The founding force was Virginia (Doña Pepita) Geffroy de Bitterlin, daughter of a French engineer working at the Santa Rosalía Boleo copper mine in Baja California Sur Territory and his Mexican bride, Refugio (Cuca) Pozo, from Mulegé, 43 miles south of Santa Rosalía, where Pepita was born on Mar. 17, 1910.

In 1920 the Geffroy children were sent to France to live with relatives, where they stayed until they made French marriages. Doña Pepita remained abroad for 18 years, during which time she married the French artist Jacques Bitterlin and gave birth to her first child, Jacqueline. Two daughters and a son were later born in Mexico.

While in France, Doña Pepita became interested in cooking and delighted her sisters, cousins, and aunts with delectable repasts from her kitchen. She took classes in French cuisine at the famed Cordon Bleu cooking school in Paris. She experimented with inventions of her own and gradually became a very fine chef.

By the 1940s the copper mine at Santa Rosalía had declined, so Pepita followed her sister to the Baja California port town of Ensenada. Her sister Mayo and husband Gastón Flourie, along with some others, had founded a new motel there, the Motel Casa Del Sol, on the town's sandy thoroughfare. Pepita was encouraged to develop a restaurant in the new motel, and El Rey Sol was born.

The décor of the original restaurant was done by Jacques Bitterlin, by this time a professor at the Universidad Autónoma de Baja California and one of the principal artists of the peninsula.

The family established Rancho Las Animas in the Santo Tomás area, where to this day, fresh herbs, fruits, and vegetables are grown for the restaurant.

The establishment prospered under the day-to-day attention of the family members, including Pepita's mother, Doña Cuca, who provided personal attention to the clientele.

A hit from the beginning

The eatery was a hit from the beginning. The 1953 book *Baja California* by Ralph Hancock, Ray Haller, Mike McMahan, and Frank Alvarado states: "Restaurant El Rey Sol is in the latter motel [Casa Del Sol]. It is reputed to be one of the best in town, serves French, American, and Mexican food and advertises a specialty or two: lobster a la cardinal, coquilles Saint Jacques, *vol-au-vent* and filet mignon."

In just a few years the restaurant was forced to move to larger quarters across the street, its present site on Ave. López Mateos and Ave. Blancarte.

Pepita trained Cándido Pacheco, an Ensenada farm boy, and discovered he had a natural flair for cooking. For over 35 years, Candido and his two brothers have presided over the kitchen at El Rey Sol.

Employee loyalty at the family-run restaurant is evident from the fact that at the 50-year anniversary, 12 employees had been at El Rey Sol for 25 or more years, and one waitress, Aldegunda Beltrán, had retired with 45 years of service.

The restaurant celebrated its 25th anniversary with another expansion in 1972. The contemporary Mediterranean redesign now offers seating for 240 and features two elegant and intimate banquet rooms and a modern stainless steel kitchen. The main dining room has plates and copper pans hanging from thick beams overhead.

The thick, padded wallpaper and stained glass windows, complete with the French fleur de lis, lends the restaurant an old-world ambience. Cushioned footstools repose nearby and freshly cut roses enhance every table. The restaurant's extensive wine list features primarily local, Ensenada-grown vintages.

A host of awards

El Rey Sol began garnering a host of culinary awards and honors, including the coveted Grand Mexican Award in 1981, 1983, 1986, 1988, and 1989. It became the only restaurant in North America to win the award five times. In 1996, owner Jean-Loup Bitterlin, Pepita's son and current proprietor, was summoned to Madrid, Spain, to accept the Gran Collar de Oro (Grand Collar of Gold) award, one of only 11 restaurants in the world to receive the honor.

With the recognition came a host of luminaries to dine there. Six Mexican presidents have sampled the French cuisine in the humble port city of Ensenada. On my last visit, my waiter, Marco, recalled greeting four of them: José López Portillo, Miguel de la Madrid, Carlos Salinas, and Ernesto Zedillo.

Other international celebrities who have dined at El Rey Sol include John Wayne, James Garner, Anthony Quinn, Jacques Cousteau, Mario "Cantinflas" Moreno, Hulk Hogan, two Miss Universes, and Vikki Carr (who also headlined the restaurant's 40th anniversary banquet and concert). When James Cameron's blockbuster movie *Titanic* was being filmed up the coast at the Fox Baja Studio, numerous cast members enjoyed the El Rey Sol experience.

The oldest French restaurant in all of Mexico has established a nonprofit foundation to give to the community in the form of the Don Bosco Ciudad de los Niños orphanage. After establishing the fund, Virginia "Pepita" Geffroy passed away in January 1989. Later that year the Don Bosco "Children's City" opened to provide a permanent home to 43 boys under age 15.

My father once mentioned that his favorite restaurant was Ensenada's El Rey Sol. I shouldn't have been too surprised. He loved Mexico and he loved good food. Apparently the place sated both his appetites.

While the restaurant does not share its recipes, it has made public a couple of them:

Pumpkin Soup (for 6 servings)

1 1/2 lbs. fresh pumpkin	5 cups water
1 pint unsweetened whipping cream	Salt and white pepper
Pinch of sugar	4 1/2 oz. melted butter
Croutons	

Peel the pumpkin and cut the flesh into cubes. Place the cubes in a large heavy pan with water and salt and simmer slowly until soft, about 25 minutes. Puree in a blender or food processor. Thin with whipping cream, season with salt and pepper, and sweeten with sugar. Heat 5 more minutes.

Pour into soup tureen or hollowed-out pumpkin and swirl in melted butter. Sprinkle with nutmeg or fresh mint and serve with croutons.

Clams: Style Coquille Saint Jacques

Cook the soft edible parts of fresh Pismo clams whole with onion and parsley in a little dry white wine (about 20 minutes). Grind.

To the ground clams, add chopped onion sauteed in butter, chopped mushrooms, salt, and pepper. Let cook 10 minutes.

Make a bechamelle (cream) sauce with hot butter and flour, adding hot milk and stirring constantly to make a thick white sauce. Salt to taste.

Combine bechamelle with the clam mixture. Fill the shells with this combination, and add ground Gruyére or jack cheese and ground bread. Grill until golden.

With the renovation of the main street out front several restaurants opted to put in alfresco dining gazebos. El Rey Sol's is classic, with a distinctive royal blue covering, outdoor heaters, wrought iron tables and chairs, and most importantly, a crepes bar. Crepes vary from simple to sugar-covered to mango crepes to Crepes Grand Marnier, all reasonably priced. I couldn't walk past the place recently and smugly enjoyed outstanding mango crepes and coffee as I watched the world go by.

Once while we were cooking our catch over a campfire, I was telling a fishing buddy about El Rey Sol. When I mentioned that the prices were considerably less than similar U.S. restaurants, he began to beam. "Hey, maybe we can check it out on our way home," he said, looking down at his simple grilled fish and imagining it smothered in a rich sauce.

THE SCORE BAJA 1,000

The Granddaddy of Desert Racing

The legendary Tecate SCORE Baja 1,000, the granddaddy of desert racing, brings desert racing's finest stars, along with thousands of support personnel, to Baja every November.

As long as there have been motor vehicles, people have been racing, trying for speed, distance, and endurance records or just to beat the other guy. Something about off-road racing has always appealed to certain adventurers. One early race, when just driving an auto was considered an adventure, went from Los Angeles to Phoenix.

In 1956 a Jeep derby was organized in New Mexico. In 1965 the first pro off-road race, called the National 4-Wheel Drive Grand Prix, was organized by Brian Chuchua. It was the major off-road race for several years.

The Baja California venue came into being in 1962, when American Honda created a publicity stunt to introduce a new 250cc motorcycle. Dave Elkins and Bill Robertson Jr., aboard Hondas naturally, quickly established a record from Tijuana to La Paz by making the 1,000-mile overland romp in 39 hours, 54 minutes (that was Elkins' time; Robertson was less than an hour behind).

Over the next four years numerous attempts to best the record failed, until Dave Elkins was joined by Bud Elkins, Cliff Coleman, and Eddie Mulder; on four 650cc Triumphs, they beat the old record, but only by eight minutes. The challenge was on, and there were numerous attempts trying different routes.

In April 1967 a run of 34 hours, 45 minutes was made by Bruce Meyers and Ted Mangels in a custom 4-wheel Meyers Manx dune buggy.

By June of that year speed attempts turned into a race, as two Toyota Land Cruisers and a Meyers Manx buggy diced it out. The drivers: Ed Orr, Claude Dozier, Ed Pearlman, Dick Cepek, Drino Miller, and John Lawlor did not set any records, but did set a precedent.

The next month Ralph Poole and Spencer Murray set a record from Tijuana to La Paz by covering the distance in 31 hours flat in a stock AMC Rambler American. This run got the attention of not only off-roaders, but manufacturers and would-be sponsors.

Ed Pearlman and Don Francisco then formed the National Off-Road Racing Association (NORRA) and the first Baja 1,000 was run on Oct. 31, 1967. That first field of what was originally called the Mexican 1,000 had 68 cars and motorcycles challenging the 915 miles from Tijuana to La Paz (680 miles off-pavement). North of Ensenada the speed was controlled, but south of Ensenada it was all-out racing.

Malcom Smith had a big lead

Malcom Smith, who can still be seen riding bikes in Baja (I ran into him testing some bikes near Cataviña in 1995), had a tremendous lead in that first Baja 1,000 aboard a Husqvarna 250cc to the halfway point at El Arco. There Smith turned the bike over to J.N. Roberts for the second half. The team was so far ahead that Roberts beat the checkpoint crew to La Purísima and had to sit around and wait for them.

Sitting around doesn't win a race, and the four-wheel Meyers Manx buggy driven by Vic Wilson and Ted Mangels eventually caught up with Roberts at the checkpoint. As the straight and fast roads from there to La Paz favored the car, Wilson and Mangels are credited with winning the first Baja 1,000 in a time of 27 hours, 38 minutes.

The writer Willis Tilton (*Baja California, the Last New Frontier*) was coincidentally in El Arco that historic day in 1967, reporting: "Late that afternoon excited children, who were patiently awaiting and listening, reported sounds of a fast approaching motorcycle. It appeared in the north, raced rapidly around a couple of curves, and climbed the upward sloping hill into the check point. Malcolm Smith, the rider, was first into the halfway point at El Arco and he looked tired and nearly exhausted. Riders and mechanics quickly serviced his machine, tightening spokes, adjusting the motor, filling the gas tank, and checking thoroughly a most important item here, the lights. The machine, with its fresh driver astride, leaped forward less than fifteen minutes later."

After reporting on early leaders Tilton continued, "Another day of this followed, and reports came in thick and fast of vehicles broken down everywhere up and down the peninsula. Juan towed one in that had stalled eight miles north of El Arco. The drivers appeared exhausted and badly discouraged. One of them said he doubted if they would ever come back to salvage their car. Out of 68 starting vehicles, less than

Fast and versatile Class I vehicle on Baja 1000 course.

half made the full distance. In fact, only 31 finished the race.... Most participants, though, seemed to be enjoying the rough experience, and they were saying that 'we'll be back' when another race would be held next year."

SCORE (Short-Course Off-Road Enterprises) was formed in 1973 and took over the Baja 1,000. After that first year, rather than having a controlled start, the race has begun in Ensenada, though it started once in Mexicali, and again in Tijuana, using different routes.

These days, every third year the race reverts to a purists' 1,000-mile dash from Ensenada to La Paz in the south. A special Baja 2,000 on Nov. 12, 2000 featured a demanding criss-crossing of the peninsula from Ensenada to Cabo San Lucas.

On off years it's an approximately 1,000-kilometer version looping the northern sector of the state of Baja California (Norte). The 1,000-kilometer version offers many more accessible spectator areas, is much easier to pit and support, and features a start and finish in roughly the same area.

The term "off-road" is actually a misnomer, as the race follows existing dirt roads and trails throughout Baja. I have noted on route maps from the last several Baja 1,000 races that not once has it called for racers to tear across virgin terrain.

Environmentalists are rightly concerned about damage to the fragile environment caused by vehicles. A single vehicle can permanently damage the flora and leave scars on the desert floor for decades. From my perspective, the worst damage I've seen has been caused by independent, casual users who on their own just romp all over the place, oblivious to the environment.

The Baja 1,000 is a mixed blessing. While the race itself adheres to roads, there is still some environmental damage, mostly caused by support people and spectators. On the other hand, the event definitely helps swell the economy, as the restaurants and hotels boom for several weeks surrounding the race.

Regardless of the route, each year the excitement begins to build Thursday afternoon as visitors wander among the cars and product booths on "contingency row" downtown. Friday the race starts. Many spectators choose to leave early Friday morning and head out of town to find a place where the highway nears the race course. There they position themselves for the arrival of the race.

It's one thing to see these powerful vehicles on television, but to have them blast by is an experience one never forgets. The booming roar of the finely-tuned big engines as they approach cannot be duplicated electronically, and the speed with which they travel over marginal trails is awesome. The vehicles are sturdy and specifically designed for the rough stuff, yet they still take an incredible beating, with parts and fenders littering the course.

Most admirable is the daring of the drivers, with life-or-death decisions made in micro-seconds and the demanding course constantly bruising backs, spleens, and kidneys.

At every Baja 1,000 I've attended, I've always been amazed by the crowds. Mexican officials estimated that the 1993 Baja 1,000 from Mexicali drew over 400,000 spectators to watch the race from some vantage point. For a one-day event, it was speculated that this likely outdrew the Indianapolis 500 as the largest spectator crowd ever assembled for a sporting event.

"Baja Tested" and "Baja Proven"

Suppliers, ranging from manufacturers of tires, spark plugs, oil, wheels, and shocks to fuel, as well as other sponsors, are always out in force. They are well aware of the marketability of the Baja 1,000. If successful, their future advertising can boast "Winner of the Baja 1,000." And if not, well, they can still advertise "Baja Tested" or "Baja Proven" with the magic of the land transferred to all that the name "Baja" implies.

At checkpoints are major pit areas, most of them close to the highway. The contours of sagebrush, ocotillo, chaparral, and cactus are dwarfed by the mini-cities that spring up in their midst. Large semis, trucks, trailers, and campers are strategically placed to await the racers. Generators keep the "cities" alive as riders and drivers blast by through the night.

While the motorcycles start the race earlier, many are still on the course, especially the quads and smaller bikes, when the first of the powerful cars come roaring into view. You can tell the 4-wheel leaders are nearing by the distant clouds of dust being kicked up and the helicopters that thump-thump overhead following the lead cars.

Baja 1,000 participants have a big following in Mexico. Their *machismo* is respected and their vehicles admired. While I see Americans in every crowd, the majority are the locals, who arrive from even distant locations to line the route.

Throughout the years the Baja 1,000 has drawn racing's best. Former Indianapolis 500 winner Parnelli Jones has won the Baja 1,000. SCORE pioneer and off-road racing promoter Mickey Thompson also raced. Once, in 1971, Thompson had a close call as he and partner Dick Landfield rolled their Chevy pickup onto its side while swerving to avoid an oncoming bus. Undaunted, the pair just righted the pickup and continued the race. Hollywood personalities Steve McQueen, James Garner, and Clark Gable's son have all raced the Baja 1,000.

The Baja 1,000 increasingly lures a broad range of entrants from all over the world. Each year riders and drivers from 15 or 20 states are joined by entrants from numerous countries such as Canada, Denmark, France, Israel, Japan, Mexico, England, and Wales. Media representatives from even more countries are always in attendance.

A large Japanese contingent now includes a record number of motorcycle entrants where "Beat the Baja on a Bike" has become a cultural vendetta. Riders come on junkets from Japan, buy a specially-prepared Honda in the U.S., and make time for one quick pre-run before tackling the big race. Then they take their dust-laden motorcycles back home to display in local Japanese businesses. They purposely don't wash the bikes, still encrusted with Baja dirt and mud, to further prove they did indeed survive this historic Mexican adventure.

The international flavor has brought some of the world's finest racers. Some who had raced Europe's country roads definitely did not know what to expect. One year British racer James Tenant said, "The course was great, but it was absolutely exhausting."

Anita Espinoza of the outpost village of El Rosario has told the story about a Frenchman driving a Citröen in an early Baja 1,000. Apparently, he hopelessly underestimated the race and had not even prerun the course. He then got lost in the mountains and survived on crackers and candy before some cowboys found him six days later. He then distastefully but gratefully ate some jackrabbit the cowboys caught and cooked over an open flame before being helped back to "civilization."

After one race, British driver Graham Roberts summed up why the legendary Baja 1,000 is still considered the world's premier off-road race. "This is definitely rougher than Paris-Dakar," he said, referring to what had been the world's most prestigious off-road race through the Sahara Desert.

There you have it. It appears the Tecate SCORE Baja 1,000 has earned its reputation as off-road racing's new Number One, "The Granddaddy of Desert Racing."

NEWPORT OCEAN SAILING ASSOCIATION

The World's Largest Yacht Race

The legendary Newport-Ensenada Yacht Race sailed right on past its historical half-century mark a few years back and is still going strong. Billed as the "World's Largest International Yacht Race," the 125-mile voyage from the upscale shores of Newport Beach to the bustling Mexican seaport of Ensenada is a major happening each spring for some 600 yachts that take part.

It started back in the 1940s when there were a few summertime sailboat races off the mainland of southern California, mostly to and from Catalina Island. Then at a 1947 board meeting of the Newport Ocean Sailing Association (NOSA), board member George Michaud dropped a bombshell by suggesting a race to Ensenada.

A committee looked into it and recommended to go ahead with the race, preferably in the springtime so there would be no conflict with the summer races. It was approved at the Dec. 12, 1947 general meeting, and the first trial race was scheduled for Apr. 23, 1948.

Now it's true that sailboats have been coming to Ensenada ever since Juan Rodríguez Cabrillo dropped anchor back in 1542. But the old bay had never seen the likes of the 117 sails that all arrived that same day back in 1948. Each year since, on the last weekend of April, people all along the southern California coast and Mexico's Gold Coast can look out to the horizon to see hundreds of colorful and traditional white sails heading south. The Ensenada harbor quickly fills up with sailboats, and their crews rejoin their families and support people for a weekend of celebration.

What began as a small amateur race for southern Californians wanting to fill their springtime race schedule quickly evolved into an international event that attracts some of the sport's biggest names. The race has increased in speed over the years with the record set in 1994 by San Diego's Dennis Conner aboard the catamaran *Stars and Stripes*. Conner covered the 125-mile distance in a blistering 8 hours, 29 minutes.

Along with some of the top skippers, the race has also attracted its share of celebrities. Humphrey Bogart, Roy Disney, Walter Cronkite, and Buddy Ebsen have all participated.

The record number of participants was 675 yachts in 1983. The number of different classes of boats has steadily increased each year, with 27 different classes entered in the April 2000 event.

Many take the race very seriously, always looking to garner a trophy for their class. But to numerous other participants those first-to-finish honors each year become secondary. Many skippers have entered the race for decades, and to some it's the event that seizes the moment. It is camaraderie over competition; it is memories over a sterling silver cup.

The Newport-Ensenada Yacht Race has become not just a Baja legend but a yachting legend as well.

Bahía Hotel
Baja's Biggest Swimming Pool

When it was built, the modest swimming pool at Ensenada's Bahía Hotel was billed as Baja's biggest. That was 1954 and lots of pools have been built in Baja since then. The well-known Ensenada importer Carlos Tavárez, in building the Bahía, first toured all of the then-famous resorts on the Pacific Coast and retained architect Frank W. Green for the job.

The Bahía Resort Hotel "On the Sands of Todos Santos Bay" opened in June 1954, featuring 73 rooms and suites for the princely price of $9 per couple. At that time, before there was a broad Lázaro Cárdenas Blvd., the "three heads" park, and the naval docks between it and the ocean, the Bahía did indeed sit on the sand. In fact, the original brochure boasted sand volleyball courts right outside and "horses brought to your door."

The Bahía occupies a whole block of downtown Ensenada, fronting on Ave. López Mateos with its own gift shop, restaurant, and bar. The Bahía's delightful La Tortuga restaurant on the corner is seemingly always packed for breakfast and offers a wonderful fruit platter. The bar looks out over what was once Baja's largest swimming pool and can get really crowded during major events like the Rosarito-Ensenada 50-Mile Bicycle Ride and the Newport-Ensenada Yacht Race. In fact, for years the yachting crowd has used the Bahía for its base.

Carlos Tavárez Mesa is still the owner of the Bahía. I ran into a nephew of his way down south of La Paz in the tropical village of Todos Santos, where Carlos Amador Tavárez and his wife Rosa run a small restaurant.

In keeping up with the times at the Bahía, current manager Juan Carlos Pacheco now offers special packages for tourists that include fishing and/or Spanish-language immersion programs. The bar offers dancing, karaoke, and folkloric shows, but its pool is no longer Baja's biggest.

K2 BIG WAVE CHALLENGE
Giant Surf at Todos Santos

When K2 Surf promoted its Big Wave Challenge back in winter, 1998, everyone expected the winning "biggest wave" ride to take place along the North Shore of Hawaii, or maybe even at Maverick's in northern California, both areas known for huge surf.

The contest offered $50,000 to the surfer who could ride the winter's biggest wave, bringing top big-wave surfers out in force to win the mid-January to mid-March, 1998 event.

World pro surfer Taylor Knox of Carlsbad, California won the contest by successfully riding an amazing 50-foot wave at Todos Santos Island, out in Ensenada Bay. That the world's biggest ride that year was just off Ensenada may have surprised a lot of surfers around the world, but locals have known of giant, gnarly surf off the island for years.

In a 1989 *Baja Traveler* magazine article, writer Dean Karnazes noted: "Because of the island's position, oncoming swells are focused in toward the points, magnifying the size and power considerably. It's not uncommon for Todos to be sporting a solid six-foot swell, while beaches on the mainland are completely flat."

Karnazes adds, "The huge winter storms generated in the Aleutians unleash all their fury on this island's north-facing beaches. Not only does it get giant — it gets perfect! The prevailing question is not whether Todos can handle the swell. It's 'can you handle Todos?!'"

Nine years later, the fury of El Niño storms pounded the Pacific coast with huge waves. Big-wave surfers were even leaving Hawaii and coming to the California coast, most notably Mavericks, for the action — and a chance at the $50,000 prize. At Mavericks near Half Moon Bay south of San Francisco, Pete Mel, a big-wave surfer and board shaper from Santa Cruz, rode a monster wave estimated at between 45 to 48 feet.

Those in the know realized that Todos Santos would also get some big wave action, and Orange County photographer Les Walker, who earned $5,000 for shooting the winner, caught Taylor Knox on the world's biggest successful wave ride.

The winning ride was just a couple of feet larger than second place, but at 50 feet, that's like falling off a five-story building.

Baja has some legendary surf spots along the Gold Coast between Tijuana and Ensenada, like Baja Malibu, Power Plant, Mushrooms, Calafia, K-38, La Fonda, Salsipuedes, and San Miguel. But the one that made the record books is the island called Todos Santos, across the bay from Ensenada.

SANTO TOMÁS WINERY

The Legend of Baja Wines

California wines are famous all over the world, but their inauspicious beginnings can be traced to the missions of Baja California, because the Spanish padres gave birth to the wine industry by introducing grapes to Baja California.

The first grapevine cuttings were established at Mission San Javier in Baja California 300 years ago by Padre Juan de Ugarte. Founded in 1699, it was the second mission in the Californias, and beginning in 1701, a rudimentary wine was produced there.

The later Baja mission of Santa Gertrudis became known as the birthplace of the California wine industry. In 1752 Padre Jorge Retz, a German Jesuit, made vast improvements in the wine quality by his ingenuity. He enriched his soil with a fine loam brought in from distant arroyos. As there were no casks available, he had containers hewn from blocks of stone filled with the juice of the grapes. He covered these containers with boards and sealed them with a gum from the *pitahaya* cactus plants.

Ensenada region leads Mexico's wines

Currently, over 90 percent of Mexico's wines come from vineyards in the Ensenada region of Baja California. This includes the Santo Tomás and San Vicente Valleys to the south and the popular Guadalupe Valley just north of Ensenada. The region affords the ideal vineyard climate: warm summers and mild winters, bright sunny days and cool nights, with frequent marine moisture. The porous soil, composed primarily of decomposed granite, is also perfect.

The padres took grape cuttings from the southern missions with them as they established new missions to the north. Mission Santo Tomás was founded in 1791 in a valley just 26 miles south of Ensenada by Padre José Loriente. It turned out that the fertile valley was perfect for grape growing, and the vineyards prospered, eventually producing the mission system's finest wines, including the one to be called the Mission variety.

By 1800 there were 5,000 grapevines in Santo Tomás. With the end of the mission system in 1840, the vineyards were abandoned. But in the 1880s, a couple of Spanish immigrants took over the property, reestablished the vineyards, formed the Bodegas de Santo Tomás, and in 1888 began selling barrels of wine in the town of Ensenada.

Mexico's oldest winery

Mexico's oldest winery later moved to Ensenada, but the original winery still stands in the Santo Tomás Valley, a little farm building on Rancho Los Dolores, an old country estate of General Abelardo Rodríguez, a former President of Mexico.

Vineyard in Guadalupe Valley.

Today, the 110 year-old Bodegas de Santo Tomás in Ensenada offers daily tours and tastings at their Ensenada Winery and Cultural Center, 666 Ave. Miramar, in downtown Ensenada (between 6th and 7th). Soon, their new winery in the Valley of Santo Tomás will open.

The Bodegas de Santo Tomás produces a popular St. Emilion Chianti, an all-purpose table wine; Seco Rosado, a fragrant rosé; a Cordon Bleu Champagne; and a fine Extra VSOP cognac, along with many other varietal wines.

Fiestas de le Vendimia

Each August the grape harvest is celebrated with much fanfare by all the Ensenada area wineries. The Fiestas de la Vendimia is sponsored by the Baja California Wine Society; each of the eight major wineries in the area participates and has its unique way of celebrating. There are feasts and picnics and much more at the wineries and street fairs in downtown Ensenada. There are wine competitions and samplings, wine and art auctions, dinners, seminars, a paella contest, a golf tourney, and of course music and dancing. The fiesta usually lasts about 10 days and some of the activities are elaborate parties.

It took many years for Mexico's wine industry to earn international acclaim, but the wines of Baja California are now considered to be among the finest in the world. Baja California wines were previously only exported to Europe. The open trade inspired by NAFTA finally opened the doors for Mexico's wines to be sold in the U.S. and Canadian markets. Over the past two decades there has been a greater involvement of capable vintners in Baja's fine wine-growing region. The results include greater competition, enhanced quality, and a more viable industry.

Now in the days of free trade, Americans can head south and sample wines from "that other California," where it all began.

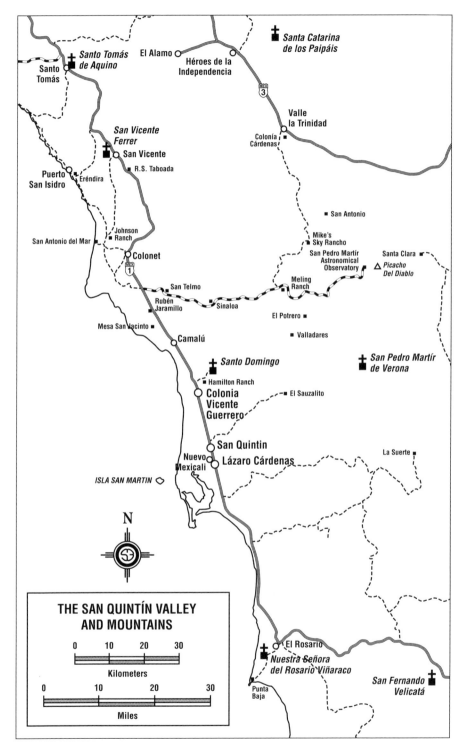

THE SAN QUINTÍN VALLEY
AND MOUNTAINS

0   10   20   30
Kilometers

0   10   20   30
Miles

Chapter 9:
The San Quintín Valley and Mountains

El Palomar Motel/Restaurant, Santo Tomás

A Landmark in Wine Country

It's hard for Baja travelers to drive past El Palomar, a roadside refuge just 30 miles south of Ensenada, without stopping. It's a welcome respite in the first village south of the suburban sprawl of Ensenada, and a shady one at that.

You drop down into the lush, green Santo Tomás Valley, cross the valley floor on a road bordered by olive trees, pass a palm-fringed curve amid some weathered old buildings, and soon the El Palomar motel and restaurant are immediately on the right. Large pepper and olive trees across the street shelter the accompanying El Palomar RV Park and campground.

El Palomar was developed by Señor Enrique Villareal Cantú, whose family members on both sides were Baja pioneers. His mother owned a ranch at Puerto Santo Tomás, where Don Enrique Villareal ran a fishing camp. In 1942 he opened a small store in front of the Santo Tomás school. In 1948 he moved to his present location, a long building tucked up against the hillside, that became known as *Parecía un Palomar*, meaning in English, "It resembles a pigeon coop." Shortly thereafter he opened a small one-pump Pemex gas station.

Villareal later added a restaurant in which he delighted customers with his personal attention. He was quite a dancer, and sometimes *El Bailarín* (The Dancer), as he was called, would show his guests a few steps.

Later he added a few hotel rooms and built the RV/campground complex across the street. The campground features a pool, outdoor dance floor, volleyball courts, scores of barbecue pits, and tennis courts, all nestled snugly in an olive orchard. Many of the gnarled old olive trees have graced the site since the days of the missionaries. After all, the crumbling adobe walls of the old Mission Santo Tomás are on a knoll just west of the grove.

A mission established in 1791

The Mission of Santo Tomás de Aquino was established on Apr. 24, 1791 by Padre José Loriente. The viceroy had previously asked the Dominican padres to locate an intermediate establishment between San Vicente and San Miguel. The original location was much closer to the ocean. It was moved up-valley to about three miles from the present Santo Tomás in 1794 and to the present location in 1799. The missionaries planted olives, pomegranates, pears, and the grapes that gave birth to Mexico's oldest winery.

A Santo Tomás legend, according to Marion Smothers' book *Vintage Baja*, involves the origin of the grapes. Don Enrique Villareal Sr. told her that the original grapevine stock had come from the foothills of the Italian Alps, home of the founding padres' Dominican Order. He added that they also brought their native heritage of viticulture and winemaking.

Other sources indicate that the grapevines were cuttings from missions to the south established by the Jesuit Order. As it was almost 100 years since those first cuttings were planted in Baja (1701, San Javier), it is possible the Dominicans added additional cuttings and winemaking skills. The current El Palomar brochure, incidentally, indicates that in 1791 the Dominicans brought vineyard root stock from Spain.

Santo Tomás appears a peaceful place in a bucolic setting, but its history is anything but peaceful. Hostile Indians constantly made threats and attacks. On different dates in 1803, Padre Miguel López and later a newly-arrived priest, Padre Eudaldo Surroca, were murdered in their beds by ostensibly friendly Indian domestics. Then in 1815, two baptized Indians were murdered. Several reports from that time indicated that the padres were extremely harsh with the Indians and according to some, deserved what they got.

Treasures stolen from mission

Another legend reports that in 1849 an Indian stole the candlesticks, chalice, and other treasures from the altar to sell to a gold-seeker passing through. The mission's last padre, Agustín Mansilla y Gamboa, left immediately thereafter. Was he disgusted or was there a connection between his departure and the missing treasures? Who knows?

The mission ruins are hard to see from the highway, but if you go through the RV park and make a left on the tree-lined road bordering the park, you will come to the adobe ruins at the end of the grove.

More than 100 years after the padres, different hosts welcome travelers to the Santo Tomás Valley. For at least the last half-century, the Villareals have brought a sense of permanence to the pretty valley. Don Enrique's children, Enrique Villareal Jr., Rogelio Villareal, Emma Villareal Montemayor, and Juan Villareal continue to run the roadside business known as El Palomar.

Over the years, many Baja travelers have stopped there. Their guest list is full of luminaries, and the Villareals consider many legends of the Baja 1,000 to be good friends. Other famous guests have included John Wayne, Alan Ladd, and Errol Flynn.

The Baja 500 off-road race traditionally ends on the other side of the campground, and for me the El Palomar is most often a brief stop on my way south, but occasionally I've made it a destination while I cover the race. The SCORE officials use El Palomar as a communications center.

El Palomar Restaurant, Santo Tomás

Jack Smith and El Palomar

Author Jack Smith recalls a visit to El Palomar in his classic book, *God and Mr. Gómez*, which tells of the travails of building a home in Baja. The Smiths' house was built at La Bocana, some 18 miles of dirt road away from where the Santo Tomás Valley funnels into the Pacific. During the late '60s when their home was under construction, the Smiths had arrived late to the area one Saturday evening and chose to stay at El Palomar.

Smith wrote, "It was a quaint little outpost; a combination little curio store, grocery, restaurant, and motel beside the paved road half-a-mile north of the village of Santo Tomás."

Securing a room from the proprietor, a Señor Villareal, and looking forward to a quiet dinner and relaxing night away from the bustle of Ensenada, Smith continues...

> "It was a bucolic setting, dimly lit by candles and an electric light globe which was energized, evidently, by the generator whose muffled clatter we could hear. The waitress moved with the grace and quiet of the jaguar. Either she spoke no English or chose not to waste words. We ordered from a handwritten menu. 'Gracias,' she whispered, and vanished into the kitchen...."

After an enjoyable dinner, the Smiths went upstairs to their room only to be disrupted by the sounds of firecrackers and music from across the road.

> "...the jukebox blasted on at the dancefloor across the road, pouring out a barrage of Mexican rock....
>
> "The bombardment continued without letup. It was impossible to sleep

133

and hard enough to read. Then the lights went out and the jukebox fell silent. It was only ten o'clock. Mr. Villareal, evidently, had an ingenious way of imposing curfew. He simply turned his generator off. Without lights and music, his festive customers would be obliged to pursue less noisy diversions in the soft Baja night."

Years ago, when the curio shop had a large outdoor section, the outstanding display of shells, rocks, and desert artifacts made browsing there almost mandatory. Over the years the motel has been modernized and expanded. The restaurant and bar have grown, and in May 1999 the Villareals completely renovated the aging Pemex gas station.

El Palomar refers to itself as the "Golden Gate of Baja," an apt name, as it is the first town south of the busy tourist/border area. The Villareal family has brought a peaceful charm to the idyllic valley and continues to welcome travelers with gracious hospitality.

CASTRO'S CAMP IN ERÍNDIRA
User-Friendly Fishing

Fishing in Baja can be an intimidating experience for the novice. The newcomer has heard stories of huge tuna, seen photos of Hemingway look-alikes posing next to marlin bigger than they are, and listened in awe to old-timers swapping yarns about tackle, resorts, reefs, seasons, or tides.

It's all a bit much for that occasional fisherman who just likes to "give it a shot" every now and then. Where can *he* go and not feel like he should have bought the book *Fishing for Dummies*? Where can he go to just have a good time — *and* catch fish?

In southern California there are party boats where you're elbow to elbow with the next guy (some of whom are pretty serious fishermen) and you spend most of the day getting untangled under their stern glare. In Baja, you might go to Ensenada, where similar party boats can take you out to Todos Santos Island. They still get crowded, filling up on busy weekends, and during the week will combine smaller parties into one or two boats to ensure your getting tangled.

There *is* a place where a neophyte angler can take his children on a first fishing experience just a couple hours drive from the border. Cabins are inexpensive, and *pangas* fish four people to a boat. And there's lots of fish.

It's called Castro's Camp, and is about 60 miles south of Ensenada, just north of the mission village of San Vicente. From Highway 1, a marked paved road follows a pretty valley about 12 miles down to the coast and the agricultural village of Ejido Eríndira. Incongruously, the drive through the town of about 1,000 people is on a bumpy dirt road. The road makes an abrupt right turn at a bluff over the pounding ocean. Fortunately there are large caution signs, lest one continue straight ahead to do a swan dive, car and all, onto the cobbled surf.

About a mile north is San Ysidro Cove, where a boat ramp angles down the face of the cliff. The buildings above the cliff are the Castro family's fishing camp. In 1949

Vicente Castro began his fishing operation, and since his death in 1970, his children Fernando and Adela have run the operation.

The Castros now have 10 boats and take out four fishermen on each. The inexpensive cost per person includes rod, reel, and bait.

In *The Baja Book III*, author Tom Miller waxes enthusiastic:

> "Skiffs from Castro's Camp will take you out for some of the finest rock cod fishing you have ever experienced. It is not unusual to catch 100 pounds of excellent eating fish in a short time. In fall and winter schools of yellowtail, white sea bass and barracuda occasionally move in here."

In Miller's other book *Angler's Guide to Baja California*, he continues along those same lines:

> "And what fishing! Many times I've returned from Castro's with an ice chest full of filets.
>
> "Drawn by the cool ocean upwelling which occurs south of Ensenada, the nearby reefs are loaded with many varieties of rock cod, white fish and large ling cod. In season, white sea bass, yellowtail, black sea bass, barracuda and bonito also make their presence known. Fishing from large skiffs, the best action is usually obtained with yo yo type jigs over the 150 foot deep reefs, although some prefer to bait rock cod ganglions with pieces of squid."

For the neophyte angler, just let the skipper do it all. He'll prepare the bait, depending on the type of fish, which varies with the season. You will catch fish!

The accommodations are perfect for a couple of dads and a few kids. The Castros offer seven different rooms, each with nine beds (three triple bunks). All rooms have a bathroom with hot water showers and a kitchenette area. There's a refrigerator and stove, but I can't say "all the comforts of home" because the pads on each bunk require that you bring a sleeping bag or bedding. And somebody's got to cook, because the restaurant was closed on my last visit. But the nine-sleeper rooms are inexpensive and offer a tremendous view out over the ocean, where in season whales can be seen migrating south.

The brother-sister team are hard workers and know how to make their guests comfortable. Adela runs the rooms, which are in small rustic buildings, while Fernando concentrates on lining up his guides with the fishermen. Both, however, are comfortable taking care of all aspects of the operation. There are also trailer sites at Castro's and many camping opportunities in the area.

According to Shirley Miller, former editor of *Mexico West Travel Club Newsletter*, "Castro's Camp is a legend with any fisherman who has ever caught a fish in Baja."

Forget the improbable *Fishing For Dummies*. Castro's sounds like *the* place for user-friendly fishing.

MELING RANCH, SAN PEDRO MÁRTIR

Where the Stars Dazzle

Meling Ranch is ensconced in an oak-dotted valley in the San Pedro Mártir, Baja California's highest mountains. At 2,261 feet elevation, the 10,000-acre working rancho is about midway between the Pacific Ocean far to the west and the mountain crest, topped by the 10,156-foot summit of Picacho del Diablo.

The Meling Ranch, (Rancho San José), was part of an 1834 land grant given to Juan Ignacio de Jesús Arce, a descendant of Juan de Arce, one of the oldest settlers of the peninsula. Arce was an Englishman who acquired a Spanish surname after being raised in Mexico. He arrived in Loreto as a soldier in 1698, one year after Baja's first mission was established there.

His descendant Juan Ignacio raised cattle in the Meling Ranch area from his base at San Telmo. Later, in 1893, Texas miner Harry Johnson acquired the property.

Baja buff David Kier passes on a good story about how Johnson got title to the ranch. David ran into a 59-year-old man named José who was born in San Telmo. José said that his grandfather and grand-uncles lost the ranch to Johnson over a $30 poker bet. Good story if it's true. *¿Quién sabe?*

Regardless, five years previously (in 1888), Johnson had bought ranch land by the beach at San Antonio del Mar and developed the Johnson Ranch there. Then at his new mountain site, he built the Rancho San José as a base for gold mining operations. He even built a canal in 1896 to transport water from Arroyo San Rafael to the nearby Socorro mine.

The mountain ranch he built was destroyed during the 1911 *Magonista* revolution. His daughter Alberta, "Bertie," and her husband, Norwegian immigrant Salvador Meling, rebuilt the Rancho San José (also now called Rancho Meling). "Salve" Meling came to Baja from Norway in 1908 with his parents and seven brothers.

The four children and 18 grandchildren of Bertie and Salve have kept the ranch in the family ever since, though some of them have left mountains to seek careers elsewhere. Son Phil later became a Mexican Forest Service warden, and son Tom went to work as a printer in San Diego. A nephew, Henry Jolliff, was a leading rancher in the nearby Valle de Trinidad for over 50 years.

The guiding lights for decades were Aida Johnson Meling Barre (daughter of Salve and Bertie Meling) and her husband Bill Barre. Aida, like her mother Bertie, was well known to Baja California travelers for gracious hospitality. After Aida's death, her daughter Duane took over the place, and occasionally Duane's sister comes from San Diego County to spend time there.

The Meling Ranch has evolved into more of a dude ranch, specializing in introducing groups of tourists to the "wild west," even though it is still a working cattle ranch.

They do welcome drive-in guests if there is space. Rooms include dinner, breakfast, and the normal ranch activities. European and Oriental tourists love it, according to her guest book. Here their visions of a wilder, untamed West become reality.

Meling Ranch

"We get mostly package deals," Duane said, "and a good many of our visitors are from abroad. It's sometimes almost comical to see some of these city people really get into it and strut around wearing big 10-gallon hats," she added with a laugh.

Rooms are rustic and simple, with butane lamps and fireplaces. There is a spring-fed swimming pool and a recreation room. Here tired "cowboys" can shoot pool, play table tennis, or grab a book from the shelf to relax in oversized ranch furniture in front of the big rock fireplace.

Horseback riding, pack trains, quail hunting, and visiting the national park provide daytime diversions, taking guests past mountain-fed streams and into idyllic meadows rimmed with pine trees. There is a 3,500-foot uphill dirt airstrip behind the rancho. Meals are family style in the mess hall.

After dinner the biggest attraction is "nature's own television set." There's no story line, disrupting news, or silly sitcom. The dramatic black sky itself has come alive, with millions of stars so bright and dazzling it demands your attention. It's such an awe-inspiring display of nature at its finest that if you lived there you'd have a stiff neck from looking upward.

It will be a long time before light pollution will mess up this view. That's why the San Pedro Mártir was the chosen site of the National Observatory, which is on the mountain crest another 30 miles up the road. The observatory is Mexico's largest, with a 2.1 meter (83 inches) diameter reflector.

Heading up the mountain, the landscape turns lush with pines, boulders, meadows, and ponds, once you enter the Sierra San Pedro Mártir National Park. About a mile from the 9,286-foot-high observatory is a ranger station, a series of domed buildings which include a small restaurant and library for the few employees.

The view from the observatory is sublime; you can see across to the rocky summit of Picacho del Diablo (also known as La Providencia and by other names), and straight down to the vast expanse of the San Felipe Desert and gulf far below. Here the eastern escarpment drops vertically to the desert floor. While it is a slow, long winding drive from the west, to the east it looks like you could throw a rock and it would drop over a half mile.

Ladybug on the rock

Back at the ranch, the main part of the Meling operation sits in a valley that is a caldera of an ancient volcano. The area abounds with mine shafts and caves and has long been the natural setting of a diverse range of flora and fauna — including ladybugs.

"In fact," according to Duane, "the ladybugs have been around a long time, because we found an ancient Indian petroglyph of one on a rock up by the runway."

The rocky crag with the ladybug is found halfway up the airstrip on the left side. High up on one rock face is the ladybug etching, complete with spots, about 18 inches long.

I heard through the Baja Grapevine that the ranch had closed down, and indeed it had during the summer of 1999, during which time family members discussed its future. The Meling Ranch reopened in 2000 with Duane Barre Meling as manager and can now accommodate 27 persons in the rooms and ranch house.

A companion business, Meling Adventures, which involves four-day saddle trips into the mountains for cattle drives, roundups, and branding, is run by Soren Meling.

MIKE'S SKY RANCH — A MOUNTAIN LEGEND

Mike's Ranch in the Sky

Mike León, an American citizen whose family came from Jalisco, Mexico, had owned a couple of bars in Tijuana, including one called Mike's Go Go Bar, but by the mid-1960s, he began looking for a more pastoral setting. In 1967, he bought several thousand acres and opened Mike's Sky Ranch, a guest resort in the foothills of the San Pedro Mártir, Baja's tallest mountain range. The ranch sits on a knoll above the San Rafael creek in a picturesque and wooded valley.

Steep, brush-covered mountains rise in the background to the pine-covered 7,100-foot summit of Cerro San Matías, visible off to the east. The crystal-clear San Rafael stream winds through the valley floor, and must be forded to reach the ranch.

Sycamore-shaded campsites are snuggled both upstream and downstream from the incoming road. The San Rafael is one of the few trout streams in Baja California, yielding small rainbow trout. There're even photos on the walls at Mike's of people holding trout caught in the stream. Hunters will find deer, rabbit, quail by the hundreds, and mountain lion.

In addition to the occasional hunter and angler, the off-road racers have been attracted to Mike León's dream in the sky. Mike himself was quite a racing proponent, driving a desert racing Volkswagen bug and also an Isuzu in the SCORE races that have now become part of Baja folklore and legend.

As several of the Baja SCORE races go through the area, including the Baja 500 and on some years, the Baja 1,000, Mike's fills up on race weekends, and the campground becomes a large pit stop. For weeks in advance of the big races, riders stop by Mike's while out prerunning the course.

The racers leave their mark, too. The tranquil vision of a restful mountain hideaway, complete with swimming pool and well-manicured grounds, changes on busy weekends. The community room is the only place not taken over by the race enthusi-

San Rafael Creek at Mike's Sky Ranch.

asts. The *sala* (living room), bar, dining room, and recreation room are all covered with off-road business cards, stickers, posters, T-shirts, and photos.

Racing lore decorates walls

On the front door is a signed poster of Honda's off-road motorcycle star Johnny Campbell. There are several signed posters of top Baja 500 and 1,000 drivers, including Toyota's ironman, Ivan Stewart. There is one Mike's Sky Ranch 1996 Commemorative T-shirt hanging on the wall that would be quite an off-road enthusiast's souvenir. That shirt was signed by the famous drivers and riders Corky McMillan, Curt Le Duc, Ivan Stewart, Larry Roeseler, Rod Hall, Jeff Lewis, Rob Gordon, and a few others.

There is a photo montage on a wall of the Aug. 1, 1997 wedding of Tim and Jennifer Morton, which took place at Mike's. It was only fitting they wed there — buried in a bar corner is a brief mention announcing that the couple's happy engagement took place in that very bar, on Dec. 14, 1996.

Mike León was not only a racer's friend, he too shared their enthusiasm. For example, León took a first place in the 1984 Baja 1,000 SCORE off-road race and followed that feat six months later with another victory in the 1985 Baja 500 Internacional. An Isuzu T-shirt hangs in the bar at Mike's commemorating numerous victories and adding "In Memory — Mike León, a Baja Legend."

León, who rarely left the ranch, died in a traffic accident in 1990. Other mementos of his largesse grace the crowded walls of Mike's Sky Ranch. In one corner of the bar behind a large glass frame is the actual door from León's racing Volkswagen, a bright red door with No. 519 markings.

In the large adjacent dining room complete with six or seven family-style dining tables under soporific tropical fans, another vintage photo of Mike León hangs just above a pot-bellied stove. And across from that is a framed photograph of a waterfall just two kilometers upstream on the San Rafael, with the inscription, "In Memory of Mike León Sr. May his memory be as fresh as the Rio San Rafael."

Mike is gone, but Mike's Sky Ranch lives on. Mike's is now run by León's sons, Mike León Jr. and José de Jesús León, both of whom live in Tijuana with their families. The brothers make weekly three-day trips to the ranch, where they welcome their guests each weekend. Ten-year employee David Loya lives on the ranch with his family and manages it in the brothers' absence.

Groups arrive every weekend

The new breed of tourist has not only rekindled the off-road spirit, but brought continued profitability to the legendary Mike's Sky Ranch. Off-road "wannabes" are brought in by tour group operators every weekend. Groups of as few as 10 people to 20, 30, and even 65, as was the case the weekend before my last visit, have brought new life to a Baja legend.

Baja Tours, Trail Boss Tours, Baja Off-Road Adventures (BORA), Baja Bound and EmBAJAdor Adventure Tours all shuttle people up the mountain for a weekend of outdoor fun and off-roading.

There are 27 sleeping rooms, including singles, doubles, and triples, at Mike's, all surrounding the refreshing swimming pool. Breakfast and dinner are included in the per-person rate and meals are large and wholesome, usually featuring steak and served family style. There are no phones, and the power goes off each night at 10 p.m.

I should have brought fishing tackle

During the week only an occasional traveler passes by, and I enjoyed the beauty and quiet of the high country during my last visit. I walked down to the San Rafael, half-wishing I had brought some fishing tackle. But I dismissed the thought, realizing the trout were probably an anomaly and the place had been fished out for years. Just then movement caught my eye. Three small fingerling trout darted across a pool to an overhang on the other side. I'll be darned. They're small, but they're there.

Getting ready to leave, I looked at where the bad road came into Mike's from the south and Meling Ranch. It appeared that a car might have been over it recently. I asked Loya, who said that it had finally been graded during the summer of 1999. He added that after years of non-use, in recent months even a few passenger vehicles had come through. The easiest way to Mike's Sky Ranch, however, is still the better 22-mile dirt road from Highway 3 near San Matías.

STOCKED BY MULEBACK

Trout Streams in Baja

Back in 1905, a native species of rainbow trout was discovered in the San Antonio Creek and a few streams of Baja's Sierra San Pedro Mártir by Edward W. Nelson, and was subsequently called the Nelson Rainbow Trout (*salmo nelsoni*). Nelson was a biologist who later published *Lower California and Its Natural Resources* for the National Academy of Sciences in Washington, D.C.

Later, in 1925, the University of California Museum of Vertebrate Zoology sent an expedition to Baja to study the rare new species.

Expedition member Chester C. Lamb, assistant curator of mammals for the museum, said, "So far as known, only one stream in Lower California is inhabited by trout, namely the Santo Domingo River. This stream heads on the west slope of the San Pedro Mártir Mountains, and the trout exist chiefly in one of its branches, San Antonio Creek, and in that branch almost altogether above Rancho San Antonio.

"At the time our fish were collected, it is believed that the species existed in only about five miles of the course of the stream, for the reason that at least 15 miles of the lower course was, at that season, dry. About five miles above Rancho San Antonio are waterfalls above which no trout are known to occur."

A 1926 University of California Press booklet *The Trout of the Sierra San Pedro Mártir, Lower California*, by John Otterbein Snyder, detailed the findings of the expedition. Snyder wrote, "The cañon of the river in which these trout live is narrow and deep, and the water, according to Mr. Lamb, at times becomes warm. Insect life, too, is plentiful. The trout were found to be extremely abundant and easily caught. About 150 were taken on two fly hooks, one a brown hackle and the other a royal coachman."

While the scientists offered pages of measurements and comparisons, in layman's language they concluded that the new trout is most closely related to the Kern River trout and various species of the golden trout of the Kern River region. The similarities are the position of the dorsal, and the bright tips of the dorsal, anal, and ventral fins.

It is a wonder that the fish survived and proliferated, given their limited habitat.

Responsible for resurrecting the Baja fishery was Charles E. Utt, a person who could make things happen. Based in Orange County, he owned the Tustin Water Works and was president of the San Joaquin Fruit Company. He had a hard time selling his grapes, so he founded the Utt Juice Company. His son, James B. Utt, went on to become a U.S. Representative in Congress, serving all of Orange County (1953 to 1970).

The senior Utt had bought a ranch in Baja, and during the 1930s, he found some of the native trout living at the foot of a series of falls in the Santo Domingo Arroyo.

Over the next decade, he and the Meling brothers, Phil and Tom, had transported Nelson Rainbow Trout fingerlings to eight permanent streams including the San José, San Pedro, and San Rafael streams (Mike's Sky Ranch). They did it by muleback, pumping air into the cans every 30 minutes, day and night. The San José later dried up and the fish in that stream were lost. Trout in the other locations have survived.

The author Tomás Robertson reported that back in 1939, he joined his illustrious father-in-law Charles E. Utt in fishing the area, including the stream at the current site of the San Pedro Mártir Mission.

In the early 1980s, a group of Mexico City naturalists also transported trout to area streams to help preserve the native trout of Baja.

THE REMAINS OF THE HAMILTON RANCH
Former Ranch Hosted Celebrities

Certain old ranches have become part of Baja California folklore, especially those that had small airstrips and catered to Americans in the 1950s and '60s. As the primitive roads of Baja were used by only the hardiest adventurers, guests could literally drop in to remote locations for fishing, hunting, or relaxing.

Old books and maps list several such hideaways, including Meling Ranch, Mike's Sky Ranch, Johnson Ranch (San Antonio), Santa María Sky Ranch, Cielito Lindo, Santa Ynez, Casa Díaz, and farther south, the Serenidad in Mulegé and the Flying Sportsman in Loreto.

There was also the Hamilton Ranch, in an agricultural area about three miles in from the main road near Colonia Guerrero, north of San Quintín. It was primarily reached by the accompanying airstrip for medium-sized planes. There is an alternative route crossing the arroyo by the big red rock off the Santo Domingo Mission road.

A 1966 Auto Club guidebook notes that the ranch offered 12 rooms at $10 per person, including meals. The book also mentioned good fishing nearby, with good deer and quail hunting, and also a fair amount of duck and geese in the area.

Erle Stanley Gardner was a regular

Author Erle Stanley Gardner, whose pilot Francisco Muñoz landed many times at Hamilton Ranch, refers to it several times in his books, including this passage from 1961's *Hovering Over Baja*: "Margo Ceseña, who operates the Hattie Hamilton Ranch, is a remarkable character. Tall, vital, competent, freedom-loving and independent, she operates the ranch just as much by herself as is physically possible.... Margo is a colorful character and it is well worth a trip to the Hamilton Ranch simply to visit with her and hear her cheerful laugh...."

The ranch was originally part of an 1845 land grant to José Luciano Espinosa, who received what was then called the San Ramón Rancho and the neighboring Santo Domingo Rancho, where the 1775 Dominican mission was established. After Espinosa's widow died in 1897, San Ramón then belonged to Señor Richard Stephens, who worked as a civil engineer with the colonization companies in Baja. It later became the Randall Young Ranch, where fruit and high quality vegetables flourished, and was the major produce supplier for the entire San Quintín Valley. It then became the Hamilton Ranch.

The Hamilton Ranch

I'd read so much about this place I had to find it. After a few initial wrong turns in my Explorer, as I neared the site it became easy to spot, with its numerous wooden buildings in a grove of eucalyptus trees. The ranch dwellings rest on a high spot on the south flank of the big red rock that was the first location of the Santo Domingo Mission. Farmland spreads out on three sides below the ranch.

As I approached, the setting appeared more and more ominous. A fine layer of dust billowed about as I came to a stop. I heard and saw a generator running, but could not roust a human. The entire place was in disrepair. A worn, weather-beaten old ranch house seemed held together by the rock chimney, from which it had become partially separated. Furniture, books, and household items from a half-century past lay about the rotting wooden floors, a fine layer of dust covering it all. A couple of old cars lay rusting outside. The guest rooms, now boarded and empty, once faced a compact courtyard, today overrun by weeds. The entire place looked as if its occupants just walked away many years ago and never came back. Inside the main house near the back door, I could see books on the floor, books in English, helping to validate that this was indeed the Hamilton Ranch. I would have loved to have had the time and the permission to search the premises, but just respectfully peered in the windows.

Out back was a grave, prominent and well marked. It was that of Margarita Henkel Ceseña, born in 1907, interred in 1977. That would have been Margo.

A few of the legendary old ranchos that welcomed Baja's early visitors have survived through the years. Most, like Hamilton Ranch, did not. The grand old places had served as a vital link, bridging a desolate, remote Baja of yesteryear with the tourist developments of today's Baja California.

Gaston's Restaurant at the Old Mill, San Quintín

OLD MILL HOTEL/RESTAURANT

Developers Eye San Quintín

For uncertain reasons, back in 1542 the first European to see the San Quintín Bay, Juan Rodríguez Cabrillo, called it *Bahía de 11,000 Vírgenes* (Bay of 11,000 Virgins). Why he chose to call it that is a moot point anyway, because in 1602 Sebastián Vizcaíno renamed the place "San Quintín."

The broad fertile valley hugging the Pacific coast had been home to numerous Indians, most of whom later hooked up with the Mission Santo Domingo to the north. The beautiful, sheltered San Quintín bay, where level flatlands meet the volcanic domes of the promontory, has long been coveted by developers.

Between 1880 and 1889 the Mexican government granted several large concessions of land to foreigners to develop. The largest of these became the International Company of Mexico, organized in 1885 and managed and financed by Americans. It had a concession for all the public domain on the Baja California peninsula north of the 28th parallel.

The International Company chose Baja's two finest ports, Ensenada and San Quintín, and set about to develop them by offering future colonists lots of six and a half, 25, and 50 acres at attractive terms. A fledgling colony was thus established at San Quintín. Railroads were planned, and the company had two steamers, which made three trips weekly from San Diego.

Despite the best propaganda efforts of the International Company and their steamships, they had trouble attracting quality colonists to help settle their property.

English settlers in Baja

So the International Company sold out to an English firm headquartered in London. The subsidiary English company, the Lower California Development Company, took over 160,000 hectares (about 65,000 acres) in San Quintín and promised to settle 1,000 colonists there. They began to dig wells and create irrigation. They set about dredging the harbor and building a pier. They built a flour mill, brought in a lot of machinery, and started the construction of a Yuma-San Quintín railroad.

The enterprise failed, however, as much of this fanfare was a charade to attract investors. Neither this railroad nor the San Diego-Ensenada line was ever built.

Those 200 colonists who did emigrate to San Quintín were further devastated by drought. Despite the prodigious amounts of rainfall reported in the previous decade, nature showed how fickle she can be — between the years 1892 and 1896 there was not one inch of rainfall in San Quintín!

The San Quintín valley eventually did become an agricultural center, but development around the bay never really took off. The bay is shallow; one arm is even called False Bay because 19th-century sailors continued to get mired in the mud there.

The old mill machinery lay rusting, and the pier the English built began to deteriorate. The train trestle that crossed the channel came down, and the area for the most part had been ravaged by marine dampness, hot afternoon sunshine, and neglect.

The Old Mill attracts sportsmen

In 1951 Al and Dorothy Vela from Chula Vista took over the old English mill and opened a small motel. The Velas ran the Old Mill Motel for 30 years, themselves becoming Baja legends. Al had been an outstanding chef at the Waldorf Astoria in New York. According to Baja buff Shirley Miller, "He could even make black brant taste good and that has to be an accomplishment." The old mill building became a cannery that packaged tuna, mackerel, and sardines.

The small motel was an ideal rustic retreat. I thought that if I wanted to drop off the face of the earth, this might be a good place to hang out. As it was, on one visit I met a writer on an extended stay who admitted she enjoyed the seclusion the place had to offer.

Baja author Gene Kira notes that Ernest Hemingway's son spent time writing there. Jack Hemingway, who died in December 2000 at age 76, wrote four books on fishing, including the 1986 memoir *The Misadventures of a Fly Fisherman: My Life With and Without Papa*.

Along with the occasional recluse, the Old Mill (Molino Viejo) attracted sportsmen, who were rewarded with outstanding fishing just outside the bay.

San Martín Island is only three miles offshore and a 30 to 40 minute run north of the bay entrance. The area's catches run from "zip" or just a few rockfish to "outstanding" with tremendous yellowtail, albacore, and dorado action. The summer is usually excellent and the fringe seasons spotty, but you never know.

Long-range boats from San Diego offer two- and three-day trips to San Martín Island; sportsmen can drive the 190 miles from the border to San Quintín Bay in about five hours. The Old Mill is off the highway about three miles on a good, all-weather graded road.

The Old Mill Motel.

The Velas retired and Al and Nolo Gastón from the San Gabriel Valley bought the historic place in 1991 and immediately began restoration. Gastón's daughter and son-in-law Brenda and Joe Hayes got into the act and manage the property on a day-to-day basis.

In 1993 Gastón's Cannery restaurant opened, occupying the old cannery site. The restaurant is a delight, with thick, heavy beams, tons of old milling and canning equipment built into the décor, and a dramatic view of the inner harbor. The restaurant serves steaks, but specializes in seafood and serves excellent lobster, halibut, seabass, huachinango (red snapper), and the fish of the day.

The Gastóns added a new wing of rooms to the hotel and refurbished the older section. Not content and continually improving, they've added an RV park with full hookups across the road, several sportfishing *pangas*, a tackle shop, a dock, and an upgraded boat ramp.

To devote time to new endeavors, the Gastóns sold the hotel to Jim and Nancy Harer, who along with their son David, have seen the grand old place become a favorite destination for many sportsmen. The rooms are reasonable and comfortable.

The Old Pier is a classic

The nearby Muelle Viejo (Old Pier) Restaurant and rustic San Carlos Motel look out from the bluff over a few remaining pilings from the old pier. The Old Pier has become one of my favorite restaurants in the area, and I often pop in to visit the gracious owners, Carlos and Lupita Martín, who serve an excellent fish dinner and offer reasonable rooms with a spacious view.

Ernesto's Motel just to the north of the Old Mill did not fare so well as the others, going out of business a couple of years ago. During 2000, Ernesto's changed owners and was totally renovated. It reopened as Don Eddie's Landing. There's a restaurant, an upstairs bar with an outstanding view, hotel rooms, and charter fishing, with fishing packages available.

Developers throughout the years have often cast an interested eye at San Quintín. Over 100 years ago, first the Americans and then the English tried. Smaller-scale enterprises like the Old Mill have bucked history, but it has not been easy. The Old Mill Motel continues to advertise in stateside sporting publications and other Baja-related guides.

Now another set of developers has eyes for San Quintín; their plans are so enormous there is no way they could have avoided criticism from environmentalists, residents, and concerned Baja buffs.

Plans call for the construction of a huge tourist resort along the bay and the eight-mile-long volcano-fringed peninsula. On the drawing boards are eight hotels, three golf courses, condominiums and other residences, shopping centers, and a 350-slip marina. It is at least a $700 million project, proposed by a group of Mexico City and American investors. Of course an airport and other infrastructure would have to be built too. Now that's considerably more grandiose than the earlier English attempt.

Many people close to the situation feel that the struggle of environmentalists and others will delay the proposal for many years, if not forever. "I don't expect to see it in my lifetime," said Juanita Fitzpatrick, owner of the Cielito Lindo in San Quintín.

More likely for development is the broad Santa María beach on the outer bay. The Mexican agency FONOTUR wants to build a marina there, as they are attempting to build marinas in certain areas of Baja, equidistant from each other.

We don't know how the attempted major development of San Quintín will play out. It could make the area into another Cancun or Cabo San Lucas, to the revulsion of many long-time Baja buffs. The conservationist "Pro Estero" movement is presently digging its trenches to oppose the massive "Cabo San Quintín" project.

Just south of the Old Pier Restaurant is an old graveyard. The weathered wood crosses and concrete headstones are sometimes hard to read, but you can read enough to recognize the burial site of English-born settlers who died in Baja in the 1890s. They were a hardy group of adventurers who sought a better life in a small Mexican colony. They worked on their dreams and farmed and irrigated and built a flour mill.

They're gone and the old mill is gone, but memories of them live on. No matter what happens to the San Quintín area, those determined English settlers will have left their mark upon it.

Cielito Lindo, San Quintín

Animals in Heaven

Cielito Lindo is a Baja Legend even without the current owners' penchant for animals, which stroll the grounds unfettered. South of San Quintín, just a few hundred yards inland from the sand dunes and the broad, sweeping beach called Playa Santa María, an airstrip and a few buildings were built and the place was named Rancho El Mañana. Owned by Italians, the El Mañana enterprise was allegedly used to smuggle illegal booze — and also illegal Italians, for that matter — into southern California.

In the late 1960s it went Hollywood. Mark Armistead, producer and inventor of television's Instant Replay, bought the Rancho, and it became a hideaway for a number of his celebrity friends. John Wayne, John Huston, Ward Bond, and Henry Fonda were among the Hollywood luminaries who sought refuge at the beach hideaway.

Armistead even modeled the bar and restaurant, which are still in use, after his favorite Newport Beach, California watering hole at the time.

An ad in the Wall Street Journal

By 1975, Highway 1 had opened and an El Presidente Hotel (now La Pinta) was constructed just a quarter mile down the beach. Too many people were in the area, and Armistead's refuge no longer held the same attraction for him. He looked to sell, and thumbing through the *Wall Street Journal* one day, he saw the following ad:

> *"Wanted: Nice place to raise kids. I need a 2 or 3 bedroom house or ??? in Mexico. Call Juanita."*

He called and met Juanita Fitzpatrick, who had placed the ad. Soon Cielito Lindo (Pretty Little Heaven) would be hers, and the animals would follow.

Cielito Lindo now boasts a fine restaurant, whose specialty is a cracked crab dinner, with an historic bar, motel, airstrip, and RV park. In fact, there are devotees who claim the restaurant serves the best Blue Shell Crab dinner on the Pacific Coast. Sportfishing can also be arranged through the Cielito Lindo.

The animals are part of the lore of Cielito Lindo. My fishing buddy Don Lund and I learned about the animals a little at a time. Shortly after check-in, a goat crossed in front of us as we walked across the lawn to our room. I looked back to reassure myself that this was indeed a motel. I then noticed a couple of miniature burros munching alfalfa in a small pen against the building.

Ahead, resting against the fountain in the center of the compound, the owner, Juanita, was talking to another guest. Just then two peacocks strolled by. A larger colorful male, with puffed chest and full plumage, and a smaller female, slowly strutted past us with the assurance of propriety. They knew it was their turf.

"Nice peacocks," I said as the large birds continued around the bend.

"Thanks. They add a lot around here," the friendly, down-to-earth woman commented with a contented grin.

The other woman broke into a chuckle and added, "You ain't seen Porky yet!"

"Porky?"

Juanita beamed with pride. "Yeah, my pot-bellied pig," Juanita added. "Everybody loves Porky. He's such a dear."

Deer? I half expected to see antlers popping out of the bushes surrounding this strange motel until I realized she was still talking about Porky.

"Sounds great," I said. "With the animals this place has become so relaxing. It's been years since I've been here."

Huge numbers on motel doors

Don and I chatted a little more with them about the menagerie and then headed across the lawn toward our room. Now I couldn't miss the room as each door has a huge room number painted on it. It is so large you could spot your room from an airplane flying in (There is a small airstrip behind the Cielito Lindo). I suppose the three-foot high number also might aid those errant souls who stay in the bar too long.

As we reached the door to our room, Juanita's husband David approached and asked us to come on over to their house when we had a chance. "I want to show you something," he said, like a child withholding a surprise.

Don and I joined him at the larger house on the other side of the courtyard. We entered and I was immediately impressed with the floor: shiny and dramatic with square blocks of polished onyx, which we found also in our large motel room. But it was not the floor he wanted us to see.

Rather it was what was on the floor. After pointing out an immense "doggy door," he took us into the bedroom, where curled up on cushions at the foot of the master bed was a huge black pig.

"This is Porky," David said as he began to massage the swine's considerable belly. Porky snorted a little and continued to wallow in its luxurious "pen." "He loves to be petted," said David, beaming with almost parental pride.

I gave Porky a good rub

Okay! I reached down and touched the beast's snout. Then I moved my hand lower and gave Porky a good rub. He liked it. Like my former dog Taco, he tried to shift a little to maximize the treatment. "Nice," I said tentatively, afraid there might be a boa constrictor in the closet.

As we walked outside, David explained that the 200-pound pig was housebroken and a real member of the family. As if I couldn't tell.

The twilight sky was filled with small birds, pumping and twitting their small wings, and flying in virtual corkscrews about the grounds. They looked like the square-tailed cliff swallows of the San Juan Capistrano Mission legend. "Swallows," said David, explaining that the swallows arrive for their San Quintín rendezvous about a week before their heralded March 17th appearance at Capistrano, some 275 miles farther north.

As the small birds darted this way and that, I could see their mud homes constructed under the eaves of several motel rooms. David beamed, "We like 'em. When we paint, we even paint around their homes. In fact, the mosquito population drops to zero once they arrive.

"I tried to attract bats to stay here when the swallows go south, but they didn't seem to appreciate the homes I built for them," he continued as darkness enveloped the area. Fickle bats.

Before we left, David pointed to a small house being constructed on a nearby lot. "Now that it's just us, we're going to move to that smaller house being built over there." He went on to explain that it would be similar to the environmentally-conscious buildings that Roy Mahoof and Becky Aparicio had built at Eco Mundo, south of Mulegé. That is, made out of bales of straw and mud.

But with Porky around, I don't know if I'd want a straw house. What was it about that legend of the three little pigs?

Apparently, it's not a problem, as the house is now finished. According to a March 2001 e-mail from Juanita, "Dave and I have finally retired to our straw bale house here at Rancho Cielito Lindo with Poncho our dog, Porky Pig, and Charlie the cat. Esteban Valdez Espinoza has purchased the 12-acre business portion of the rancho and has taken over its operation. This portion is basically the bar and restaurant, motel, RV and camping area, and the big house. Dave and I will still be running the rest of the 400 acres, including homesites and monthly RV sites."

Casa Espinoza, El Rosario

Mama's Welcome Mat

Many travelers do not feel free of the U.S. influence that lingers some 200 miles south of the border until they drop down the winding road from the plateau that separates El Rosario from the Pacific. The busy border towns and frenzy of gringo developments are replaced by the vast San Quintín agricultural area. Many feel that the real Baja begins at El Rosario.

It's just a small dusty town at a bend in the road, but has always had great significance. As the next town of any consequence is another 220 miles south at Guerrero Negro, most travelers stop for fuel and other supplies. There are a couple of small modest motels, a few stores and bakeries, and several restaurants.

El Rosario was the first and southernmost mission established by the Dominican padres. From the south, the missionaries brought horses, mules, donkeys, cattle, sheep, goats, and swine. The fertile valley was suitable for planting grain and large olive and fig trees, as well as date palms and grapevines — the variety imported by the missionaries still exists.

The Indian population at El Rosario numbered 557 in 1777, but disease had reduced the population to 150 by 1824. Today there are no known full-blooded Cochimí in the area, but their heritage is evident in the current population.

In 1849, El Rosario even briefly served as the capital of the Northern District and was its largest town until 1870. Until 1900, it was still larger than either Tijuana or Mexicali.

Just down from the new Pemex at the town's entrance on the left is a little brick-red stucco building smothered in bougainvillea. For years travelers have been welcomed there by a small wooden sign nailed to the building that said, "Espinoza's Place, Gasoline, Beer and Soda, Meals, Rooms, Information, English Spoken." It has been replaced by a red wooden sign nailed to the pole out front that says simply "Mama Espinoza's."

Mama Espinoza has been serving lobster burritos, omelets, and other fare to travelers, most notably off-road enthusiasts, for years.

Casa Espinoza, El Rosario.

These days, the dining room has been enlarged and a nook set aside as a small gift shop. Both it and the restaurant are full of artifacts, and Mama's original guest book has grown to several volumes sprawling along a table. Old photos, maps, and memorabilia line the walls, including a plaque signed by NORRA President Ed Pearlman proclaiming Mama Espinoza to be a Charter Member of that off-road association.

An old deer head seems out of place on the wall overlooking the busy establishment, surrounded by posters of famous off-roaders. Adding to the eclectic décor are an old pot-bellied stove from Chihuahua, Mexico and colorful crepe piñatas that hang from the ceiling like technicolor bats in a cave.

Mama Espinoza

Anita (Mama) Espinoza has become a legend among Baja wayfarers. She was born on Oct. 16, 1910, the youngest child of the half-French, half-Italian mining engineer Eugenio Eduardo Grosso Boitare and his wife, a Pima Indian Chief's daughter, Tecla Peña.

Grosso, who earlier worked for El Boleo mine in Santa Rosalía, had developed copper mines throughout Baja and was working out of El Rosario when Anita was born. Over the next couple of years, the Mexican government was overthrown and bandits threatened raids, scaring the owners of foreign-run mines.

So Grosso sent Tecla and the youngest children to Calexico, California, where Anita lived from 1913 to 1922, learning English in school. The family later returned to El Rosario and leased a ranch.

In 1932 Anita married Heraclio Espinoza, the oldest son of the village patriarch, Santiago Espinoza. As early as 1800 one of the first land grants in the area was made to Carlos Espinoza, a retired Spanish soldier. The Espinoza family became prominent in the fertile El Rosario valley, four miles from the sea, and still is.

While Heraclio managed the family cattle ranch, Anita raised flowers and vegetables, when she wasn't raising children, that is. She gave birth to 15 children. The family moved to their present site in town right after World War II, and Anita opened a small restaurant shortly thereafter.

Doña Anita also became the Postmaster for El Rosario, a part-time job she held for 22 years. For 10 pesos a month, she would receive weekly mail in a canvas pouch for the entire valley. People would come to pick up or mail their letters and buy stamps. Outgoing mail left on that same weekly trip.

Mama Espinoza

For years, increasing numbers of expeditions had been arriving at El Rosario. (In 1905 only two parties, the author Arthur W. North and the biologist Edward W. Nelson, made the journey; by 1927 the Auto Club of Southern California made its first trek there.).

After World War II, many more cars were attempting the trip and all of them stopped at the modest building that has hardly changed over the last half century. Anita's guest register is filled with names that comprise the lore that is Baja. Almost all of the off-road racers, including such celebrity drivers as Steve McQueen and James Garner, have signed her register.

In the early years she kept tabs on those who drove south, monitoring their progress through the informal Baja grapevine. For example, her older brother Arturo Grosso owns the rancho at Laguna Chapala about 125 miles away, and if someone hadn't stopped there, it was cause for concern. Contacts like that and primitive but effective communication helped them keep track of travelers.

One of Anita's sons, Heraclio Manuel Espinoza Grosso, became a teacher. After assignments in Sonora and La Paz, Professor Espinoza returned to El Rosario and its grade school. He wanted a secondary school for El Rosario and saw his opportunity in 1974, when President Luís Echeverría rode through on the new highway. Seizing the moment, he and the schoolchildren linked hands and formed a chain across the road, forcing an unplanned stop for the presidential caravan. When young Heraclio explained the demonstration, the President was so moved he committed to establish a middle school and even gave the town an immediate cash deposit of 20,000 pesos on his promise.

Professor Espinoza was soon appointed superintendent of the vast school district, which extends from San Quintín to Guerrero Negro. He died in an auto accident near

Mexicali in 1980 at age 35. Not only was the new middle school in El Rosario named for him, but also the schools in San Quintín and Guerrero Negro as well.

Doña Anita has seen it all, including the paving of the Transpeninsular highway and the resultant increase of visitors. Her succinct comments about the road are echoed by many a longtime Baja buff, "Bad roads, good people; good roads, all kinds of people!"

Mama Espinoza's daughter, Rolli Espinoza Grosso, now manages the restaurant. She's a smart lady who speaks perfect English and runs a friendly place, continuing in the tradition established by her mother.

On an October 2000 visit I saw that another Espinoza restaurant had opened in town. Anita's granddaughter Libya Espinoza, along with her husband Martín and daughter Yasbeth, opened Baja LYM, a colorful restaurant on the left as you drive south out of town. She said that LYM was an acronym for Libya, Yasbeth and Martín.

The place serves great food, and the youthful-looking Libya and her teenage daughter Yasbeth are gracious hostesses. However, I noted Yasbeth only spoke Spanish, understanding very few words in English. At first, I thought she was kidding but when I realized she was not, I admonished her to learn. After all, her illustrious great-grandmother Anita Grosso Espinoza became part of Baja folklore partially due to her command of the English language.

Flying Samaritans

Angels on Wings

The e-mail from the Flying Samaritans advised me, "Whatever you think, perhaps cover some of the political history like in your book, and of course anything about Mama Espinoza since she was our founder." I was in the process of preparing a slide presentation for the Orange County Chapter of the Flying Samaritans, and Joan Scully was responding to my query so I could tailor the presentation to the audience.

Mama Espinoza! I didn't realize that Mama Espinoza was considered the founder of the Flying Samaritans! I'd long admired that organization of medical doctors, dentists, and nurses who pay their own expenses on frequent forays into Mexico, and now I learn that another person I'd respected, Mama Espinoza, was credited with their existence.

It appears the connection began on Nov. 13, 1961 when a group of El Rosario locals were sitting around a table at Espinoza's Place while a furious dust storm raged outside. They heard an airplane; it circled and then the sound stopped.

Some of the men jumped in a truck and headed off over the rocky road to the mesa where they correctly figured the plane had landed. The twin-engine Bonanza that was forced to put down was dangerously short of fuel, and the five shaken occupants were happy to be safe.

The pilot was Aileen Saunders Mellot, who would go on to win the world-renowned Powder Puff Derby twice. On board that day were her son Frank and friends Evangelia Hanlon, Polly Ross, and Roberta Ridgley, then of *San Diego Magazine*.

Safely ensconced in Espinoza's Place, they were delighted to meet the proprietor, Anita "Mama" Espinoza, who was fluent in English, having learned it in California as a young girl.

After Mama Espinoza fed the grateful group, her husband Heraclio and another villager drove them about 30 miles north to Santa María Sky Ranch (near present day Cielito Lindo) to spend the night and pick up some aviation gas. Mrs. Hanlon was ill, but there was no way to help her in El Rosario. El Rosario residents had earlier built a clinic, but with no supplies or equipment, nor any medical team to staff it, it had been abandoned.

Returning to El Rosario the next day to refuel and depart, they learned more about the difficult situation in the little village of El Rosario. The current drought had ruined crops and left animals to die. The village was having a tough time.

Shortly after the incident, Mama Espinoza received a letter thanking the villagers for their much-appreciated assistance, including a promise to return on December 6 to bring some things for Christmas.

It was not an idle promise. "It was beautiful when they came," said Mama Espinoza. "Nine planes formed stairsteps in the sky."

The planes brought toys and donated Christmas gifts. A Boy Scout troop from La Jolla even got into the act by gift-wrapping every package. They brought dry food, clothing, 100 pounds of candy, and medicine. According to the *San Diego Union*, "It was accepted with true Mexican dignity and low *gracias*."

The trip also brought a doctor/pilot, a last minute substitution. While the others passed out supplies, Dr. Dale E. Hoyt noticed people who needed medical attention.

It started on Mama's kitchen table

Using Mama Espinoza's kitchen table, they hung some sheets for privacy, and the townspeople came. They used candles and flashlights for illumination. It is reported that a San Diego reporter held the flashlight. They didn't know it at the time, but that was the birth of the Flying Samaritans. After treating 22 people and running out of supplies, Dr. Hoyt closed shop, but promised to return in two weeks.

He and his wife Jessie began regular trips. Then his associate, Dr. Diane Trembley, began alternating weekends. Soon other doctors, dentists, optometrists, and nurses caught the enthusiasm and began to make trips. Even craftspeople came along to help rebuild the El Rosario clinic.

By early 1962 a formal organization called the Flying Samaritans was formed in San Diego, and monthly trips to El Rosario were being made. Aileen Saunders Mellot became the first president. A second clinic opened in Colonet in 1963 in facilities provided by Andy Bradley, a retired Mexican-American living there.

Soon other clinics were opened in other Baja California villages lacking medical facilities. Their arrival is always anticipated by the rural *bajacalifornios*, some of whom make long, arduous journeys by horse, cart, or truck to get medical attention.

The Flying Samaritans grew and is now organized in 12 chapters, mostly in southern California, but also with chapters in northern California, Arizona, and Rosarito

Beach. They regularly serve 17 clinics throughout the state of Baja California, with each chapter maintaining one or more clinics.

A typical Flying Samaritan trip includes about 20–22 volunteers, each paying a portion of the aviation fuel as well as their own expenses. They each have specialized duties; most chapters have the following coordinators: Pilot/Trip, Clinic, Nurse, Optometrist, Pharmacist, Dentist, Dental Hygienist, Chiropractor, Audiologist, Translator, and Support. One or two members fill each role on the regularly scheduled monthly trips.

Each chapter has officers and regular meetings, plus there is an annual International Conference.

Altruistic men and women

The altruistic nature of those dedicated men and women who make up the Flying Samaritans is well noted in this quote from their brochure:

> "Just seeing the look of gratitude on a patient's face, knowing that you have helped relieve their pain or worry is more than enough thanks. The feeling of satisfaction that comes from helping someone see better with a pair of glasses or watching as a child hears for the first time are the priceless rewards of one person helping another.
>
> "In the evening after a hard day's work we sit around the dinner table or campfire and reflect on the friendships that were made with each other and the people of Mexico, remembering that as individuals, we are the most effective ambassadors to our neighbors to the south."

In their many hundreds of hours of air time, the organization has had remarkably few accidents, but one great tragedy took the lives of volunteers. In the early days, a plane was leaving El Rosario when a wing came off, and it crashed and burned. Aboard were the hard-working Julian Burchett, the American nurse Linda Cox, and two local girls who were headed to the U.S. to work as babysitters.

The tragedy was a great personal loss for those who helped get the Flying Samaritans off to a start. The two girls, Gloria and Yoly, were both Espinozas, sisters of Mama's husband Heraclio.

The gracious Señora Anita "Mama" Espinoza praises the wonders performed by these selfless Americans. After a couple of decades of service, she said, "The Samaritans have saved many lives, and many mothers in their delivering. They need only wings to fly and be Angels."

Francisco Muñoz

Baja's Best Bush Pilot

Poor and nonexistent roads throughout the Baja California peninsula gave birth to legendary bush pilots during the middle years of the 20th century. During the decades from the 1930s to the 1970s, flying was in many cases the only way to visit some ranchos, towns, remote sites, and most of the new resorts.

The greatest of the Baja bush pilots was unquestionably Captain Francisco Muñoz. The mystery writer Erle Stanley Gardner, better known for his Perry Mason series than his seven books on Baja California, often called upon Captain Muñoz to get him into and out of some extremely remote locations. That Gardner spoke in awe of the pilot is putting it mildly.

Muñoz was a former lobster pilot who transported live lobsters in all types of weather and conditions. Because of this, Gardner explains in *Hovering over Baja*, his 1961 Baja book, "So these Baja California pilots learn to fly by instinct, the seat of their pants, an inherent skill and a daring resourcefulness which puts them out in front as the world's best and most daring fliers. My friend Francisco Muñoz is one of these pilots."

Later, Gardner describes Muñoz taking off from an extremely short mountainous strip,

> "I watched with my heart in my mouth as Muñoz took off from that landing strip. From our vantage point in the helicopter poised a couple of hundred feet above the landing strip, we could see the whole procedure, and as Muñoz started lifting the plane into the air, I felt certain he wasn't going to make it.
>
> "As Muñoz explained to me later, on a short landing strip it is always advisable to take advantage of all the landing strip there is. Some people, he explained, get nervous and try to use only half or three-quarters of the strip. Muñoz takes it all."

By his seventh Baja book, Gardner had offered many instances of Muñoz's flying prowess. In *Off the Beaten Path in Baja* Gardner tells of being caught in a storm over northern Baja on a trip from Tijuana to Mulegé. Along with Muñoz and Gardner were Jean Bethell and the writer Choral Pepper, who was editor of *Desert Magazine*. Gardner describes an adventure in which Muñoz tried different altitudes, circling and circling waiting for the weather to break, and finally dropped down very low to follow the coastline to where he could safely land at the Hamilton Ranch.

"We taxied up to the Ranch — just about the most welcome sight I have ever seen in my life," admitted Gardner, who immediately asked where the men's room was.

Francisco Muñoz not only had known Hattie Hamilton, but was a longtime friend of the Meling family and knew the proprietors of all the other remote ranchos.

At first he had only one plane, but branched out until he ran a small airline serving Baja and parts of mainland Mexico. He also chartered flights like those for Gardner. He used to fly the parents of author Marion Smothers to Bahía de los Angeles. He last worked for Exportadora de Sal at Guerrero Negro as their chief pilot.

Tom Miller's *Baja Book III* calls Captain Muñoz Baja's "Numero Uno" pilot:

> Few people become legends in their own time, but captain Francisco Muñoz became one nearly a half-century ago. ...A large percentage of the small dirt strips in Baja, and some of the paved landing fields, would probably not exist

had it not been for this amazing man. His expertise in getting in and out of tight quarters has led to many stories, one of which is that Captain Muñoz can make a wheelbarrow fly and can land a DC-6 in a sand trap. But his true exploits are in the supplying of remote ranchos and fishing villages, and his roles in countless search and rescue missions.

Erle Stanley Gardner's books featured numerous photos of Señor Muñoz. You could easily identify the dapper pilot, as he was the only guy in Gardner's remote camps wearing a tie. He still has an impressive presence and these days, Captain Francisco Muñoz and his wife, Lisle, live in the San Diego area.

Fellow Baja authors and writers Fred Hoctor, Ann Hazard, and Lynn Mitchell are among those who have their own Francisco Muñoz stories. I've never been fortunate enough to have flown with him, but I have met Señor Muñoz and realized I had shaken hands with a true Baja legend.

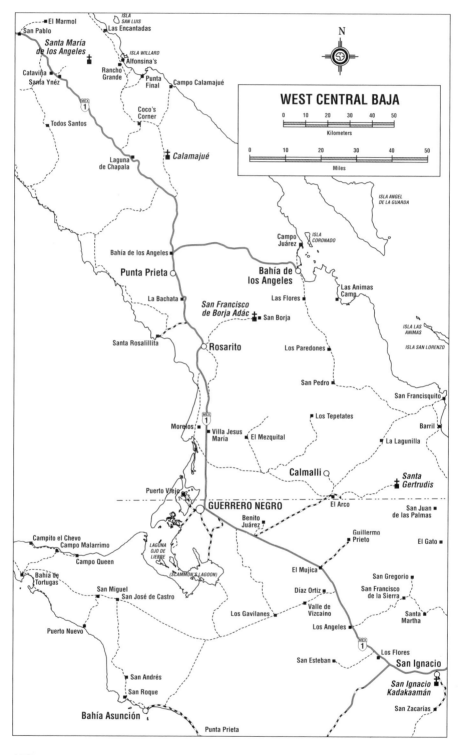

Chapter 10: Central Baja

Cirios cover the hills of central Baja.

Cirios, the Boojum Trees

As you drive south from El Rosario, the highway crosses the riverbed and starts winding into the hills, where the traveler will first glimpse the strange and unusual cirio tree.

The cirio grows only between latitude 30 and 29, between El Rosario on the north to a hilly area just north of Guerrero Negro on the south, approximately a 250-mile range. There's a small colony of cirios on the Mexican mainland, and nowhere else on this earth can you find it.

The cirio is a round stubby plant that grows to what looks like a tall, thin thorny-stubbed exotic-looking upside-down carrot. Some grow to almost 60 feet, straight and tall like tapered telephone poles. Others bend and loop in bizarre contortions. It's a member of the ocotillo family and often has other branches that look like the arms of an octopus. In the winter cirios have dark green leaves. In the summer you can note small pale yellow or white flowers.

Baja's Mexicans, due to their Catholic nature, call it a cirio or wax candle, as it tapers like a religious candle. The earlier Cochimíes called it *milapa*.

In 1922 an expedition led by Mr. Godfrey Sykes of the Desert Botanical Laboratory in Tucson saw the strange plant. Sykes called it a "boojum" from the Lewis Carroll story *Hunting of the Snark*. Carroll calls a legendary creature in a far-off corner of the world a boojum, also using the term as one who dwells on distant desert shores.

Call it whatever, cirio, boojum, or even *milapa*. Once you've seen this strange plant, you'll never forget it. It's another oddity of that distant desert called Baja.

El Mármol Mine
The Onyx Capital of the World

While El Mármol means "marble" in Spanish, the product of the central Baja quarry of El Mármol is actually the more valuable onyx. At one time this quarry was the world's largest producer of onyx.

El Mármol is off Highway 1 some 70 miles past El Rosario on a nine-mile dirt road. It's now a deserted mine where you can marvel at the immense slabs of onyx and the old schoolhouse, which was made entirely out of blocks of the creamy stone. Most of the schoolhouse is still standing, but inconsiderate people have taken chunks off the building, which is not only unfortunate but unnecessary. All around the area there are many slabs and chunks of the luscious stone, there for the picking.

"Lush and creamy" describes the stone, as much of it is milky white; some stones contain streaks of Venetian red or burnt umber, making them look like caramel topping mixed with French vanilla ice cream. When cut and polished for ashtrays, bookends, paperweights, penholders, knickknacks, or figurines, the stone shines like smooth marble and is an object of beauty.

Making the difficult commonplace

The mining operation at El Mármol was a lesson in determination and making the difficult commonplace, so typical of Baja legends.

For millennia the onyx has bubbled out of the ground in this remote section of central Baja, some 300 miles south of Tijuana and about halfway between El Rosario and Punta Prieta. At nearby El Volcan the bubbling carbonated springs still produce the onyx that similarly formed long ago at the El Mármol quarry.

Because of the unusual conditions required for its production, it is an uncommon stone, and for years, North Africa was the world's chief source.

In Baja, the surface around the arid country at El Mármol is mostly mica schists and silicified limestones. After the springs flowed, erosion exposed travertine on the lowest layer and above that, alternating bands of limestone and onyx.

The deposit was discovered in the early 1890s by gold prospectors and the find was announced in scientific journals. That attracted George P. Merrill, head of the Geology

A school made from onyx.

Department of the Smithsonian Institute, to visit the site. A piece was polished for display at the then-current Colombian Exposition, and that prompted development by an American company.

The company changed hands several times, but the American Southwest Onyx and Marble Company, based in San Diego, had the most success. Early on, large slabs of El Mármol onyx were shipped to grace the lobby of San Diego's new Spreckels Theater.

The resident managers for the San Diego-based company were first George P. Brown and then his son, Kenneth Brown, both legends of the El Mármol onyx operation. George P. Brown, an engineer, took charge of the operation in 1919 and trained his son to assist. The younger Brown took over in 1934 and was the mine's driving force for 25 years until it went out of business in 1958.

Even though the nearest drinking water was at Rancho San Agustín eight miles away, a small mining village consisting of crude wooden buildings was constructed. There were some 300 people living there by the late 1920s, all Mexican workers and their families, with the exception of the manager. Water was brought in regularly in a 3,000-gallon truck. Even under these conditions, Mrs. Brown, a former society debutante from Kansas City, was able to tend a small flower garden.

The world's only onyx school

The one-room school was built for the employees' children and can boast of being the world's only school to be constructed entirely out of blocks of onyx. In the late 1950s when visited by the writer O.W. Timberman (*Mexico's Diamond in the Rough*), 16 students were being taught by one 18-year-old teacher. I counted 24 students in an earlier photo (1953). Now the wooden roof is gone but 3 and a half of the walls still stand.

The mined onyx lies in thick layers near the surface. Large slabs were pried loose by six or eight men with pry bars, then lifted to the surface by a huge derrick run by two other men. These large blocks, some weighing as much as several tons, were then numbered for shipment.

Getting the onyx to port

But getting the onyx out of the mine was not the only onerous task. Getting it to market was a very difficult process, as Tijuana was just over 300 miles away. The Pacific Ocean was 48 miles distant; the mining operation established a port there at Santa Catarina. I have driven the road to Puerto Santa Catarina some 40 to 50 years later and can only label it very bad. It couldn't have been any better in the days when the ponderous old Reo and Commando trucks carried the heavy onyx to port. The old trucks used hard rubber tires that even then had not been in production for years. Visitors to El Mármol during the 1950s noted many hard-rubber wheels stockpiled for the arduous, rocky journey.

At Santa Catarina the onyx awaited the cargo ships. When one came in, 50 or 60 miners went there to load. Flat-bottom lighters (like long canoes), just 14 or 15 feet long with 8-foot beams, were specially designed to carry the onyx to the ship without tipping over. A lighter could carry 10 tons on each trip to the ship anchored approximately a quarter mile offshore. Optimum tides and calm seas were required to get the job done. Because of big waves and rough seas, some days only six to 12 tons could be loaded, while on other days they could load from 50 to 100 tons. It usually took about 12 days to load a ship, with the ship's booms lowering the cargo into the holds.

Previous to El Mármol, onyx from Algerian quarries had added many luxurious touches to Europe's cathedrals, churches, and public buildings, including the grand staircase of the Paris Opera House.

During the heyday of El Mármol, Baja onyx found its way around the world to markets in England, Belgium, the Orient, and the U.S., most of it used for mantelpieces, tabletops, and smaller ornamental objects. Mr. Brown even supervised the cutting, loading, and hauling of a statue for the St. Paul, Minnesota courthouse that weighed over 120,000 pounds. It was 85 feet tall and 21 feet wide.

There was one moment of glory for El Mármol onyx, as legend has it that early Hollywood's "Vamp Girl" Theda Bara ordered one huge block from which to have her bathtub carved. According to an old press release, the smooth-stoned onyx bathtub was graced with gold faucets, naturally.

The quality of onyx taken out of Baja's remote outback was considered the finest anywhere. However, due to the post-World War II advent of plastics and other inexpensive materials, demand for the pricy onyx dropped. The mine closed down in 1959, and Mr. Brown went to live in San Diego.

Behind where Highway 1 passes the Rancho San Agustín there is a dirt road to El Mármol. I often take the time to drive the 18-mile round-trip dirt road and look around or add a few new pieces to my gardens. Mostly, I just like to be there to feel another remarkable part of Baja's history coursing through my veins.

The rustic rooms at Rancho Santa Ynez.

RANCHO SANTA YNEZ

A Rustic Respite in Cataviña

Because of its strategic position far from anywhere, many Baja travelers spend the night in the Cataviña area, an enchanting, ethereal, boulder-tumbled landscape about 120 miles south of San Quintín.

There's the La Pinta Hotel, but for campers or travelers on a budget, they might try Rancho Santa Ynez. Less than a mile south of the La Pinta, after Highway 1 crosses the shallow creek bed dappled with native blue palms, there's a short half-mile road off to the left that leads to a typical Baja rancho.

Rancho Santa Ynez has been welcoming travelers to this desolate location for years. Indeed, before the highway was paved nearby and accompanying accommodations built, everyone who drove the old road stopped at the remote and restful Rancho Santa Ynez. They even arrived by plane, stopping at the paved airstrip built on the nearby knoll.

Off-roaders have been stopping at Santa Ynez for years, and the windows of the small kitchen/dining area are covered with their signature stickers. Santa Ynez has always been a good value, with typical ranch fare served: *tacos, enchiladas, machaca, huevos rancheros*, sodas, and beer. Breakfasts include the wonderfully spelled "huevos con hotkeks."

Wayfarers meet on hard dining room benches and compare notes from the road under the illumination of a propane lantern, which the owners turn off early. No problem — there's a large level grassy field where their guests can set up camp, complete with a plumbed restroom in its center. They also have a handful of small rooms at the rancho for rent at excellent rates. I've found their lodging to be as comfortable as the nearby hotel at a fraction of the cost. Of course, all the power goes off at 9:30 p.m.

While the original owner of the land was a Señor González, it was Señora Josefina Zúñiga Ramos who developed the rancho. In 1904, she had been born to an upper-class family in Sonora, Mexico that fled to Arizona and Calexico, California during the revolution. At age 17 Josefina moved to San Diego where she went to work in a department store.

By World War II, Josefina bought and managed apartment houses in San Diego. Speaking good English by this time, she also became the U.S. buyer for the Mexican Army stationed in the northern part of Baja California.

According to an article in the *Mexico West Newsletter* by Marvin Patchen (Sept. 1989), in 1956 Josefina was shown home movies of Rancho Santa Ynez and bought it sight unseen. She also acquired the adjoining land creating a rancho of 854 acres. Then she helped develop Punta Final, a small mostly-gringo development on the gulf. As Mission Santa María is in the mountains behind Rancho Santa Ynez, perceptive Josefina also bought 47 acres surrounding the mission site to help protect and preserve the site.

She became a true Baja pioneer and also established a clinic between the rancho and the highway — the only medical help for miles around. Patchen also reported that the clinic was built by the famous off-road racers Bill Stroppe and Parnelli Jones in her honor.

Josefina died in August 1989 at the age of 86. Off-roader Brian Chuchua used his helicopter to erect a large cross on the mountain overlooking the rancho as a tribute to her. Her nephew and other family members still own Rancho Santa Ynez, but live in Ramona, California and have others as resident managers.

Señor Oscar Valdez Romero has now been managing the Santa Ynez Rancho for 20 years. He and his wife Matilda de Valdez are assisted these days by their daughter Yesenia Valdez Rodríguez and her husband José Lucas Gómez Sánchez and their family.

Marion Smothers in *Vintage Baja* mentions Santa Ynez before the road was paved,

> "After a sumptuous dinner that could include quail, deer, carne asada or sea turtle — always with the Señora's famous enchiladas — we would share a campfire and music before turning in for the night. My fellow travelers were mostly truck drivers hauling live sea turtles north to Ensenada, trucks heavy with onyx from El Mármol, stake trucks loaded with cured hides, a Baja Buff or two, sometimes a prospector with his burro train, once in a while a goat herder and his charges going God-knows-where, or a scientist, such as a botanist doing field collecting. A real mixed bag sharing the courtyard, sleeping under the stars."

A sparkling ceiling overhead

The first time I camped in the field I discovered that in this clear, dry desert the brightness of the stars created a sparkling ceiling so bright we didn't need the flashlight. Then in the morning we enjoyed a hot breakfast before continuing our trip.

While I have rented rooms at Santa Ynez, in December 1996 son Ken and I camped out again, sleeping in his truck on a rainy night, hearing the drops pound the metal above our heads. It was muddy in the morning, but not quite the quagmire I'd feared.

Over dinner we met a couple of German bicyclists who had come to "Challenge the Baja." The camaraderie of diverse strangers sharing experiences and warmth is part of what lures many to explore Baja.

While nowadays, the larger tourist hotels have allowed more people to drive the length of the Baja California peninsula, the ranchos like Santa Ynez and their star-studded sleeping quarters are the Baja legends that will endure.

Rancho Laguna Chapala

A Dry Lake Legacy

Before 1973, in the days before the Transpeninsular Highway, sometimes the only place any speed at all could be reached was at Laguna Seca Chapala, a dry lake bed in Central Baja. But the exhilarating ride was short-lived and first earned by traversing a maze of dirt tracks.

From the north the old road entered deep, flour-fine silt, where drivers had created many tracks while trying to find a smoother, less-dusty section. As many as 40 or 50 roads took off in seemingly every direction over a couple of miles, crossing and recrossing each other, and no matter which one you took, you wished you had taken one of the others.

All the roads through the deep powder, however, invariably ended at the Rancho Chapala on the edge of the dry lake bed. There a rancho was founded by a hardy Baja pioneer, Señor Arturo Grosso Peña.

Grosso, the oldest son of an Italian mining engineer from Santa Rosalía and his Indian wife, became a central Baja legend in his own time. Born in 1892, the oldest brother of Señora Anita "Mama" Espinoza of El Rosario, Arturo Grosso had also aided travelers for years. His modest rancho allowed travelers to camp, offering small guest rooms for just $1 per person, and meals. He even encouraged campers to unroll their sleeping bags on his dining room floor if it was too windy outside. There was a 2,000-foot packed dirt airstrip between a nearby hill and the rancho.

Grosso was a soldier and became known as the person who could get things done. Baja's Northern Territory Governor Abelardo Rodríguez turned to Grosso in 1925 for a special project, to build a road for cars through the most impossible terrain of Baja California.

The road would extend from El Rosario in the north to El Arco in the south, a link of about 250 miles. With no engineer or other supervision, "Jefe" Arturo Grosso led a team of only six or seven workers and got the job done in one year. They had a 1924 Ford to shuttle the workers, their tools (rudimentary picks and shovels), supplies, and food. Years later the paved road would closely follow Grosso's original work. The building of the road is just one story attributed to the indomitable Mr. Grosso.

Erle Stanley Gardner in his 1961 book *Hovering over Baja* describes Grosso's broad influence: "Grosso is an intelligent man, an energetic man, and, according to Baja California standards, a rich man. He has many head of cattle and he has the ability to look and plan ahead.

He has sufficient cash margin to hire cowboys and all through this section of the country Arturo Grosso is a power. Grosso is friendly, speaks good English and is keenly interested in people and in events."

There are several stories and photos about Arturo Grosso in the Museum at Bahía de los Angeles, but another notable and true Grosso tale describes his creation of another road, the San Felipe-Calamajué road.

Baja California became a Mexican state in 1952 and was attempting to attract tourists. San Felipe, on the gulf, was just being developed, and in 1955 the state government offered a 10,000 peso reward (about $800 at the time) if someone could create a road from San Felipe south to tie in with the old main road (built by Grosso thirty years previously) near the dry lake bed.

Arturo Grosso-Peña

Arturo Grosso rose to the challenge, got some dynamite, and blasted a road he could drive his truck through. The road, through Gonzaga Bay and Puertecitos, became known as the "three sisters," for three major summits and was considered one of Baja's more difficult roads until it was graded about a decade ago.

But it was a road nonetheless, and it led tourists to the once-secluded Gonzaga Bay area and to connect with the main road south. The rancho at Chapala also became an important rest stop for participants in the early Baja 1,000 off-road races.

There are many legends surrounding Grosso; he was so adept at getting things done that it became hard to separate fact from fancy. He was a practical joker and delighted in shocking people who asked what they had just eaten by taking them back into the storeroom and pointing at some dried strips of various game, sometimes with the hair still on it. According to his sister, "Any animal that had legs was fair game for Arturo's stews."

He loved to talk to American visitors in English. He'd drink beer with them and then often talk them into a footrace, which the wiry rancher would win almost every time.

Admittedly, he used to help people smuggle illegal parrots into the United States. The smugglers would land at the Chapala airstrip and pay Grosso to water, feed, and care for the parrots while awaiting their journey north. One story he loved to tell was about how once he was shopping on Market Street in San Diego and heard someone say, "Arturo Grosso, Arturo Grosso." He looked and saw a pet store with two parrots on perches. One said to the other one, "Isn't that Arturo Grosso from Chapala?" He told the story so many times that even people close to him began to wonder if it could be true.

When the Transpeninsular Highway was paved in 1973, it bypassed Grosso's Rancho Chapala. No problem. He just moved his rancho — lock, stock and barrel — two kilometers west to the new road.

Grosso and his wife had five children, a son, Eugenio Grosso, and four daughters. Eugenio, now forty-five years old, his wife Hortencia, and their three children presently run the Rancho Chapala. It's rustic, a holdover from a time gone by, but the friendliness lingers. Truck drivers who ply the highway stop for coffee and good basic food. The old wooden walls are decorated by a lot of framed jigsaw puzzles; the incongruous lush mountain scenery and European buildings were obviously attractive to the Grossos, who painstakingly assembled them.

Three of Grosso's daughters have left the arid Laguna Chapala area, but have not migrated far. One moved to Bahía de los Angeles, another to El Rosario, and the third to San Vicente. Eight years ago the fourth, Naty, established her own Rancho Laguna Chapala one kilometer north of the older one.

The original legendary rancher and road-builder Arturo Grosso died on his 85th birthday, Apr. 15, 1977. All the family members I've met throughout Baja, including a grandson, Javier, share the pride of their illustrious grandfather. It was good to learn that the simple life led by this man out in the middle of one of the driest, most desolate corners of the universe could have such an influence on people.

Dick Daggett, Pioneer

The Legend of Las Flores

Mining for gold, silver, and copper began about 1880 in the Bahía de Los Angeles area near the Sea of Cortez. The area's first mine was called the Santa Marta. Then capitalists from Sonora, Mexico developed the San Juan silver mine, which became the largest producing mine in all of Baja California.

The San Juan mine was eight miles back into the mountains, so a narrow-gauge railroad using a scaled-down engine and cars was built to transport the ore from the mine to a mill. A small town called Las Flores came into being at the mill site. The town and milling operation provided a contrast to the flat desert floor about nine miles south of Bahía de los Angeles.

Heavy mining and milling machinery was brought into the bay by boat. Mule, burro and wagon trains then transported it all to Las Flores, with much of the machinery having to be dismantled and reassembled.

The mine flourished for a time, and legend has it that $2 million worth of silver was recovered. They even strung up a telephone from the loading dock to the Las Flores processing area and on up to the San Juan mine. The mine has not been worked since the Mexican Revolution of 1910, so the mill town of Las Flores lost its reason for existence. After the town died, most of the buildings were torn down for the lumber. Today visitors who drive down the dirt road from Bahía de los Angeles can find rusting hunks of machinery, pilings, and even an historic old adobe jail.

They wrote the area's history

I'd been to the Las Flores town site several times, but hadn't noticed the small cemetery until last year. There, inscribed on modest headstones, were the names of those who wrote the area's history. The most prominent marker simply said, "Richard Daggett, 1893–1969,

Don Lund with mining equipment at Las Flores Mine

En Paz Descanse (Rest In Peace). That would have been Dick Daggett Jr., I mused, knowing that his father had arrived in the early 1880s.

Other markers tied an early Anglo family with another family of early settlers, and connected the past with the present: "Reyes de Daggett, 12-12-1897, At Age of 23 Years," "Isabel Arce," "Germana Arce, 1901, 30 Years Old," "Josefa Arce de Daggett, 19 March 1888–3 December 1972,"and "René Daggett, 30 August 1962–2 October 1994." Also buried at Las Flores is the family patriarch himself, Dick Daggett Sr.

Daggett jumped ship

Daggett Sr., an Englishman from Oxford, England, was a junior officer on a German ship that came to the port with bricks for the new mine buildings. He disliked his captain and jumped ship. The German captain came ashore and searched for the deserter, but Daggett's new Mexican friends hid him in a cave. The captain unknowingly hired the same man who hid Daggett to search for him, and that man led the German on a wild goose chase. Frustrated, the captain sailed off without his English junior officer.

Daggett got a job at the Las Flores mining operation and married a young girl from the Arce family of San Ignacio. He became mine superintendent in 1892. For a while he was partners with Señor Eduardo Grosso, an Italian whose children Anita (Mama) Espinoza and Arturo Grosso have also become Baja legends.

Dick Daggett became a true Baja Character. In the 1910 book *Camp and Camino in Lower California*, author Arthur W. North mentions being impressed by the "fascinating Englishman." According to North, he was "an irrepressible, good-natured, daring, devil-may-care adventurer."

One of Daggett's duties was to build the jail. Made out of stone, it has two small barred windows, still intact, and two heavy iron doors. His son Dick Daggett Jr. said that the majority of the jail's offenders were drunk miners.

Joseph Wood Krutch in his 1961 book *The Forgotten Peninsula* confirms that statement by relating an interesting legend about the Las Flores jail: "The liquor bar, of which nothing now remains, was located some little distance further from the settlement in such a position that the Mexican workers returning from refreshment there must pass by the jail to get back home. If they had drunk too deep they could be halted by the jailer without the necessity of pursuit and could be confined until morning — by which time, it was hoped, they would be sober enough to go back to work."

Las Flores Jail

A skilled, improvising mechanic

Señor Dick Daggett Jr., "Diquito," who was very skilled at improvising, a preeminent trait of Baja mechanics, became known for his mechanical wizardry. He was said to have always walked around with a wrench in his hand. Whenever word reached him that a traveler needed help, he'd drop what he was doing, grab whatever rescue equipment he thought might be needed, and head out to help. He came to the rescue of many gringos whose vehicles were stalled by the infamous Baja roads.

In one of his books, Erle Stanley Gardner even commented, "In 1962, Dick Daggett consented to go with our expedition to show us the way. And it was well he did because, without a man who knew the country, exploring this tract of desert where there is no vestige of a road might have been disastrous."

Dick Daggett Jr. had also married a girl from San Ignacio, Josefa, and they had two children; the one who died as a baby was also named Dick. The other, Trinidad Daggett Arce, married and had six children, three boys and three girls.

One of the three boys, Rubén Daggett, now runs Daggett's Beach Camping. On the beach two miles north of town, Daggett's offers beach spaces, RV parking, showers, guides for fishing and whale watching, and kayak rentals. With an engaging smile and typical Baja grace, Rubén Daggett often works the fishing Tackle and Boat Shows in California and encourages Baja visitors to "Come on down."

Rubén and his brothers and sisters, the great-grandchildren of the original sailor, are only one-eighth English. Las Flores, a long-forgotten chapter of Baja lore, lives on through the memories of many early Baja pioneers. And the Daggetts in the Bahía de los Angeles area enjoy a link with the area's history through their adventurous patriarch, Dick Daggett Sr., an Englishman who jumped ship to seek a better life.

Casa Díaz, Bahía de los Angeles

Mama and Papa Leave Legacy

After the mine and mill at nearby Las Flores closed down, the pretty little bay of Bahía de los Angeles languished. Later on, an energetic young man named Señor Antero "Papa" Díaz had a dream that he might attract American sportsmen to the midriff fishery on the picturesque bay.

Unfortunately the area was an arduous three-day overland journey from Ensenada. Undaunted, by the 1950s Papa Díaz had scraped a small airplane landing field, built six small cabins with primitive showers and opened a dining room that would be presided over by his wife, Cruz Rosas Ortiz "Mama" Díaz. Calling the enterprise Casa Díaz, the pair soon became enduring Baja legends.

Both born in the Mexico City area, they got married in 1939 when 25-year-old Antero came to Baja California to work in the mines. He worked at Calmallí to the south and Desengaño just to the north of Bahía de los Angeles. Times were tough, and the pair moved back and forth from Baja to Mexico City several times between 1939 and 1945, when they returned to Bahía de los Angeles to establish their legacy for good.

There were just a handful of families in the area at the time. In addition to Díaz there were mostly the Daggetts (the children and grandchildren of the Englishman Dick Daggett Sr.) and the large family of mine worker Tilongo Smith. Tilongo's grandson Fermín Smith is currently the village *delegado* (mayor). In addition there were the Ocañas, Navarros, Verdugos, and Corderos. Even today, almost the entire populace of about 800 is from one of those families.

In 1941 just a small group of villagers at "Angeles Bay" greeted writer John Steinbeck and marine scientist Edward Ricketts when their *Western Flyer* made anchor there: "The *Coast Pilot* had not mentioned any settlement, but here there were new buildings, screened and modern, and on a tiny airfield a plane sat. It was an odd feeling, for we had been a long time without seeing anything modern. Our feeling was more of resentment than of pleasure. We went ashore about three thirty in the afternoon, and were immediately surrounded by Mexicans who seemed curious and excited about our being there. They were joined by three Americans who said they had flown in for the fishing, and they too seemed very much interested in what we wanted until they were convinced it was marine animals...."

By the 1950s it was still a small settlement of 60 people, and Antero became *delegado* of Bahía de los Angeles.

Fly-in sport fishing

Antero "Papa" Díaz gradually began to develop his fly-in sport fishing business, and by the 1950s he operated the general store, a small service station for autos and planes, and two landing fields, one along the beach (north-south) and the other about a mile away on a mesa (east-west).

With the profits, he built the distinctive stone buildings of Casa Díaz, opening the original buildings in 1960. Today's main complex, which includes the arched store,

The village of Bahía de los Angeles.

restaurant, and some of the guest rooms, was completed in 1963. Papa and Mama Díaz offered a family-style restaurant, boats for rent, clean quarters with showers, ice plant, and a smokehouse for fish. Antero also ran a large turtle business back then, sending 60 to 80 turtles each trip to Tijuana and points north.

To develop his community, Antero Díaz built the one-room original schoolhouse, even encouraging American sportsmen to kick in. He also built the little chapel outside of Casa Díaz, using blocks of onyx from the El Mármol quarry. Señor Díaz regularly read stories from a Spanish newspaper to groups of illiterate men who would gather outside his store.

Home-cooked meals at Casa Díaz

Rooms at Casa Díaz included meals, and Mama Díaz became a legend, preparing sumptuous banquets from the sea. In 1961 Marion Smothers said in *Vintage Baja*, "You've never really had yellowtail until you've sampled Mama's, only hours from your jig to her pan to your plate. And if Antero ruled the *campo*, Mama ruled Antero — make no mistake about that!"

In 1961 Erle Stanley Gardner wrote of Bahía de los Angeles, "It is known to scores of sportsmen having private planes, and on weekends plane after plane will come in bringing adventurous fishermen or people who simply want to make the trip and relax in the warm sunshine of the gulf, or perhaps to get in a little fishing; but above all, to sample the fabulous cooking prepared under the direction of Señora Díaz."

Six years later, he continued the compliment in a different book by writing, "Bahia de los Angeles has some of the best home-cooked food anyone could ask for. Señora Díaz cooks lobster and fish so sweet and tender they will melt in your mouth."

An interesting sidelight that few people are aware of is that one of America's greatest heroes and by far its most famous aviator, Charles Lindbergh, flew a small plane into Bahía de los Angeles. He spent the day, but only one known photograph recorded his visit. At the village museum, it shows Lindbergh with Mama Díaz.

Antero "Chubasco" Díaz Jr.

The road to Bahía de los Angeles was paved in October 1974, a 40-mile one-way road off Highway 1. That same year Cliff Cross in his book *Baja California* wrote: "Casa Díaz has a unique feature. When the evenings are warm, the indoor innerspring beds are given up for Mexican cots on the cooler porch where guests can look up at the stars."

My first visit to Bahía de los Angeles was in the 1970s. A friend and I enjoyed Mama's family-style dinner, and we too slept out among the stars. I've been to the area many times, and even this past summer noted many guests dragging their bunks out to the porch to catch the breeze from the gulf.

Antero Díaz, the village founder, who was born in 1914, died in 1989. A eulogy written by Baja author Tom Miller explains the attitude of many: "The relationship of Papa Díaz with the Baja old-timers — the pilots, off-roaders, fishermen and other adventure types who entered his always open door — was special. I am richer for having known Antero "Papa" Díaz, as are thousands of others."

His widow, Cruz Rosas Ortiz "Mama" Díaz, who was being cared for by family members her last few years, died in Ensenada in October 2000. Casa Díaz is still being run by the Díaz family.

The seven children of Antero and Cruz — Rosa María, Rafaela, Aurora, Anita, Elvira, Sammy, and Antero Jr. — were all born between 1937 and 1952. Only two still live in town. Sammy, the oldest boy, and his two sons run the fishing operation and the fuel supply and tire shop. Sammy also has two daughters, Anita and Rosa. Antero Jr., who has three daughters, runs the store, restaurant, and guest rooms. Antero Jr. is known as "Chubasco" to the townsfolk because he was born during a violent storm or *chubasco*. The family members continue the tradition of Mama and Papa.

Guillermo's and Las Hamacas

The town has grown up around the original Casa Díaz. Now there are several markets, restaurants, and other modest motels. There's Guillermo's, a great restaurant and motel complex on the bay, run by Guillermo Galván and his sister Lucy Galván. Guillermo's son Ygor and mother Socorro also help out at Guillermo's.

There's also Las Hamacas, which keeps getting bigger every time I see it, and is owned by the enterprising José and Delia Ortega and family.

The old airstrip has, in the interest of safety, been abandoned, and a new paved airport is north of town.

I am mostly in awe at the fine quality of the Natural History and Cultural Museum of Bahía de los Angeles. There are fossil and shell exhibits, extensive exhibits from the indigenous Cochimí and other Indians, the missions, and mining and ranching activities. T-shirts, postcards, and historic photos are available; outdoors are whale skeletons and a native botanical garden. It's open from 9 to 12 noon and 2 to 4 p.m. daily from October to June.

Bahia de los Angeles is, for the most part, still a sleepy little town, but those of us who've been drawn to the area for years have seen it grow. Perhaps 400 Americans have homes or winter in the area. Casa Díaz is no longer the center of town, but everyone knows that that's where the town began. Bahía de los Angeles is the legacy left by Papa and Mama Díaz.

Charles M. Scammon

To the Brink of Extinction

Conservationists of today shudder when they recall the mass slaughter of the California gray whale in the mid-1880s. But at the time, while it was a bloody business, no one gave a thought to slaughtering the species to the brink of extinction, and whaling was considered a romantic and adventure-filled life.

While his name is synonymous with the carnage, Charles M. Scammon was not only one of the most successful whalers of his time, he was also one of the most literate. He was a very fine artist, a self-trained naturalist and an accomplished writer. He was keenly intelligent, self-confident, and destined to command.

Born in Maine in 1825, he took to sea on the East Coast and came to California with his wife in 1853. For ten years he commanded his own whaling vessel all along the Pacific coast, hunting the gray whale from his home port of San Francisco.

He began to astonish other whalers by returning to San Francisco with a ship full of whale oil after only being out a short time. What did he know or discover that they didn't?

Legend grew that Scammon had accidentally discovered a lagoon halfway down the Baja California peninsula that could be entered only through a long narrow mouth. He tried to keep his lagoon secret, but whalers from San Francisco followed him to discover where he found all the whales.

The shallow Ojo de Liebre Lagoon (which incorporates Scammon's Lagoon) and the San Ignacio Lagoon are the breeding grounds of the California gray whale. Prior to the discovery by the whalers, an estimated 18,000 to 22,000 whales migrated there each year from colder Alaskan waters.

Into the Baja lagoons

Filling the public demand for whale oil were the adventurous whalers, who now could increase their profits by increasing their yield. They headed into the Baja lagoons in record numbers. Scammon soon had competition.

Scammon wrote in 1860:

"The following year found us again in the lagoon, with a little squadron of vessels, consisting of one bark and two small schooners. Although this newly discovered whaling ground was difficult of approach, and but very little known abroad — and especially the channel which led to it — yet, soon after our arrival, a large fleet of ships hovered for weeks off the entrance, or along the adjacent coast, and six of the number succeeded in finding their way in.

"The whole force pushing the whales that season numbered nine vessels which lowered thirty boats. Of this number, at least twenty-five were daily engaged in whaling. The different branches of the lagoon where the whales congregated were known as the 'Fishpond,' 'Cooper's Lagoon,' 'Fort Lagoon,' and the 'Main Lagoon.' The chief place of resort, however, was at the head-waters of the Main Lagoon, which may be compared to an *estero*, two or three miles in extent, and nearly surrounded by dunes or sand-flats, which were exposed at neap tides.

"Here the objects of our pursuit were found in large numbers, and here the scene of the slaughter was exceedingly picturesque and unusually exciting, especially on a calm morning, when the mirage would transform not only the boats and their crews into fantastic imagery, but the whales, as they set forth their towering spouts of aqueous vapor, frequently tinted with blood, would appear greatly distorted. At one time, the upper sections of the boats, with their crews, would be seen gliding over the molten-looking surface of the water, with a portion of a colossal form of the whale appearing for an instant, like a spectre, in the advance; or both boats and whales would assume ever-changing forms, while the report of the bomb-guns would sound like the sudden discharge of musketry; but one cannot fully realize, unless he be an eyewitness, the intense and boisterous excitement of the reckless pursuit, by a large fleet of boats from different ships, engaged in a morning's whaling foray.

"Numbers of them will be fast to whales at the same time, and the stricken animals, in their efforts to escape, can be seen darting in every direction through the water, or breaching headlong clear of its surface, coming down with a splash that sends columns of foam in every direction, and with a rattling report that can be heard beyond the surrounding shores. The men in the boats shout and yell, or converse in vehement strains, using a variety of lingo, from the Portuguese of the Western Islands to the Kanaka of Oceania. In fact, the whole spectacle is beyond description, for it is one continually changing aquatic battle-scene."

The slaughter seems repugnant

While Scammon's description of the slaughter seems repugnant to most people a century and a half later, the 19th century was not known for its sensitivity in such matters. Indeed, the American bison was almost totally wiped out by "sportsmen" who shot into herds of the beasts from trains, leaving their carcasses to rot in the plains.

When Scammon left whaling, he returned to San Francisco and in 1874 published *Marine Mammals and the American Whale Fishery* and *Marine Mammals of the Northwestern Coast*. His wonderful pencil and watercolor sketches and systematic description of marine mammals were considered scientifically sound and used for decades.

Later he entered the U.S. Revenue Service and commanded a cutter in Alaskan waters until he retired in 1882. He died in 1911 at the age of 86.

International agreement formed

Once the slaughter of the California gray whales began it never stopped completely until 1937, when Mexico and the U.S. forged international laws to protect the whales. The international agreement of 1938 protects all members of the species wherever found.

It appears the agreement came just in time. One source estimates that by the 1930s the whale population was down to only about 250 animals. By all accounts, the current California gray whale population is now back to its strength of 150 years ago. A September 1999 *Orange County Register* article estimated there are 24,000 whales.

Scammon found a lagoon that now bears his name. He was a man of his times who did what society wanted and did it well. His name should serve as a reminder of the precarious balance of nature.

CALIFORNIA GRAY WHALES
The Friendly Whales

When a gray whale first approached the boat of some local fishermen in San Ignacio Lagoon almost 30 years ago, it did more than precipitate a friendly encounter between a leviathan of the deep and mankind. It spawned an entirely new and exciting Baja industry.

The whale came up to their boat and rubbed against it. One of the fishermen, Francisco Mayoral, later said, "The whale would allow me to touch it, rub it. It almost seemed to relish the contact. It would submerge only to resurface on the opposite side of the boat and approach as if it wanted me to lean over the side and touch it again."

Then in 1976 a whale surfaced next to the vessel *Royal Polaris* while it was in the Laguna San Ignacio. At first, the crew thought it was an institutionalized whale released from study at Sea World, but it was just a curious wild animal, going from one side of the boat to the other as if greeting the observers.

The playful California gray whales, descended from those hunted in large numbers, have never been hunted nor even learned to fear humans. Nor do humans have a reason to fear the whales, even though they reach lengths of 35–50 feet and grow to weigh as much as 40 tons.

The California gray whales have been called "friendly whales," as they've learned to interact with humans, especially in Laguna San Ignacio. Sometimes mother whales even show off their young by pushing them right up to boats. The phenomenon of these playful, friendly whales has given birth to a broad whale-watching and whale-petting industry.

The world's longest migration

In October, gray whales begin their 5,000 to 6,000 mile journey from Alaska to Laguna Guerrero Negro, Scammon's Lagoon, Laguna San Ignacio, and Bahía Magdalena, along the Pacific coast of Baja California. It is the longest migration route of any mammal.

Around half of the mature females, those who conceived the previous year, are about to give birth. As the females are fertile every other year, most of the others are ready for breeding. About 1,500 grays are born in the Baja lagoons each year, about half in Scammon's Lagoon.

Between April and October the grays feed off protein-rich waters in Alaska. They begin to arrive in the Baja lagoons by late November. A few calves are born en route, but most are born in the lagoons. From late January to mid-February they start to head back, with most departing by late March. A few stay through April and as late as May or June.

The 5,000-acre San Ignacio Lagoon, the number one spot for interaction with the "friendly" whales, is part of the El Vizcaíno Biosphere Reserve, United Nations Educational Scientific and Cultural Organization (UNESCO) designation, making it a world sanctuary deserving of international protection.

As such, the Mexican government has afforded the lagoons its protection. Special permits are required to enter the lagoons. Thus several locals and a few other commercial operators have permission to take visitors out in small *pangas* to encounter the whales. To keep the wild contact manageable, people bringing boats without permits are not allowed out on the lagoon during the season.

Numerous providers and tours

The Central Baja area is a whirlwind of activity in the wintertime, as more and more Americans come to experience contact with the "friendly" whales. There are numerous providers and tours that make an expedition of the experience by providing transportation, lodging, boat guides, etc. from the border.

Those who drive into central Baja on their own will notice several guides and whale-watching tours from the nearby towns of Guerrero Negro and San Ignacio. Or those willing to head over dirt roads directly for the small lagoon-side village can hire a local guide and go out to encounter the whales.

Another option is arranging a trip through the hotels in San Ignacio or Guerrero Negro. San Ignacio only has four hotels, the La Pinta, two inexpensive ones (La Posada and the Oasis on the highway), and Ricardo Romo has good medium-priced rooms at Rice and Beans in adjacent San Lino. There are also a couple of RV parks and campgrounds.

Petting a friendly whale.

One Guerrero Negro example is the Whale Watching Tour provided by Malarrimo Eco-Tours out of the Malarrimo Restaurant/Hotel in Guerrero Negro. Offering tours since 1990, during January, February, and March they provide bilingual guides, round trip transportation to Scammon's Lagoon, a three-hour boat trip, and a box lunch with beverage.

There are numerous package tours from not only southern California, especially San Diego, but also Ensenada. One quick tour arranged through the San Nicolás Hotel in Ensenada offers transportation, two nights in a motel, lunch, snacks, sodas, and a guided *panga* trip into the lagoons for $300.

Others are Baja Expeditions, Discover Baja Travel Club, and Baja Discovery Tours. There are many others, offering numerous choices, from quick trips of a few days to a week or more, from roughing it to more comfortable accommodations. Those who demand first-class resorts, however, might best watch the whole thing on television.

Obviously, the cost is less for those who must make the most effort on their part. Those willing to drive the 532 miles of Highway 1 to San Ignacio and then 42 miles of dirt road (one and a half hours) to the San Ignacio Lagoon can find several local guides more than willing to take visitors out. And quite a few people do just that.

Last March, by asking around in San Ignacio I was directed to Antonio Aguilar Osuna of Antonio's Whale Tours. The boats usually take off about 9 a.m., so I left town around 7 a.m. Finding him at the lagoon was no problem. He added me to his boat while dispatching others on other boats. The approximately three-hour encounter cost only $30. For an additional few dollars, his wife will have lunch waiting.

I shared the whale-watching boat with two couples from different parts of the U.S. The couple from Mississippi was making it their second day out in a row. The other couple from northern California had flown their private plane to a strip right on the banks of the lagoon. While the pilot, Tim, had been out in the lagoon several times in the past, he kept saying he'd never actually touched a whale.

He got his wish on that trip. There were so many whales that unless one was within 50 yards, we wouldn't even bother to point it out. Many came real close, and we learned that you don't choose the whale encounter — it chooses you.

Finally, a large whale came right up to the boat with her calf, rolling over so we could pet her stomach. "Wow," said Tim, his eyes as big as saucers and his smile like a kid on Christmas morning, "She keeps coming back for more!"

When I leaned over to pet her, her eye, a little bigger than my fist and just inches from my hand, opened up to stare at the human she'd trusted. I stared back. She rolled a little and spouted from her nostril as if to recognize the bond that had just taken place. It was awesome.

These days, the "friendly" whales seem to enjoy being petted. It's like a zoo without bars, an incredible interaction with some of the earth's largest creatures in the wild. The whales of Baja are a reflection of the people of Baja — and that's "Friendly."

Exportadora de Sal, S.A.

The World of Salt

In addition to water, of which there is precious little in Baja California, another substance necessary for life is sodium chloride (common table salt) and Baja has plenty of that. In fact, the salt in the vast tidal flats of Scammon's Lagoon (locally called Laguna Ojo de Liebre or "Eye of the Jackrabbit Lagoon") makes the area the world's number one salt producer.

In order to expand, the salt producers have wanted to build an even larger saltworks operation on the shores of the nearby San Ignacio Lagoon, a pristine habitat for the California gray whales. And that was "salt in the wound" for a number of conservationists.

Commercial salt around the world comes from brine, salt beds, salt pans, or salt domes. The first to exploit the saltworks at Guerrero Negro were the British. During the early 1950s their interest was acquired by the Compañía Exportadora de Sal S.A. (ESSA), owned principally by American shipbuilder Daniel K. Ludwig. Originally from New York, Ludwig personally had over $12 million invested in the project by 1963.

A colorful quilt of salt pans

His company diked the shallow tidal flats, creating evaporating ponds approximately one meter deep and 100 meters square. After sea water rushes in and is evaporated by the sun, the salty brine solution is moved to another pan for further drying out. The man-made salt pans on the shores of Scammon's Lagoon cover some 113 square miles and from the air look like a colorful quilt that never ends.

After the brine has completely evaporated, the harvest machines are able to collect 2,000 tons of salt precipitate per hour and load it into huge 60-ton triple-trailer bottom-dumping trucks, which drive to loading docks for shipment.

A company town grew up around the enterprise, which is located midway down the Baja peninsula just south of the 28th parallel at the northern border of the state of Baja California Sur. Named for an old whaling ship wrecked in the lagoon back in 1858 called the *Black Warrior (Guerrero Negro)*, the company town now has over 10,000 residents, most either employed by the company or directly influenced by it.

At the loading docks the salt is lightered by 6,500-ton barges to Cedros Island; from there, it is transported around the world to the U.S., Canada, Mexico, and Japan. The first large shipment was made in 1957, and by 1962 the firm had exported one million tons of salt.

Enter Mitsubishi and the Mexican Government

In 1973 Ludwig sold his interest to the Mitsubishi Corporation of Japan. Early on, the Mexican government acquired 25 percent of ESSA and in 1976, added another 26 percent, making them the majority shareholders.

In what is today the world's largest salt operation, an incredible five million tons of salt are shipped each year to ports around the world.

But the worldwide demand for salt was so great that ESSA had planned to build an even larger $120-million industrial salt facility to the south, specifically at Laguna San Ignacio, the last remaining pristine calving lagoon of the California gray whale.

This announcement came in 1994, one month after the gray was removed from the "endangered species" list and upgraded to "threatened." The plan was initially rejected, but in 1997 passed a governmental review.

With the existing operation in Scammon's Lagoon and a planned 2,000 hectare (809 acres) tourist resort slated for Bahía Magdalena, the opponents of the new plan alleged it could wipe out one of the whales' few remaining nurseries.

One of Mexico's most prominent environmental groups, El Grupo de los Cien (Group of 100), brought the proposed saltworks to international attention, effectively halting the hasty construction. Instead, Mexico undertook more stringent environmental impact studies, which didn't ignore the threat to the whales, as the earlier report did.

Mexico actually has more stringent requirements for environmental impact assessments than does the United States. Reports are required more often and on more levels.

But anything could have happened. Mitsubishi, at 49 percent ownership, actually has greater control of the company, because they have the capital to fund operations and expansion. Japan is the main beneficiary of growth, due to the fact that Japan's strategic industries are the main users of salt in chemical compounds.

According to the environmentalists, only 208 jobs would have been created, only half of these going to Mexican nationals, creating a minimal economic impact. It could have even had a negative impact if the new plant replaced Guerrero Negro. But the Mexican government gets tax revenues and its share of profits from the sale of the salt.

Proponents of the new facility stated that a saltworks operation in one location at the edge of a lagoon would have minimal, if any, impact on animals inside the lagoon. They also refuted the minimal job impact, which did seem rather hard to believe considering the bustling economy of Guerrero Negro.

Both sides tried hard to get their story out, with proponents pointing to the minimal impact the salt operation at Scammon's Lagoon has had on the whales. Also, they noted that big ships would not be entering the lagoon, but putting in at a new pier to be built at the nearby village of Abreojos.

How did the scenario play out? If it weren't for the concern of environmental groups like the *Grupo de los Cien*, the new salt operation would already be in effect. It looks like the whales have a friend — in fact, at least 100 of them.

The day after I wrote the first draft of this story, I received an e-mail from Baja author and colleague Ann Hazard (*Cooking With Baja Magic*). It was sent to her from another Baja author, Judy Botello (*The Other Side*), and I share this partially to illustrate how quickly the Baja drums beat these days, so unlike an earlier era when travelers passed messages up and down the road:

> "I just got a phone call from a friend who works in Senator Boxer's office in Washington D.C. He has been a long time *compañero* on my Baja trips, and he has just learned that President Zedillo today vetoed the San Ignacio salt plant that Mitsubishi has been pushing. If Mexico's out, the project is clearly dead. *Que vivan las ballenas, y que viva Baja!* Thought you might like to circulate the news to your network. *Con cariño*, Judy."

The *New York Times* a few days later (Mar. 5, 2000) did a detailed story, indicating that Mitsubishi had received at least 750,000 letters calling for it to scrap the project. It noted that since NAFTA, Mexico has become more global, and the effort to stop Mitsubishi crossed borders, adding that Mexican and foreign conservationists united behind the campaign.

It read, in part: "'It took a million people to do it,' said Jacob Sherr, a Director of the Natural Resources Defense Council, a U.S. group that led the campaign, 'but we showed that we can work together worldwide to compel even the largest corporations to respect nature.'"

In consolation, the Exportadora de Sal (ESSA) was granted several million dollars to modernize their existing operation, but regardless of major or minimal impact, there will be no expansion into San Ignacio, the lagoon of the friendly whales.

MALARRIMO BEACH
Junkyard of the Pacific

Mal means "Bad." *Arrimar* means "To pull in." The aptly named Malarrimo Beach is a bad-to-pull-into-place all right — except for the junk that arrives by current, that is.

The 9,000-mile equatorial current makes a clockwise loop around the Pacific Ocean, going up past Japan and Alaska and back down the Pacific Coast. That same current helped the old Spanish galleons return from the Philippines. Floating flotsam and jet-sam gets caught in the current and would probably continue down to Antarctica, except for a land hook that juts into the Pacific and catches much of the debris. That hook is called the Vizcaíno peninsula of Central Baja California, and on its northern shoreline is the famed Malarrimo Beach. Explorers and other adventurers for years have told of finding cases of Scotch whiskey, oars, entire dinghies, full bottles of assorted liquors and wines, and valuable items from all around the world — all washed up at that lonely windswept beach at Malarrimo.

Over a decade ago I traversed the 72 miles of bumpy graded road from the farm town of Vizcaíno and Highway 1. Then I turned north onto a 27-mile dirt track to Malarrimo, winding through some narrow arroyos and crossing a rocky plateau. Off to the side of the rocky road I passed a skeleton of a horse, its bones bleached white by the unremitting sun, reminding me of the area's isolation.

Taking me three hours, the 27-mile track finally ended at some large sand dunes rimming a long, blinding-white beach. No other people would be at Malarrimo this week, and the virgin beach awaited its explorer.

The sand was strewn with goodies from afar and near. I found light bulbs with Japanese writing on them, old hatch covers, large wooden telephone line spools, fishing floats, oars, wooden boxes, ropes, rubber sandals, caps, helmets, plastic glasses from a cruise ship's New Year's Eve party, plastic shampoo bottles, a half-intact *panga*, and much more.

There was nothing of immense value, but it was fun to collect. Like a grab bag, you never knew what some colorful, half-buried thing in the sand might be.

It was the kind of place where you could allow your imagination to run rampant, reflecting on the past use of the discovered items. Was it a couple rekindling a romance who discarded their New Year's Eve party glasses? Who were they? They never dreamed an old Baja bum like me would wonder about them, especially while standing on a broad windswept beach that was "bad" "to get near to."

MALARRIMO RESTAURANT/HOTEL

Dining in the Desert

The Malarrimo Restaurant in Guerrero Negro is considered by many to be the best place to dine between Ensenada and La Paz. It's on the north side of the main street near the entrance to town and offers good value motel rooms and a gift shop, along with its signature restaurant.

It seems incongruous finding an upscale dining room after driving past so many small cafes and ranchos, so the Malarrimo is a welcome stop. They offer great seafood, fresh fish, shrimp, clams, *calamar*, and a very good seafood combination. Americans also like their breakfasts at Malarrimo, which can include lobster omelets, *machaca*, and *chorizo y huevos*.

Malarrimo owner Enrique Achoy is considered by many Baja buffs to be one of the Baja legends. He had previously worked in a restaurant in Ensenada before relocating to Guerrero Negro in 1963. He became a cook, and later a chef, for the ESSA saltworks. He also served as a translator for the company. In a few years he left and became the owner and operator of the old El Pollo restaurant in downtown Guerrero Negro.

He opened the larger Malarrimo Restaurant in 1974 and has long directed travelers to the best whale-watching sites and the remote Malarrimo Beach. Before he built the motel rooms, he added some RV sites for his guests, most of whom arrived to visit the whales.

Some of the Malarrimo Restaurant menu items include Breaded Abalone, Octopus Spanish Olive Oil (sauteed), Blue Crab Casserole au Gratin, Deep Sea Scallops (broiled in butter or abalone style), Half Broiled Lobster, and my favorite, Halibut Filet Broiled with Crispy Garlic. For carnivores there are Sirloin Tips au White Wine, Sirloin Steak au Milanaise, New York steaks, and Filet Mignons. You can also get the classic Mexican broiled steak (carne asada) and chicken tacos and burritos.

Adjacent to the restaurant is the Scavenger's Bar, in which all sorts of items discovered and scavenged on the famous Malarrimo Beach are displayed.

These days the affable Enrique is mostly retired, and other members of the Achoy family help run the delightful Malarrimo Restaurant and accompanying businesses. One of his five children, daughter Elena Achoy, keeps a well-stocked gift shop next door at the Casa El Viejo Cactus.

The Malarrimo has become more than a restaurant; it's a jumping-off place for whale-watching tours and is a great place to meet fellow travelers in Central Baja.

The Fischers of San Ignacio
A San Ignacio Village Smithy

In a scenario similar to the Daggetts of Bahía de los Angeles, the patriarch of San Ignacio discovered Baja California by jumping ship. Frank Fischer, the German fourth engineer on a vessel docked in Santa Rosalía, got into some trouble with the second mate and fled ashore. It was 1910, and the 25-year-old fugitive, who was wanted by authorities for his illegal status, somehow made his way overland to San Ignacio.

The oasis of San Ignacio has long drawn visitors to its fertile valley and pools of fresh water. The plentiful Indians there had called the place Kadakaamaán (Place of Reeds). Jesuit padres had been visiting the location for years before establishing a mission on Jan. 20, 1728, which they named for the founder of their religious order, San Ignacio de Loyola.

It became a quite populous mission site, and later, after the Jesuits left, the Dominican order built a fine stone church that still stands in the town square over 200 years later.

Finding San Ignacio to be an idyllic location for his sanctuary, Fischer married a local Mexican girl, Cruz Sandoval, and became the village blacksmith. With automobiles finding their way to central Baja, he became such a good mechanic no one cared where he came from or bothered to turn him in.

He was a real pioneer Baja mechanic. As there was no electricity, he made much of his own equipment, which included belts and pulleys and flywheels. He spoke fluent German, English, and Spanish.

A 1958 book *Solo Below, a Guide Book to Lower California* by Don A. Hugh says, "Fischer, a genial German, operates a garage there and is a good mechanic. He also has a deep well where water may be obtained."

A 1961 guidebook advises travelers to look up Fischer's Garage and Blacksmith Shop. According to *Sunset* magazine's 1971 *Guide to Baja California* "Fischer is something of a Baja legend. ...His auto repair and welding shop has doctored many ailing vehicles making the trek down the peninsula."

Discovered Serpent Cave

When he was younger, Fischer covered much of the surrounding countryside afoot or by horse or mule. While on a hunting trip, Frank Fischer discovered what would later be called Serpent Cave, a painted cave in the mountains that featured the likeness of a serpent running along the entire lip of the overhang.

The cave was in an area so remote it took eight hours to get there from San Ignacio by pack train. Once when he was in the area, mystery writer Erle Stanley Gardner heard of the cave and wanted to visit it, but he could not afford the time. He returned on another trip with helicopters and picked up Fischer, who guided the famous writer and his team to the cave. Some of the locals still remember Fischer being whisked away into the sky.

The original Frank Fischer and his wife Cruz had four sons and four daughters. Their children became some of San Ignacio's most enterprising residents. In 1970 the Fischers established a small inn called *La Posada* on a San Ignacio back street. Frank Fischer died in 1972. Son Oscar Fischer took over the La Posada Inn, and son José Fischer runs a store facing the town square. At either establishment visitors can inquire about whale watching tours and/or guided trips into the mountains to view the painted caves.

Two other sons have died. One of them, Francisco, ran the old Fischer's Café, about 10 miles north of San Ignacio at the intersection of Highway 1 and the Abreojos road. It is now just a small rancho.

The two remaining sons (Oscar and José) and one of Frank's daughters still live in San Ignacio. The others have married and left, one to La Paz, one to Ensenada, and the other to Puerto Vallarta.

Oscar has nine children, with three remaining in San Ignacio. Oscar's son Dagoberto now manages the La Posada Inn. The others have scattered to other parts of Mexico: La Paz, Michoacán, Mexico City, and Tijuana.

Fischers seem to be everywhere. While visiting some caves north of San Ignacio two years ago, I had a blowout on the dirt road coming out of the mountains. I changed the tire and continued, finding the first *llanta* repair shop near the entrance to San Ignacio. The shop owner was Francisco Fischer, a nephew of the popular village smithy.

It seems the townspeople of the oasis village of San Ignacio, if they're not descendants of Fischer, still remember him. Once I was having dinner at René's, a little thatched-roof restaurant overlooking a small pond, and chatting with the manager, Victor López Arce. He related how when he was a kid he knew the original Frank Fischer well. "He was real old, a short little guy who walked all over town. He was a *mecánico* and even though he was short in stature, everybody looked up to him."

The Arces of Baja California

I mentioned to Victor that in this part of Baja if the locals are not named Fischer, then they seemed to be named Arce. He couldn't agree more, being an Arce himself.

There are Arces all over the Baja California peninsula, mostly descended from Juan de Arce, an Englishman who acquired a Spanish surname after being raised on the mainland of Mexico. Arce arrived in Loreto as a soldier in 1698, one year after the first Baja mission was established there.

The brothers José Gabriel de Arce and Sebastián Constantino de Arce had arrived in San Ignacio prior to 1764 when Sebastián's son Ignacio María Arce was born. Ignacio María become a soldier, serving in several Baja locations. His son Buenaventura Arce eventually returned to San Ignacio and by 1818 served as *mayordomo* (Indian labor boss).

It was Buenaventura Arce who later became the undisputed leader and power in San Ignacio, acquiring much property, including the land and buildings of the San Ignacio Mission. He made his home in the former priest's quarters for over 30 years. Don Buenaventura, who died in 1870, and his wife Romualda Murillo had at least eight children who, in turn, have continued to populate the area with the Arce name.

It was Eustacio "Tacho" Arce and his son Ramón Arce who helped author Harry W. Crosby find and photograph prehistoric cave sites all over central Baja. When I drove to the mountain village of San Francisco, before I could visit the painted caves I had to register with the coordinator. His name was Enrique Arce, and my guide that day was his brother-in-law, Jorge Guadalupe Arce.

If you're in the San Ignacio area and are looking for either a Fischer or an Arce, you better know the full name, because a lot of people will answer if you only use the surname.

CASA DE LEREE, SAN IGNACIO

First Inn in the Oasis

Time seems to stand still in San Ignacio. Highway travelers enter the town to walk around the square and photograph the old mission church, but outside of the gringos the town seems slow to change.

Manuel Meza's store on the corner opposite the mission looks about the same as when he first established it back in 1945. He once gave me some wonderful old black-and-white photos depicting a San Ignacio of years gone by. When I'm in town, I often pop in to say hi, or maybe buy some dates from Manuel.

And Meza's the newcomer! The store on the other end of the square has "1939" etched on the stone entrance. Behind that store is a blue-and-white building that also has an interesting history.

For many years, there were no inns at San Ignacio, so local resident Señora Leree created one. In the mid-20th century she opened part of her home on Calle José Morelos, one block north of the plaza, to travelers.

In his 1943 book *The Land Where Time Stands Still*, Max Miller reports on a 1941 trip,

> "We had been told to ask for Mrs. Learie [sic], a long time resident of San Ignacio. Her name sounds Irish, but she is mostly French. She runs a clean little hotel for travelers in connection with her home. We had some gifts for her, some cloth and patterns, sent by the Griffing Bancrofts of San Diego. I asked for her as soon as we hit town and was directed to her house near the plaza."

Her small boarding house that served as a hotel was aptly called the *Casa de Huéspedes Leree* (Leree Guest House). It was inexpensive and simple, and welcomed visitors for years. By 1961 Señora Leree was also able to acquire guides to take her guests to nearby caves.

The next chapter in the history of Casa Leree was written by the founder's daughter, Rebecca (Becky) Carrillo. When young, Becky had left the village of San Ignacio for the bright lights of Hollywood and worked for many years at MGM, where she not only honed her English but met many of tinseltown's luminaries in her behind-the-scenes capacity.

Becky returned to San Ignacio during the late 1960s to help her mother, who was by then 98 years old, run the Casa Leree.

Bruce Berger, in his 1998 book *Almost An Island: Travels in Baja California*, notes how during a 1968 adventure, he encountered the Casa Leree: "Ten miles before town we had come upon a flat rock lettered 'Casa Leree Good Food English Spoken Ask For It.'"

Upon arriving, he noted,

> "...The gate opened on a large courtyard covered by a five foot high grape arbor. We crouched beneath it and straightened our spines in a cool kitchen... Becky Carrillo, whose English, good or not, was precisely like ours. Plump, bespectacled, sixtyish, with a quietness that drew us close, she invited us to sit and produced beers from the refrigerator."

> "...Becky returned and showed Katie and me to a sectioned dormitory, one partition of which was ours. Overhead was a thatching of fan palms intricate as a carved ceiling. This room, Becky's kitchen and a table under a grape

arbor became our midpeninsula headquarters during the three consecutive springs we traveled the MTH (Main Transpeninsular Highway)."

By 1974 when the highway came through, Fischer's La Posada had been open a few years, and the new (now La Pinta) El Presidente was built on the road in from the highway, but the venerable Casa Leree still provided rooms, refreshments, and good meals. Señora Carrillo also served food, requesting that arriving travelers let her know ahead of time if they wished a meal.

Becky's son Eduardo was a UCLA art instructor and director of the regional Arts Center in La Paz. When some paintings from the main altar of the San Ignacio Mission church were taken and not returned, Eduardo painted several of the replacement paintings.

Becky Carrillo has passed away, and one neighbor told me that the pretty building that formerly housed the Casa Leree is now owned by "a gringo." A distinctive royal blue colonial-style building with white trim, it peeks invitingly at travelers from the end of the narrow street just off the town square.

Its history can best be illustrated in a statement made by Señora Becky Carrillo when asked by author Berger why she kept the grape arbor so low that guests had to strain their backs to get in from the street. She simply said, "It is well that people humble themselves a little when they enter someone else's home."

MEXICO'S ROADSIDE ASSISTANCE
The Green Angels

Longtime Baja travelers know that when you develop car trouble in the middle of nowhere, you hope the next person who comes along will be a Mexican. In the "Amigo Country," the custom of genuine courtesy and friendliness almost demands that they stop to render help to a total stranger.

And if you're really lucky he will be a professional, driving one of a fleet of 20 radio-equipped green trucks that plies the Baja highways daily. Affectionately dubbed "Green Angels," these Samaritans of the open road have earned their heavenly reputation.

They are the Tourist Assistance Service, created by Mexico's Ministry of Tourism in 1960 to aid all travelers in Mexico. The highway assistance personnel in their distinctive green trucks are not selected lightly. They are all bilingual, are all accomplished mechanics, and also all trained in first aid.

Service is rendered free of charge, except that motorists must pay for any gasoline or parts. These "Angels" will change flat tires, diagnose your problem, make repairs on the spot if possible (like replacing a fan belt), radio others for assistance, provide you with enough gas to make the next station, or even go get spare parts for you.

Each of the drivers in Baja's green fleet assists three to five motorists a day. Together they help about 1,500 vehicles, including both foreign and domestic tourists and even local ranchers. They're on the road from 10 a.m. to 8 p.m., seven days a week.

I always make a mental note when I see a "Green Angel" and calculate where he might be later in case I might develop a problem. And one other thing — I always give him a friendly and grateful wave.

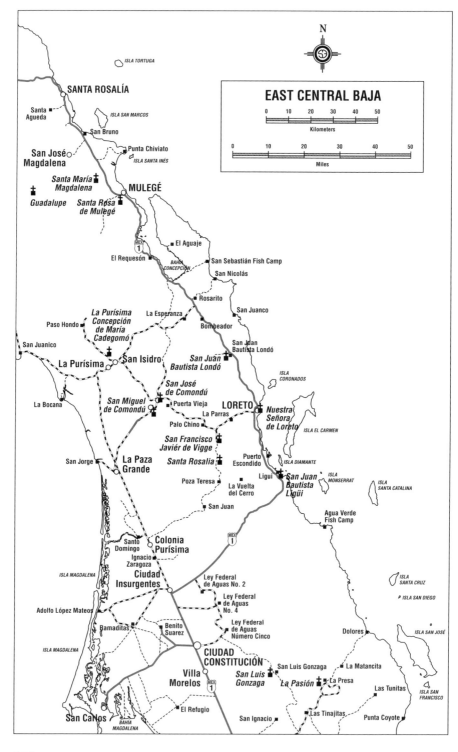

ISLA TORTUGA

SANTA ROSALÍA

Santa Agueda

ISLA SAN MARCOS

San Bruno

San José Magdalena

Punta Chiviato

ISLA SANTA INÉS

Santa María Magdalena

MULEGÉ

Guadalupe

Santa Rosa de Mulegé

El Aguaje

El Requesón

BAHÍA CONCEPCIÓN

San Sebastián Fish Camp

San Nicolás

Rosarito

San Juanco

La Purísima Concepción de María Cadegomó

Paso Hondo

La Esperanza

Bombeador

San Juanico

San Juan Bautista Londó

La Purísima

San Isidro

San Juan Bautista Londó

ISLA CORONADOS

San José de Comondú

La Bocana

San Miguel de Comondú

Puerta Vieja

LORETO

Nuestra Señora de Loreto

La Parras

Palo Chino

ISLA EL CARMEN

San Francisco Javiér de Vigge

Santa Rosalia

Puerto Escondido

ISLA DIAMANTE

San Jorge

La Paza Grande

Poza Teresa

La Vuelta del Cerro

Ligui

San Juan Bautista Ligüi

ISLA MONSERRAT

ISLA SANTA CATALINA

San Juan

Agua Verde Fish Camp

Santo Domingo

Colonia Purísima

ISLA MAGDALENA

Ignacio Zaragoza

Ciudad Insurgentes

Ley Federal de Aguas No. 2

ISLA SANTA CRUZ

ISLA SAN DIEGO

Adolfo López Mateos

Ley Federal de Aguas No. 4

Bamaditas

Benito Suarez

Ley Federal de Aguas Número Cinco

Dolores

ISLA SAN JOSÉ

ISLA MAGDALENA

CIUDAD CONSTITUCIÓN

San Luis Gonzaga

La Matancita

Villa Morelos

San Luis Gonzaga

La Pasión

La Presa

Las Tunitas

ISLA SAN FRANCISCO

San Carlos

El Refugio

BAHÍA MAGDALENA

San Ignacio

Las Tinajitas

Punta Coyote

N

EAST CENTRAL BAJA

0 10 20 30 40 50
Kilometers

0 10 20 30 40 50
Miles

Chapter 11: The Sea of Cortez

THE FEROCIOUS SERI INDIANS
Cannibals on Tiburón Island?

In 1905 Professor Thomas Grindell and a party of three others never returned from a gold-seeking expedition to Tiburón Island and the coast of Sonora, Mexico. They had ventured to the heart of Seri Indian country, a small tribe then characterized by outside visitors as "savages," "beasts," "animals," and even "cannibals."

Grindell's brother Edward searched in vain for the party; his adventure was published in 1907 in *The Wide World Magazine*. According to the story, "It is well known that the Seri are treacherous, and because of their crude manner of living and their fondness for raw food, they are believed to be cannibals."

The Seri, whose culture had clashed with the European attitude of superiority, were nomadic Indians, long considered wild and fierce and unwilling to be assimilated. They had never been agricultural. Instead they switched directly from a sustenance existence to today's handcrafting of tourist products, particularly heavy ironwood sculptures.

It is not surprising that in the time of European occupation, the Seri attacked and killed domestic horses, burros, and cattle brought to the area by their victors. They craved flesh, particularly of horses and burros, and loved fat and bone marrow from the animals. These practices helped establish the cannibal legend.

"Warlike gentiles"
The ship carrying a Jesuit group in 1709 was driven far to the north by a storm in which some of their party drowned. According to Clavigero in *History of (Lower) California* those survivors who clambered ashore were "...exposed to another not less serious danger because that coast was inhabited by the Series [sic] who were warlike gentiles and implacable enemies of the Spaniards."

The report continues that Mission President Padre Juan Salvatierra, upon hearing of the shipwreck, traveled to the area, where he won the goodwill of the Seri, "So the dominating sweetness of the character of Father Salvatierra, aided by the grace of the Master, triumphed over the ferocity of those barbarians who were so feared, not only by other Indians, but also by the Spaniards."

John Steinbeck visited the Tiburón Island area in 1941. In his book *Sea of Cortez*, he commented on Clavigero's report, "The 'dominating sweetness' of the character of Father Salvatierra did not, however, change them completely, for they have gone right on killing people until recently."

Explorer Lt. Robert William Hale Hardy of the British Royal Navy made numerous trips to Tiburón Island in the 1820s. While he found neither gold nor pearls on his trips, he did encounter the fierce Seri. "These people have always been considered extremely ferocious," Hardy wrote, "and there is little doubt, from their brave and war-like character, that they may formerly have devastated a great part of the country…"

Hardy went on to explain that the Seri had developed a method of poisoning their arrows. Hardy, who brought gifts and provided medical assistance to the Indians, was unusual in that he was so well received he was given free rein on the island. He even allowed a young woman to paint his face like the warlike Seri. He also was able to return in one piece.

The reports of Seri fierceness continued. By the 1890s the Mexican-Seri relationship had deteriorated badly. The Seri had been not only ravaged by disease, but methodically exterminated, and only about 200 remained from a group that may have been as high as 5,000. Again the Seri survived by killing and eating the Mexican cattle and horses that had come into their homeland.

Disappearing in Seri Country

At least four other outsiders had disappeared in Seri country before the ill-fated Grindell party. The deaths were attributed to murder by the Indians. One of them, a Mr. Robinson, went to Tiburón in 1894 to search for gold and never returned.

Luckier was U.S. anthropologist William John McGee from the Smithsonian Institute, who in 1895 was studying the nearby Pápago Indians. He learned of the warlike Seri and decided they would afford a better and more aboriginal subject. He built a small boat about the size and shape of a coffin and headed for Tiburón at low tide. There he noted a lot of horse bones and teeth in the Seri campfire ashes, but never mentioned anything resembling human bones. He and his party returned intact.

The Grindell brother in his 1907 article perpetuates the cannibal myth and even "explains" how he feels they did it. He mentions that his search party had come across a camp site where they found a "dance ring" surrounding a stake upon which were impaled only the hands of a white man, fastened by leather straps from a camera case.

In his explanation, Grindell theorizes, "The savages, I should explain, tie their wretched victim to this plank and as they dance, first one and then another will cut a piece of his flesh off … and it was into the hands of these human fiends that I feared the explorers had fallen."

The hands, it was noted from carved initials on the leather and other objects, belonged not to Grindell's brother and his party, but to two miners from Los Angeles, Miller and Olander, who were certainly murdered by the Seri. It appears, however, that most of the earlier Grindell party died of thirst in the desert.

Savagely cutting off human hands and eating meat from cattle and horses do not make a cannibal. The Seri shied away from certain types of food, for example not touching coyote, hawks, and snakes. They loved seafood and pelicans, but would not eat shark (*tiburón*).

Perhaps the most thorough study of the Seri was done by adventurer/writer and naturalist Charles Sheldon in 1921 and 1922. Sheldon's considerable hunting skills were admired by the Seri, and he was invited to Tiburón. He spent time with them and documented their lifestyles as the trained biologist he was.

Sheldon wrote: "The Seri are fierce and treacherous but if one approaches them in the right way, a person with tact and previous experience with such people can get along with them. The Seri have been known to commit theft and murder, and I would not care to have landed on Tiburón Island a complete stranger to them. They are well aware that strangers fear to come on the island for, at different times, three of the men asked me if I was not afraid of them."

Yet, Sheldon concluded that even as treacherous and murderous as the Seri could be, "From all I could learn, they have never been cannibals."

Steinbeck also adds, "It is said of them [Seri] that they are or have been cannibals, a story which has been firmly denied again and again. It is certain they have killed many strangers, but whether or not they have eaten them does not seem to be documented. ...It is very curious the amount of hatred and fear that cannibalism inspires. These poor Seri Indians would not be so much feared for their murdering habits, but if in their hunger they should cut a steak from an American citizen a panic arises."

The Seri in recent years have left their mark on their handicrafts. Throughout Baja California and in mainland Sonora, visitors can find the heavy ironwood Seri sculptures. Until the recent coarse copies that have flooded the market, they have all been the beautiful handiwork of a proud and ferocious people. We know the historic Seri Indians were mean and tough, but we don't know for sure that they were ever really cannibals.

VAGABUNDOS DEL MAR
Wanderers of the Sea

One of the most enduring and endearing legends of the Sea of Cortez is that of the "*vagabundos del mar*" or sea wanderers. These fishermen, usually two to a boat, ceaselessly plied the Sea of Cortez in small crafts, staying a night or two in thatched lean-tos on islands and remote Baja beaches.

Their boats were seldom longer than sixteen feet, mostly 48" wide and 25" deep, and more often than not were carved from a single log in the manner of their forefathers. While some used dinghies of planking, favored was the boat of a single log hollowed out by Indians on mainland ports where large trees were more available.

The tall mast, carved from a single straight tree, was the most noticeable feature, with makeshift patchwork sails to take advantage of winds. Paddle-power was regularly applied.

Modern-day nomads, these sea gypsies went out in all sorts of conditions from blistering heat to chubasco-driven winds. Their knowledge gleaned from years at sea replaced charts and compasses and other devices of modern mariners.

John Steinbeck reports on a 1941 encounter with a couple of *vagabundos:* "They were barefoot and carried the iron harpoons of the region, and in the bottom of their canoe lay a huge fish. Their canoe was typical of the region and was quite interesting. There are no large trees in the southern part of the Peninsula, hence all the canoes come from the mainland, most of them being made near Mazatlán. They are double-ended canoes carved from a single log of light wood, braced inside with struts. Sometimes a small sail is set, but ordinarily they are paddled swiftly by two men, one at either end. They are seaworthy and fast. The wood inside and out is covered with a thin layer of white or blue plaster, waterproof and very hard. This is made by the people themselves and applied regularly. It is not a paint, but a hard, shell-like plaster...."

These wanderers, who numbered about seventy-five (to other estimates of between 100 to 300) fishermen in about fifty *pangas* or *conaos* in the late 1950s, tended to keep their boats far apart from each other and only made brief visits to civilization. There they would trade their fish and shark livers for a few staples.

Their complete freedom of movement and carefree existence inspired many, including the writer Ray Cannon, who admitted, "With strenuous effort, I have succeeded in evolving from a position of fame and wealth to the enviable status of *vagabundo del mar* (sea-going gypsy) and I wouldn't trade jobs with any man on earth."

One travel group founded in 1966 honored the wanderers of the sea in their name. The Vagabundos del Mar Travel Club now has a current membership of 12,000 Baja and boating enthusiasts. They and others like them are the new "wanderers of the sea."

El Boleo of Santa Rosalía
A Bit of France in Baja

After driving Highway 1 for miles and miles through barren desert, first-time travelers greet the Sea of Cortez with anticipation and look forward to the first seaside village. Most are disappointed.

Instead of a broad sandy beach and a laid-back Mexican thatch-roofed village, travelers find a rocky shoreline, lots of old smelting and mining equipment, and a dark soot that seems to permeate everything. They have arrived in Santa Rosalía, an old mining town where a French company created not only one of the world's major copper-producing mines, but a company town with a decidedly French flavor.

The town has rows of wood frame buildings, balconies and corrugated tin roofs that look more European than Baja. Even the church was shipped from France. John Steinbeck once noted that the town looked "built" whereas: "A Mexican town grows out of the ground."

Everything about the place was company-built and company-run: the homes, the smelters, the stores, the hotel, the railroad, the docks, and the ships. The product of the smelter, called copper matte, was shipped to Guaymas across the Sea of Cortez, then by rail to New Orleans and finally as ballast in steamers to France.

A pittance for a discovery

It all started in 1868 when copper ore was discovered by rancher José Villavicencio. The original ore appeared as small, round blue-and-green concretions or balls (*boleos*). Legend has it that Villavicencio was paid only 16 pesos for his discovery.

Some of these ore samples found their way to France and caught the attention of geologists of the House of Rothschild, who decided to finance the mining operations.

In 1884 and 85, they formed the Compagnie Boleo (El Boleo Copper Company) and bought up the holdings of a number of independent miners. The Mexican government granted a 200-square-kilometer claim to the company in 1885.

Later, the ownership became both French and Mexican and the name was changed to Boleo Estudios y Inversiones Mineras, S.A., but it was still referred to as El Boleo.

Getting workers to such a remote location was a problem. Some Yaqui Indians were brought in from mainland Mexico. The company recruited about 2,000 Chinese workers, assuring them they could plant rice when they came to work at El Boleo. Most left when they discovered that rice wouldn't grow in such a desert climate.

Mine workers were also recruited from nearby villages. Mulegé, 38 miles to the south, lost more than its workforce to El Boleo. Mulegé was originally named after its mission, Santa Rosalía de Mulegé. The new company town to the north appropriated the first part of the name as well as many of its citizens; neither was ever returned.

At one time, the company controlled more than 2,000 square miles of surrounding country.

An ugly reputation

They erected a huge copper smelter that deposited a dark soot all over, rendering Santa Rosalía its ugly reputation. Early on, to remedy some of the soot problem, El Boleo built a horizontal duct from the smelter in town to a huge chimney stack half a mile north. It allowed the citizens to breathe, but did not enhance the sooty character of the town.

Almost 375 miles of tunnels were dug, making the ground under Santa Rosalía more porous than Swiss cheese. They built 18 miles of narrow-gauge railroad track to move the ore. Water was another problem. They had to pipe fresh water in from the Santa Agueda oasis, about 10 miles away.

By the early part of the 20th century, Santa Rosalía had become one of the world's major copper-producing areas.

The original director of El Boleo was Monsieur Cuminges, the geologist who examined the first deposit. After him were the directors Monsieur La Farge and Monsieur Michot. Then Mr. Nopper was director for 35 years before turning the helm over to Monsieur Pierre Scalle.

It is said that Monsieur Michot was the most generous with the company's money. Along with establishing many mining safety measures, he dug numerous water wells, established ranches and farms to furnish the miners and their families with food, and constructed highways.

During Monsieur Nopper's long directorship a worldwide economic depression occurred and the price of copper dropped to an all-time low. Hard times came, ranches and farms were neglected, and credit had to be extended by the company stores to help the miners. Many of them sank deeper and deeper in debt, or to quote a song, "I owe my soul to the company store."

The company town straddles two mesas, with all the French mining officials housed on Mesa Norte. On the South Mesa lived the Mexican officials and soldiers. Most of the workers lived in the business part of town, which was laid out on straight streets in the arroyo between the two mesas.

The high-grade ore was mined out by 1930, but the company stayed in existence until it finally closed in 1953. A couple of years later, a Mexican company resumed operations. Another company, (Compañía Minera Lucifér), was organized around the same time to work the manganese deposits in the area. Both those companies operated on a much smaller scale than the legendary El Boleo.

French influence lingers on

There would be no Santa Rosalía were it not for El Boleo. It took dedicated efforts by the French to make their influence upon the distant Baja shore.

Today the most important thing about Santa Rosalía is the ferry to Guaymas on the mainland. The seven-hour crossing leaves Santa Rosalía at 8 a.m. on Sundays and Wednesdays, while the return trip leaves at 8 a.m. on Tuesdays and Fridays.

I find the town a delight. The unique European architecture may seem incongruous in a desolate corner of Baja, and perhaps therein lies its attraction. It's a wonderful walking town, up the narrow streets on one side of the arroyo and down the other, with occasional side jaunts onto the mesas.

I always find myself waving at little old ladies sitting on broad verandas or old wooden balconies with corrugated tin roofs. Or smiling at attractive young Mexican girls whose features are more European, as they contain varying degrees of French blood.

Few people would think of the House of Rothschild when they think of Baja. But they haven't been to Santa Rosalía, where a little bit of France has lingered for years.

SANTA ROSALÍA'S METAL CHURCH
Eiffel Monument in Baja

The French influence in Santa Rosalía extends to the village church, an unusual metal prefabricated job that looks more like an erector set than a house of worship. The galvanized iron church is different, even standing out in an unusual town like Santa Rosalía. It was conceived in France on the drawing board of an architect of

Iglesia de Santa Bárbara, Santa Rosalía

some renown, Alexander Gustave Eiffel, who also designed a tower that has been a symbol of Paris for over 100 years.

The church was built in 1897 for the 1898 World's Fair in Paris, put on display for awhile in the 1890s, and then broken down into sections and shipped around Cape Horn to the French settlement in Santa Rosalía. It was reassembled in 1897, opened as the parish church called Iglesia de Santa Bárbara, and has served the community ever since.

Some sources indicate that the build-it-yourself church was shipped in error to Baja instead of other supplies, but most historians feel that it was specifically ordered.

Santa Rosalía locals have told me that the first manager of the El Boleo mine was not religious and made no provisions for a church. After hearing rumbles of dissent from among the townspeople, the wives of some of the early managers convinced their husbands that the people wanted a church.

The El Boleo officials relented, but with a provision: the tower of the church could not be higher than the tower of the clock of the El Boleo Administration Building. Apparently that juvenile tactic would illustrate to everyone who the boss really was.

If the House of Rothschild was responsible for building the Baja town, the local officials were responsible for much of what went on. How could Eiffel know that his prefabricated iron church would lend an artistic signature to a dusty little mining town? And no one remembers the clock on the administration building.

Hotel Francés, Santa Rosalía

Charm Permeates Miner's Hotel

The historic Hotel Francés (*Français*), a wonderful example of Santa Rosalía's picturesque wooden buildings, has been reopened and is worth a visit. From the Eiffel Church (*Iglesia de Santa Bárbara*) take the uphill road to the north mesa. Or take the more direct cutoff from the highway north of town.

You can sit on the broad European-inspired veranda and look out past mine pilings, tunnels, and rusting machinery to the broad blue sea. It's easy to imagine you're a visitor from a century ago. The original company-owned and company-run Hotel Francés has been renovated and rejuvenated, and once again welcomes weary travelers.

The Hotel Francés was actually built over a century ago, in 1886, but it burned down over a decade later and was rebuilt by 1920. One long-time hotel manager was Señor Pierre Mayieux.

The only town in Mexico established by the French languished after the El Boleo mine ceased operations. El Boleo then deeded much of its property, including the Hotel Francés, to the Mexican Federal Government. The federal government gave it to the state of Baja California Sur, which didn't want to mess with it either, deeding it to the Municipality of Mulegé. Governments are not in the business of running hotels, and while the Hotel Francés still welcomed guests for years, it began to fall into disrepair.

By 1990 the oldest hotel in Baja was put up for sale. Enter Laura Coronado Pasas, whose family had successfully taken over and upgraded the La Perla Hotel in La Paz. She saw the hotel advertised in the paper. It had been on the market for five years and had closed, abandoned and shuttered, with old furniture and artifacts gathering dust inside. She bought it in 1995 from the municipality and made its restoration a pet personal project, renovating it with care and personal attention. "I read a lot about decorating," Laura admitted after the project was completed.

As Laura still manages La Perla and is only able to make twice-monthly visits to Santa Rosalía, she established her friend Irma (Guadalupe Irma Camacho Manriquez) as manager.

Inside are squeaky wood floors, polished high ceilings with soothing fans, and thick fabric-designed wallpaper. There is a rustic wooden desk. The adjacent dining room's tables are of finely polished wood. A couple of small tables grandly overlook the dining room from modest balconied alcoves.

The courtyard out back now has a pool surrounded by a mini-museum of mining artifacts and implements. The 17 guest rooms, which are entered from the courtyard, are a sort of floral chintz, replete with padded chairs and thick brocaded wallpaper.

The food has always been considered good, with today's menu featuring regional and international cuisine along with wonderful seafood. The hotel rooms have traditionally been reasonably priced, and still are. During summer 2000 I found the rooms and the entire place to be a throwback to an earlier era. You almost expect to see the

Mining equipment in front of Hotel Francés, Santa Rosalía.

men in muttonchops and bowler hats and walking sticks and the women in long floral dresses with parasols.

In early years there was another old hotel downtown called the Hotel Central, but travelers through the years seemed to have preferred the "French Hotel" on the hill. One writer in 1953 called the Hotel Central "primitive but convenient."

According to author Don Hugh in 1958, "The French Hotel on the bench above town is the best bet for food and lodging, although the Hotel Central downtown is okay but caters to the native trade."

Cliff Cross in his 1974 guide book *Baja* said, "The company Hotel Français offers the best accommodations in town. Charges around $4 a day with meals, and it is cleaner and quieter than Hotel Central at the plaza, which is located over a pool hall."

Many years ago I enjoyed my first meal in Santa Rosalía downtown at the Hotel Central, where I relished the fine hybrid French/Mexican cuisine. That old hotel, which has been converted into a *Casa de Huéspedes* (guest house), now has a plaque outside that reads: "In this hotel the local Chief of Police Luís Parra arrested the U.S. citizen William Cook, wanted intensively by the U.S. police, charged with 11 murders in Louisiana, Texas and New Mexico. Santa Rosalía, Baja California Sur, 1950."

Well, maybe the Hotel Francés can't boast about a desperado being captured there, but at least it's not above a pool hall.

El Boleo Bakery

EL BOLEO BAKERY

Pan Dulce and French Pastry

Panadería El Boleo occupies a fading yellow clapboard building with a corrugated tin roof, on the right side of Santa Rosalía's main street, just past the Eiffel Church. For years it was considered by many to have the finest baked goods in all of central Baja California.

The old French bakery was known throughout the peninsula for its pastries and *pan dulces*; the French rolls were especially delicious. The machinery for the El Boleo Bakery had been brought over from France in the 1880s, and much of it is still operational.

Everything is baked in mesquite-fired brick ovens built in 1903. *Pan dulces* include: *quequitos* (cupcakes), *elotes* (ears of corn), *campachanas* (puff pastries), sweet *empanadas* (filled rolls), great *bolillos* (which they call "*birotes*"), and more.

I learned the hard way that they are closed on Sundays, and I used to find a long line of people at the bakery during the week. Last year I grabbed some goodies and wasn't that impressed. My selection was okay, but certainly not better than hundreds of other *panaderías* (bakeries) .

On this last visit, I found that the bakery is but a memory of its years of glory. A small selection of what looked like day-old pastries was displayed. Worse was the "care less" attitude of the few surly clerks. I mentioned this to others in Baja; many have agreed that unfortunately, the El Boleo Bakery is but a shadow of its former self.

The Dentist of Santa Rosalía

The Legendary Doc McKinnon

Almost everybody who traveled the unpaved length of Baja before the 1970s either talked about or wrote about a legendary character who plied his trade in the remote old French outpost of Santa Rosalía.

Dr. Charles S. (Mac) McKinnon was a dentist who practiced in the Santa Rosalía area for over 35 years, from the late 1920s into the 1970s. He originally visited his patients on muleback and later bought a truck, onto which he affixed a mobile office.

According to mystery writer Erle Stanley Gardner, who first met Mac in 1947, the dentist knew every rancher, every water hole, and every twist in the road between Santa Rosalía and La Paz, where he traveled bringing relief to thousands.

Later Mac settled into his office across the street from the Eiffel Church (*Iglesia de Santa Bárbara*). It is said that no one would consider continuing on their journey without consulting road conditions with Mac, who was described as a one-man automobile club.

The author Ralph Hancock, in his 1953 book *Baja California*, said, "The man we enjoyed most in Santa Rosalía is Dr. C.S. (Mac) McKinnon, who always goes out of his way to help in a dozen little ways, who keeps us entertained with his stories of early days in Baja California (he has been a practicing dentist here for over thirty years and has never been out of B.C. in that time) and then sends us on our way with letters of introduction to everyone he knows from Santa Rosalía to La Paz. What he doesn't know about the Distrito del Sur is hardly worth knowing."

Don Hugh, author of *Solo Below* in 1958 says, "Dr. C.S. (Mac) McKinnon, a dentist from 'down under' is the man to contact at Santa Rosalía." Hugh went on to call him an ambassador-at-large.

According to author O.W. Timberman in his 1959 book *Mexico's Diamond in the Rough*,

> "Doc is a fluent conversationalist and there is never a dull moment when you are with him. He is well read and seems to know something about everything and a lot about some things. He has a beautiful and gracious wife (Rosita). One of Doc's faults is his willingness to drop what he is doing and to be helpful in many ways to the travelers who stop to see him. He is never too busy to make your visit in Santa Rosalía pleasant.
>
> "On this trip we had dinner with Doc at the French Hotel, where he knew what to order to assure us a tasty meal. He sent his assistant, Ramón, to the French bakery to procure our supply of bread and rolls while we did other shopping."

Cliff Cross's 1974 book *Baja* shows a photo of a patient in Doc McKinnon's dental chair next to the antique drill, operated by a foot treadle he was still using.

One local told me a good story about Doc McKinnon. It appears that Mac was hard of hearing and wore a hearing aid. Once at a Rotary Club meeting his fellow

Rotarians pulled a trick on him. They pretended to be talking, but just mouthed the words. They enjoyed watching Mac get flustered. He proceeded to pull out his hearing aid and bang it a few times, thinking it had failed him. That brought on a good laugh.

Marion Smothers in her book *Vintage Baja* says, "If anyone deserved nomination for 'almost-saint' it was Dr. Mac. And if there could be a celestial need, I can visualize him now going from cloud to cloud with his little black bag, filling and extracting the teeth of angels."

Mac, who was originally from Australia, had lived in Canada. He and Rosita had a son who went to work in the States. The son has himself since retired and lives in Guaymas, Mexico.

It seems obvious that this one-man Samaritan made an incredible impression on so many people. The American writers could and did extol his prowess and Baja knowledge. And there are many simple and grateful people who may not write flowery words in English, but know how to say thank you from the bottom of their hearts.

THE LEGEND OF THE MULEGÉ PRISON
The Prison with Open Doors

The tropical village of Mulegé has led an interesting life. It reposes in a lush valley, thriving off a freshwater stream that empties into a beautiful estuary on its way to the Sea of Cortez. Tropical Mulegé has long attracted visitors, from Indians to the padres, from Americans who were repelled to Americans who were welcomed.

The name *Mulegé* is derived from the Cochimí language meaning "Large ravine of the white mouth." In 1705 the popular Padre Juan de Ugarte brought Padre Juan María Basaldúa to the area to establish a mission, which they christened Santa Rosalía de Mulegé. The beautiful stone building that replaced the original mission still stands on a rocky promontory overlooking the river.

Fourteen years later, Ugarte built the first ship ever built in the Californias near the Mulegé estuary. The settlement of Mulegé was flooded in 1770 but restored. Much later, the 1847 Battle of Mulegé in the Mexican-American War found the residents of Mulegé rallying behind Captain Manuel Pineda to repel the American naval advance.

Most interesting chapter

But perhaps the most interesting chapter in Mulegé history was the territorial prison that was erected on the hill above town in 1907. This prison was different. The inmates were allowed to leave each morning to work in town, as long as they returned when the horn was sounded each afternoon.

While locally it had many nicknames, including "The University," officially it was the Territorial Prison of Baja California del Sur. Some visitors remember up to 30 and 40 prisoners.

The doors were open during the day. The prisoners would go out to earn minimum local wages, either pruning palms, fishing, or other work. For a while during the 1950s, some worked on the construction of a hospital. At 6 p.m. the caretaker would blast a loud conch shell horn. The prisoners and guards would then drift in from all directions. Roll was called, the prisoners marched into prison, and doors were closed. It was said that they were not allowed to dance or drink, but they could go to a dance if they stood on the sidelines to watch.

O.W. Timberman noted in 1959:

> "On top of this hill was the prison, surrounded by a high wall with sentry boxes placed at the corners. We were allowed to go as far as the high iron doors, where we passed out cigarettes and candy to the inmates, totaling four, who were locked inside. I bought, from one of them, a hatband he had made of braided horsehair. From the looks of the interior that we could see from this gate, the quarters could not be called luxurious. The prisoners' blankets, which were all the bed they had, were rolled on the bare ground, and the place was far from sanitary.
>
> "Any other prisoners they might have had were probably off in the town at some form of work, for it was our understanding that the honor system was used here, and those who were in good grace were allowed to work in the date groves and vegetable gardens close by — the only restrictions being that they could not enter places where intoxicating liquors were sold, and they had to be back at the prison at a specified time each evening to answer roll call. I could not help but wonder how an escaped prisoner could go very far in this wasteland and survive, considering the great distances between habitations and the frugal water supply."

From all indications, the townspeople treated the prisoners well, as if they were just like anyone else. Only a few ever betrayed the trust. In the 1960s one prisoner stole some clothes from a store in town. For this, all of the prisoners had their rights rescinded for a while. The peer pressure not to abuse the system must have been enormous.

Then, the Territory of Baja California Sur became the State of BCS in 1974, and a new prison was later built to the north of town. The new one looks more like a prison, too. And the old one, well, the distinctive large, white rococo Spanish-styled structure that dominated the town began to suffer from inattention and abuse. So a local group got the old whitewashed adobe building with four-foot thick walls transformed into a museum, and it's well worth a visit.

This group was led by Americans, by the way, who have been welcomed to Mulegé in droves. Homes along the river and south of town along the *Bahía de Concepción* are now primarily owned by Americans, who find the tropical village a paradise.

The transformed legendary old prison on the hill now serves as a reminder to a more laid-back system of jurisprudence and a more laid-back Baja of an earlier era.

Hotel Punta Chivato
Fly-in Resort on the Point

The year was 1966 and the American Dixon Collins was building a fly-in resort out on the picturesque point called Punta Chivato, a few miles north of Mulegé. Collins had a twin-engine plane which he used to commute back and forth to the States, as well as a single-engine plane he used locally.

When an Erle Stanley Gardner expedition nearby had problems and needed parts for a helicopter, Collins let Gardner use the planes to go to the States for parts and whatever else was needed. That type of hospitality seems to be the rule rather than the exception among those who spend a lot of time in Baja.

The Hotel Punta Chivato, originally named the Hotel Borrego de Oro, was a luxurious resort for its time, with stone buildings and beautiful arches overlooking the Sea of Cortez. Built with the pilot-sportsman in mind, it was acquired by Bill Alvarado in 1980 and is now under Mexican ownership. The hotel has its own airstrip, pool, air-conditioned rooms and boat ramp. Fishing *pangas* can be provided, and the area is one of the better fishing spots along the Sea of Cortez.

I drove to the place, about 14 miles of dirt road off the highway, in the early 1990s. Just past the hotel there was an outstanding camping area out on the point. On a sandy beach, there were no hookups, but about 40 sites with a disposal station, pit toilets, and cold showers.

Fishing legend Ray Cannon wrote that at Punta Chivato, he saw a couple of locals wrestling an enormous jewfish on board. Another Baja buff told me she saw waiters bring in a small marlin by hand.

When the hotel opened Cannon wrote about it, noting a stay made delightful by hostess Mrs. Barbara Collins and Marty Price. He also wrote, "The Hotel Borrego de Oro is truly elegant with spacious suites and sun areas facing the sea from atop of a low cliff. The food, service, and hospitality without the Acapulco-type disciplines, are quite deluxe. Furthermore this grand resort is located in the heart of one of the most exciting big and small game fishing areas in the Cortez."

Hacienda Hotel, Mulegé
A 200-Year-Old Building

While the present hotel doesn't date back 200 years, its old adobe building does. The colonial style building with thick walls and high doors was built shortly after the village of Mulegé was devastated by flood in 1770.

It served for decades as a guest house where visiting dignitaries and politicians could secure lodging. It's been a public hotel since 1955, when part of it was opened as the Club Mulegé Lodge by Octavio (Sal) Salazar, who helped set up fishermen with guides for snook fishing in the estuary.

Hacienda Hotel, Mulegé

After merging the Club Mulegé Lodge with the older hacienda building behind it in 1962, Salazar and his Mexican partner renamed their hotel the Hacienda de Mulegé, or the Vieja Hacienda (Old House) of Mulegé.

Today it's just known as the Hotel Hacienda. Right in the center of town across the street from the plaza, the Hacienda is a group of 26 rooms around a cozy central court-yard with colorful plants and flowers, and a small bar which doubles as a reception counter off to the side. Ten of the rooms were added in 1959 during rebuilding follow-ing a major *chubasco* (storm) that hit town. Nine rooms were just added recently.

In 1964 the Hacienda was purchased by owner/manager Alfonso "Al" Cuesta. He loved talking to American guests, and according to one source, it was "in the most broken English you've ever heard." His practice over the past 36 years has paid off, because I found Señor Cuesta, now 73 years old, to speak fluent English.

The 1971 *Sunset Guide to Baja California* talks about Mulegé's historic Hacienda and indicated that Cuesta himself must have felt his English needed some work with this report: "A sign outside the 200-year-old adobe near the plaza reads: '*Vieja Hacienda Hotel — Broken English spoken.*'"

The article continued, concurring with my assessment of Señor Cuesta's linguistic ability, "Inside the Hacienda Hotel, a spacious courtyard lined with rocking chairs is filled with colorful bougainvillea, including one purple-flowered specimen 90 years old. The rooms are enormous, with high beamed ceilings and adobe walls three feet thick. Rates are $10 a day per person on the American plan, $5 on the European plan. The owner, incidentally, speaks excellent English."

203

Reports from the '60s and '70s noted that Cuesta took pride in showing off his great treasure, a beautiful Stradivarius violin crafted in 1731. I asked him how he came by such a piece of antiquity and he laughed and said, "It's a long story." He admitted that he never did take violin lessons, having taught himself how to play the instrument.

Cuesta is one of those hands-on guys you'd almost expect to be an accomplished violinist just by practicing on his own. I heard from someone that he is an accomplished bush pilot. I met him at his newest enterprise, the Cuesta Real Hotel on the river south of town (just before the Serenidad). The hotel was still undergoing construction, growing on the lot that extends from the highway to the river. He gestured about and indicated what he was planning. "And then," he added, pointing to possible future expansion, "My children can always make it bigger."

Cuesta has five sons and a daughter. Two of the boys moved to Ensenada, and his daughter to Guanajuato, Mexico, but the others are in Mulegé. Son Adrián S. Cuesta Romero now manages the vintage Hacienda Hotel. Son Ciro A. Cuesta Romero is an authorized guide who takes tourists to Indian paintings and petroglyphs in the Mulegé area.

The Old Hacienda Hotel in the center of town is an old, high-ceilinged kind of place, with acoustics that still allow you to hear dogs barking and roosters crowing outside. The room rates are still very low. There's now a restaurant owned by Americans on a corner of the building facing the plaza.

The Hacienda attracts travelers who like old Mexican ambience and the ability to walk outside and browse around the picturesque town of Mulegé.

CLUB AERO DE MULEGÉ, VISTA HERMOSA
The Hotel on the Hill

Only two years after Mulegé's Hotel Hacienda opened for business, and almost a decade before the Punta Chivato fly-in resort, the Club Aero de Mulegé began to welcome fly-in guests. It was built high on the north hill between the town and the river's mouth by the original 1957 owners, Luís Federico, Jean Bonfantes, Don Johnson, and Paul and Joven Ortiz. Its original name was Loma Linda (pretty hill).

It's easy to be confused about Mulegé hotels, because that same hotel on the hill has had so many different names. In addition to Club Aero de Mulegé, it has variously been called the Club Aero, Club Mulegé, Hotel Mulegé, Vista Hermosa, and the Loma Linda, sometimes even reverting to older names.

It's also had various owners. The original group sold the hotel in 1963 to Dick Stockton, who relinquished his interest in 1965. In 1967 it was operated by one of the owners, George Remley, who according to the mystery writer Erle Stanley Gardner, was an "international financial soldier of fortune." Other owners have included David Galloway and Alejandro Arcos.

According to one of the original owners, Don Johnson, "We had our hearts and souls in that place. We really loved it and hated to see it go downhill."

Early on it was the most deluxe resort in Mulegé. It featured a dining room, bar, and luxurious sea-view rooms opening onto gleaming tiled walkways smothered in colorful bougainvillea. The hotel on the hill featured an 1,800-foot landing strip on the mesa out back and a modern fleet of fishing boats. By 1974 two landing strips supplied aviation fuel. It was considered a first-class resort, with a dining room and the only swimming pool in Mulegé.

I discovered the place in the mid-70s and didn't realize it was the same one recommended to me, because it had a different name. It was a pleasant drive along the cool, enticing river road from town and then up to the mesa top and the inviting sprawling hotel. It had been rejuvenated, and by 1992 the Vista Hermosa was considered in one guidebook as the best value in town.

But things change in Baja, even legendary hotels, and in 1993 there was a land dispute and the old hotel on the hill closed down. Today the hotel has been converted into what looks like several private residences. Today, walls painted salmon and fuchsia shroud the history of the old hotel on the hill. There's a water tank with the words "Loma Linda" on it, reflecting the hotel's original name. But I guess it doesn't make any difference now.

SERENIDAD HOTEL, MULEGÉ

Fly-in for a Pig Roast

Mulegé to many Baja travelers *means* the Hotel Serenidad, a tropical fly-in resort down near the mouth of the Santa Rosalía (or Mulegé) River. And when they think of the Serenidad, they usually think about its affable host, Don Johnson.

Johnson, who seemingly has been around forever, actually hasn't, only *almost* forever. He personally discovered Mulegé in 1960, arriving that first time by boat from San Felipe. Born in Springfield, Illinois, he was raised in San Jose, California. At age 35, looking for a change and a better opportunity, he left San Jose to return to Baja, settling in Mulegé.

He married a local girl, Nancy Ugalde Gorosave, the granddaughter of Mulegé area rancher Don José Gorosave and niece of Cuca Gorosave, who had opened Las Casitas, a small motel and restaurant in town, with her husband Fred Woodworth in 1961.

The Serenidad (Serenity) Hotel was developed in 1961 by Leroy Center. Johnson, who had earlier been part owner of the Loma Linda, was the Serenidad's boat manager during the 1960s. Later, with partners Fernando del Morel and Chester Mason, Johnson bought the resort in 1968.

Don Johnson has owned the Serenidad ever since, his name synonymous with the place. For a while in the mid-1990s, the Serenidad was closed during a land dispute, but Johnson prevailed and reopened the Serenidad in October 1997.

The airstrip next to the Serenidad has always been and still is the main source of travelers for the hotel. By the early 1970s the hotel offered modern accommodations,

Don Johnson (in white) with the author at Saturday pig roast.

patio dining, a bar, and a new swimming pool. The Serenidad became like its name, serene, with large, beautifully furnished rooms strung out across tropical grounds. A large outdoor patio was built and is still used for dining alfresco.

The Serenidad became known for its assistance and advice for pilots, its good boat launching, and other facilities. Even in the early 1970s they offered compressed air to fill scuba tanks. The ambience of the tropical hotel about two and a half miles from town has been hard to beat. And then there's the food.

A 30-year tradition

Johnson started a tradition that has been going strong for at least 30 years. Every Saturday night is a pig roast, and I've met Baja pilots who fly in just for the feast. The tradition began as an occasional weekend celebration.

Ray Cannon, author of the bestseller, *Sea of Cortez*, wrote about the Serenidad and the beginning of the pig tradition in 1970: "Most of our group stayed at the Hotel Serenidad, where another old friend, Don Johnson, is co-operator and where he sees to supplying gas and supplies to the boats at his pier. Don had a whole pig barbecued for us on an old style spit beside the outdoor dining veranda. The evening was a gay one...."

A special magazine put out by Four Wheeler Publications heralding the opening of Highway 1 in 1973 even had a photo of the pig roast. The magazine was simply called *Baja Highway One*, and the photo caption read, "Every Saturday night is fiesta at Serenidad. The management barbecues a whole pig for the dinner."

206

Even today, the Pig Roast is still offered every Saturday evening. The traditional dinner now features folkloric dancers, mariachis, one margarita, and all the roast pig you can eat. It's a real party-time atmosphere, and you won't go away hungry. Johnson has now even added an Italian night each Thursday. Each September, the kitchen is closed, but the hotel and bar remain open.

The comfortable sleeping rooms are spread out over a refreshing garden array of plants and flowers. There are also several two-bedroom bungalows with fireplaces. The 50 rooms are all air-conditioned and offer satellite TV. There is an adjacent trailer park with RV hookups and disposal.

Many guests fly private planes into the adjacent airstrip. The 4,000' × 125' graded strip is no longer called "Serenidad," having been renamed "El Gallito."

The current manager is Diana Johnson, the oldest of Don and Nancy's three daughters. She is assisted by her husband, Marco Luján. Diana also served as Director of Tourism for the Municipality of Mulegé, the largest county in Baja California Sur. She runs the Serenidad with competence and resolve — I even found her hard at work early on a Sunday morning. Her sisters, Sara Laura and Sandra Lynn, are both married and no longer live in Mulegé.

Her dad still serves as the unofficial ambassador at the Serenidad, constantly visiting and chatting with his guests. It's a comfortable role for him, as in 1980 he became the American consulate in Mulegé, a job he performed for 13 official years and 20 unofficial ones.

Don loves to tell stories

Don Johnson once joined me while I dined in the patio and offered me an ice cream, which he insisted his restaurant crew had made fresh. I'm sure they did; it was rich and creamy. People kept dropping by our table to say hi or make a quick joke with their host. He loves to tell stories, and sometimes they're told about him.

He once told me an ice-cream story that involved a frequent visitor to Baja, John "the Duke" Wayne. "He loved these kinds of places," admitted Johnson. "He was the most down-to-earth guy you'd ever want to meet. After he died I learned from the captain of the *Wild Goose* [John Wayne's boat] how considerate the Duke was. The captain [who still lives in L.A.] reminded me that every time Nancy and I would have dinner on Wayne's boat, the dessert was always Rocky Road ice cream. I said, 'You're right, I love Rocky Road ice cream.' The captain added that the Duke knew that and always reminded him to stock up if we were heading down to visit Don Johnson. I was pretty impressed that he would do that."

Author Jerry Klink, in his 1974 book *The Mighty Cortez Fish Trap*, tells a wonderful story about Don Johnson and his partner, Fernando del Moral, referring to the Mulegé prison where prisoners would leave for day jobs:

> Well.... Don Johnson was sitting at the bar with a couple of gringos who had just checked into the hotel. They were asking him the usual questions about the prison when Fernando, his partner, came in and sat at the other end of the bar. "There's one of the prisoners now," said Don, pointing to Fernando. Fernando, picking up on the gag, charged down to Don and the guests. His countenance was surly as he wagged his finger in Don's face. "Why you point at me?" he bellowed.

"These people want to see a prisoner," said Don.

Fernando, who speaks excellent English, rattled off some violent Spanish.

"What did he say?" asked the wary gringos.

"He's offended," replied Don. "He claims that a man has a right to cut his wife's throat when he catches her with another man. He resents being singled out as a curiosity." And with that he called the bartender and instructed him not to give the prisoner any more to drink.

Fernando then blasted Don and the gringos in Spanish, shook his fist at them, and stomped out of the bar.

The shaky Americans heaved a sigh of relief and each ordered a double Scotch. Don and Fernando will do anything to keep their guests spending money.

Don laughed when I reminded him of the story on my last visit. He said, "It's true." He also got a little maudlin as the yarn reminded him of his old partner. "Fernando was a great partner. I miss him and will always remember him. Unfortunately he passed away in 1974."

There's a caring and tender side to this icon from Mulegé. He's about the best-known hotel owner in Baja. People will be telling stories for decades about the legend named Don Johnson and his little piece of paradise down by the mouth of the Mulegé River.

ISLA SANTA CATALINA

Baja's Rattleless Rattlesnake

Yes, it's true. In the land of the weird, sinuous cirio tree, the thick-trunked elephant tree, and the social, friendly whale, another oddity appears. There is an entirely different species of rattlesnake on the Isla Santa Catalina off the southern Baja coast — a rattleless rattlesnake.

Without the natural predators that threaten rattlesnakes elsewhere, these unique island dwellers evolved without a need to develop any type of defensive warning system. They look like other rattlesnakes, and when alarmed, they vibrate their tails. But since they have never developed rattles, they do not make any warning sound at all.

The unique snake was discovered in 1952 by biologists who originally thought their first specimen was a mutant and not a new species. Further research indicated that the island does house a new species (*crotalus catalinensis*), Baja's rattleless rattlesnakes.

LORETO: MOTHER OF THE MISSIONS

The Birthplace of California

The gulfside village of Loreto is important, and the villagers know it, even though they often appear to ignore the town's significance. They move at a slow pace and enjoy a somnolent life, only having to dodge a hurricane every hundred years or so.

But every October there is an awakening. It is a time to acknowledge that little Loreto was the first permanent settlement anywhere in the Californias, including that big U.S. State to the north. That's when Loreto celebrates the *Festival de las Misiones de la Antigua California* (Festival of the Missions of Old California), a two-week affair that encompasses much of the Mexican state of Baja California Sur.

Loreto, the first 17th-century development in the Californias, came into being on Oct. 25, 1697. The "*Nuestra Señora de Loreto*" (Our Lady of Loreto) mission became the first of a system that would colonize and settle not only Baja California, but all the way up to northern California.

The 300th birthday in 1997 was a grand and historic affair that infused even more pride into those noble and proud *loreteños* (people of Loreto). But each year, the fies-

Our Lady of Loreto Mission

tas offer much for the visitor, featuring conferences, recitals, movies, *leyendas* (readings), special visits, art and photo expositions, ballets, concerts, children's programs, solemn Masses, and more. Much of the celebration spills out beyond Loreto to the towns and settlements and missions of San Ignacio, San Luis Gonzaga, San Javier, and La Paz.

On Sunday, Oct. 22, 2000, under blustery skies that dampened much of Baja just over the mountains, Loreto again assumed its dominance of the Missions Festival. A vast stage had been set up on the grand Plaza Salvatierra in front of the historic Loreto Mission and the old *Museo de las Misiones* (museum) next door.

Outside in the plaza, about 12 or 15 booths featured displays of schoolchildren's exhibits, art, handicrafts, photography, and food.

A brief shower rolled through, and while some scurried for cover in the booths, workers hastily covered speakers and video equipment. Shortly the wind and rain abated, the seats dried off, and classical music welcomed those townspeople drifting in for the activities.

Loreto is an outside kind of place, and the rain shower was but a minor inconvenience, forgotten a half hour later. Radiant light from the stately tower belfry of the old mission added importance to the scene of people milling about, visiting booths, pouring out of the well-used mission church from Mass, or grabbing rain-washed metal seats in the plaza.

A piano recital ("A Piano Recital from the Children of La Paz to the Children of Loreto") took place in the revered old Mission. The formally dressed youngsters from the state capital gave a virtuoso performance with innocence, clarity, and love. Small, tinny voices took turns, with the sounds of Bach, Beethoven, and Mozart being recreated by tiny little fingers and wafted out of the narrow mission church into the plaza.

The main performance on the outside stage that evening was a Folkloric Ballet from the La Paz Institute of Technology. The show featured beautiful señoritas, all with similar dark hair, red lips, and broad, flashing smiles, raising colorful skirts, twirling, spinning and fluttering, kicking well-toned legs, accompanied by mustachioed men with sombreros, their hands behind their backs, boots stomping, and music booming.

Loreto had earned its historical significance. The inscription above the mission door reads *"Cabeza y Madre de las Misiones de Baja y Alta California"* translating "Head and Mother of the Missions of Lower and Upper California." It dates back to Oct. 19, 1697, when the Loreto founding party of six Spanish soldiers, led by the indomitable Jesuit Mission President Padre Juan María Salvatierra, came ashore and began preparations to establish the mission. The entire California mission system began on that date.

There was an earlier short-lived settlement at San Bruno, eight leagues (24 miles) north of Loreto. In 1683 Padre Eusebio Kino, Admiral Isidro Atondo, and some Spanish soldiers and friendly Indians constructed a presidio and mission at San Bruno. It was abandoned in 1685, primarily for lack of water.

Padre Kino would get another chance after he and Padre Salvatierra helped create the Pious Fund, into which donations were made by wealthy individuals. They proposed to the Spanish viceroy that the Jesuits get another chance to colonize and Christianize the peninsula. They not only agreed to pay their own way, but also the wages of any soldiers needed for support. As there were no great riches to be taken, Spain didn't really care what happened to California and granted the Jesuits their wish. But Padre Kino had been recalled to the older mainland missions, and the foray into California rested on the shoulders of the capable and zealous Italian Padre Juan María Salvatierra.

At Loreto, under Padre Salvatierra's direction, a church was constructed of stone laid in mortar of clay, all enclosed within a hardwood timber stockade topped by cactus thorns. Thatched palm leaves made the first roof.

Later a permanent chapel, three small houses, and storage rooms were built. Hand-hewn cedar timbers were cut and dragged down from the mountains by oxen. The Roman bricks, forming a decorative motif in the mission walls, were contributed by an Italian patron and shipped over as ballast.

The mission church was completed in 1704. By this time the padres had baptized over 200 Cochimí Indians, and there were over 70 permanent colonists (Spaniards, Mestizos, and Christian Indians from Mainland Mexico). The stone Loreto mission building of today was completed by Padre Juan de Armesto in 1748.

The mission not only served as headquarters for the Jesuit mission chain for 70 years, but was, in effect, the capital of both Californias for well over 100 years. When the town was wiped out by a hurricane in 1829, the capital of Baja California was moved to La Paz, and the village of Loreto began to dwindle in importance.

The Indian population has long since disappeared. Much of the present Loreto population is made up of the descendants of the early Spanish settlers.

In the fiesta audience that night were people named Arce and Carrillo, others named

Marques and Villavicencio, and yet others named Cooper and Davis, the latter two reflecting settlers who arrived in the 19th century. The people of Loreto indeed have a proud and diverse heritage.

Luck of the Padre

Playing the lottery might have been considered a vice by some religions, but Catholics have stressed moderation in activities such as gambling and considered it sinful only if indulged in excess or if the actions neglected other responsibilities.

That tolerance waved a lucky wand over Loreto a half-century ago in the form of the enterprising padre, Don Modesto Sánchez Mayón. He arrived at Loreto in 1950 and spent the next few years cajoling the gentle people of Loreto to not only a greater interest in their spiritual lives, but a renewed interest in preserving their historic mission, the "Head and Mother of All the Missions of Baja and Alta California."

While prayers were rendered regularly, Father Sánchez occasionally purchased tickets in the National Lottery of Mexico. When the good padre hit, he hit big, winning 500,000 pesos. In his prayers, he promised that if he ever won a major prize, he would spend all of it on restoring and refurbishing his church.

He kept his word, and along with adding a new tower, made many other repairs. Writer Norman Phillips notes in 1974's *Baja Highway One* as he visited the Loreto Mission:

> "A great deal of restoration has been done on it recently. The padre at the time was Father Sánchez, a good friend of mine whom I very much admired. It was he who had the altar regilded; who had the workmen renew the gold leaf on all the statues; who had brought in religious artists from all over Mexico to freshen the paintings on walls and ceiling. A lot of stone repair was done, too, and done beautifully, quite like the original.
>
> "Father Sánchez paid for all of this work, many millions of pesos, out of his own pocket.
>
> "Where did he get the money? Well, believe it or not, he bought a couple of tickets on the Mexican National Lottery.... And he won. I don't remember how many millions of pesos he won, but it was a potfull of them. True to his word, he spent all of them over the next several years restoring his church to what it was when built by the Spaniards."

Phillips' report implies that buying the tickets was a one-time occurrence, but other reports indicate Padre Sánchez had bought lottery tickets more than once. Phillips also admits he couldn't remember how many pesos, but other documents reveal the 500,000 pesos to be more accurate. Regardless, it was enough to restore the first mission in the Californias to the prominence it deserves.

The lucky padre kept his promise.

THE OLD FAMILIES
Loreto Legacies

When Padre Salvatierra stepped ashore at Loreto in October 1697, he was accompanied by six Spanish soldiers. Over the following few months and years, more soldiers arrived to help establish the mission, presidio, and new settlement. Spanish soldiers played a vital role in helping the padres in Loreto and other missions for well over a century.

That the Loreto mission prospered is a tribute to some of these early soldiers whose descendants are now not only found in Loreto, but throughout the Californias.

For example, one Nicolás Márques landed with Salvatierra in 1697. Today there are many descendants named Marques in Loreto and many more scattered throughout southern Baja, primarily in rural areas.

Even more prominent in Baja California is the surname Arce, mostly descendants of Juan de Arce, an English-born soldier with a Spanish name who arrived at Loreto from Sinaloa in February 1698. He returned to Sinaloa on the mainland of New Spain in 1701. Later, in 1751 and 1764 respectively, two Arce brothers (José Gabriel Arce and Sebastián Constantino de Arce) emigrated from Sinaloa to Baja.

While some of the early Spanish soldiers married Indian maidens, most found wives among Spanish families of mainland New Spain (Mexico), as the padres encouraged them to.

For example, Captain Esteban Rodríguez Lorenzo, a Portuguese, who was military chief at Loreto and eventually served as a soldier for 30 years, brought his bride from what is now the Mexican state of Jalisco. One of his sons, Bernardo Rodríguez Larrea, later also became captain. And one of his daughters married a Spanish soldier, Manuel de Ocio, who made a fortune in pearls and mining, becoming one of the first capitalists in California.

Early Loreto soldier Juan Carrillo became the patriarch of the renowned Carrillo family of Los Angeles, California, which included the popular actor Leo Carrillo. The Carrillos settled in Los Angeles after Juan's two sons, Mariano and Guillermo Carrillo, accompanied Captain Portolá and Padre Serra on their historic 1769 overland journey from Loreto to San Diego.

Loreto still includes many descendants from some of its oldest families: Garayzar, Castro, and Larriñaga. Other old Loreto families have scattered throughout Baja California, including descendants of the following Spanish soldiers: Alvarado, Aguilar, Camacho, Castro, Ceseña, Cota, Gastelum, Meza, Murillo, Ortega, Ruiz, Talamantes, Vareño, and Villavicencio.

The clan of Villavicencios, many of whom are tall, slender, and sport a prominent Roman nose, can be found throughout the mountain villages of central Baja California. They trace back to the Spanish soldier José Urbano Villavicencio, who arrived in Baja in the latter part of the 18th century. He was born in 1745 and retired as a sergeant before becoming *mayordomo* (Indian labor boss) at the mission in Mulegé in 1807 or 1808.

Many of the early Spanish soldiers were given land grants as a reward for service in their difficult and demanding assignments. One Felipe Romero was given a land grant at Mission San Luis Gonzaga in 1768. There are Romeros throughout Baja, including the longtime family of caretakers of the Mission Santa Gertrudis.

Other Loreto legacies came later. Sprinkled throughout Baja are families named Smith.

The American sailor Thomas Smith, 27, from New York City, hid ashore at San José del Cabo when the Yankee ship *Dromo* left port on Dec. 31, 1808. He became the first U.S. citizen to permanently settle in Spanish California. He was baptized, taking the name Javier Aguilar, married a María Meza, served his adopted country as a soldier, and settled down in Comondú where his children eventually resumed the name Smith.

Then there was the English gentleman James Wilcox Smith, who arrived at Loreto in 1817. He fell in love with the governor's daughter, the lovely Concepción Arguello. However, the winsome lass was already in love with the Russian Count Rezanof and spurned the Englishman's offer. Smith later married a Señorita Verdugo, whose family had come to Baja California from Sinaloa. A Mariano Verdugo of that family also marched north with Portolá and Serra to Alta California. A brother, José María Verdugo, followed later and founded the Rancho Verdugo, now part of the city of Glendale, California.

In 1850 the Portuguese Antonio de los Santos Sosa is recorded as marrying one Rosario Acevedo in Loreto. And then in 1859 the Englishman John Cooper married Juana Osuna.

If there is one name that is still dominant in Loreto, it's Davis (pronounced Dahvees). It seems half the town is named Davis, as you constantly run into someone with that surname. The clan patriarch, Englishman Peter Davis, arrived in the mid-1800s and married Rosario Higuera in 1859.

Some of the Davis clan have become quite prominent. Lorella Castorena Davis is a doctor and sociologist in Latin American Studies. Estela Davis is an author/writer and longtime magazine and newspaper writer of national scope in Mexico.

Many of the early soldiers who settled on their granted lands near the old missions founded families as long-lasting as the land itself. Their progeny has multiplied and grown so much that until very recently, the descendants of those early soldiers made up a majority of the peninsula's population. To say that they have figured prominently in the history of Baja California is an understatement.

As noted, over the past 300-plus years, those original *bajacalifornios* have been joined by adventurers, pearlers, fishermen, miners, dreamers, and dropouts who have sought the solace of Baja California.

As I walk down the streets of Loreto, the village that gave birth to everything south of Oregon, I can't help noticing the attractive and gentle people and marveling that their ancestors carved a heritage out of a desolate land.

FLYING SPORTSMAN LODGE
Loreto's Original Resort

Some of Baja's legendary resorts never survived to welcome in the new millennium, but were instrumental in developing the tourism of Baja California and Baja California Sur. The Flying Sportsman Lodge, the oldest of the Loreto resorts, was of immeasurable importance during its 30-year heyday.

Ed Tabor was the founding father and guiding light of Loreto's first fly-in resort, which opened in late 1951. Tabor was a former radio broadcaster who flew civilian planes for the U.S. during World War II. He bought and ran his own six-plane DC-3 airline. He discovered the bucolic gulfside village of Loreto and sold his airline to move there and establish the Flying Sportsman.

Tabor used different planes, including a DC-3, to bring anglers from the states to Loreto, making a trip to the Flying Sportsman Lodge a fly-in charter package, although those arriving by car or private aircraft were also welcome. The lodge was on the beach about a mile south of the plaza in downtown Loreto, and had its own boat fleet and dock.

It turns out that one of the smartest promotional moves Tabor made was sending a telegram to "Fish Editor, *Western Outdoors News*" in April 1954 with a teaser about a great marlin bite and inviting a writer to visit. A writer took him up on it, and that's how Ray Cannon made his first visit to Baja California Sur. Cannon continued to write about the Flying Sportsman Lodge (and all of Baja) for years.

Along with the outstanding fishing, the lodge also took guests on dove and quail hunting expeditions and had equipment for skin divers. Air-conditioned accommodations, either in beachfront rooms or cabañas, included all meals. There was also a swimming pool, bar, and food flown in from the U.S.

Tabor married Bertha Davis Verdugo, who worked at the lodge as a secretary and later served as a flight attendant. After Aeroméxico Airlines began making scheduled stops at Loreto, the Tabors devoted their energies to arranging charters for Aeroméxico. Following property disputes with the local *ejido*, the legendary Flying Sportsman Lodge went out of business in 1982. The legend himself, Ed Tabor, passed away in 1987.

HOTEL OASIS, LORETO

Landmark in Loreto

Loreto has no shortage of landmarks. As the only California development in the 17th century, the 300-plus-year-old mission town is its own greatest landmark. The town was built around the *Nuestra Señora de Loreto* (Our Lady of Loreto) mission and was the capital of both Californias for 132 years.

But Loreto dwindled in importance following an 1829 hurricane, which caused the capital to be moved. The Indian population has long since disappeared, and the descendants of early Spanish settlers made up much of the Loreto population. For years, Loreto persevered as a sleepy oasis where summer's heat forced a slow, laid-back pace for locals and visitors alike. California's first city had changed very little until the 1960s.

Fishermen began to learn about Loreto, hearing stories about the dorado, yellowtail, marlin, sailfish, grouper, rock sea bass, roosterfish, and other species being caught there.

These stories prompted Bill Benziger, who had married Loreto's Gloria Davis, to open the Hotel Oasis. (Gloria is another descendant of the European Peter Davis and Rosario Higuera, who married in 1859). Bill and Gloria opened for business in 1963 with only two rooms. On the beach in a lush tropical setting amid towering date palms, the hotel befits

its name. The Benzigers kept adding, and now there are 40 air-conditioned rooms and suites.

Early visitors and travelers were consistent in praising Benziger's knowledge and help, some calling him a "wealth of information." Others noted that Gloria supervised an excellent kitchen. Bill and Gloria have called their resort a fisherman's paradise, and many guests have agreed. The Hotel Oasis can arrange fishing, whale watching, kayaking, and other activities.

Only five blocks from the downtown Loreto Plaza, it's easy to find. Just drive straight to the seafront, make a right, and go to the end of the road. I checked into the Hotel Oasis last year and was walking to my room when movement on the other side of a chain link fence startled me. I actually jumped back, as a huge deer was grazing just inches away.

It turns out that "Bambi" is a local deer whose mother was hit on the highway near Loreto 13 years ago. The baby buck was taken in by the Benzigers, who built the enclosure for him. The hotel's lush garden setting is as good a place as any for the well-cared-for Bambi.

The Hotel Oasis provides a home-type atmosphere, with an American Plan that features all meals. They also can accommodate travelers like me who prefer not to have all their meals in the hotel.

Most rooms face the sea and include a hammock out front under the thatched patio to change a guest's mind from day-to-day concerns to blissful relaxation. Colorful gardens attract small birds that flit around your hammock. More importantly, they provide a rich, tropical scent that mingles with the salt air from the sea. The rooms are built on polished rock floors and include a woven bamboo roof and amenities such as fishing rod holders.

The Oasis also has a heated pool and a tennis court (almost lost in the garden foliage), a bar, and a restaurant that opens at 5 a.m. to accommodate fishermen. Rates depend on the number of people and type of plan.

While Bill and Gloria are still very much involved in the Oasis, their daughter, Anna Gloria Benziger, along with Hector Gutiérrez, manages the place. Their two sons have left for the big cities, one running a clothing store in La Paz, while the other owns two shoe stores in Cabo San Lucas.

The Oasis is the oldest of the old Loreto resort hotels still around, and many of us feel, the most comfortable.

Other hotels

Also dating back to the 1960s is the Hotel Misión de Loreto, right on the waterfront a block or so north of the Hotel Oasis. It was opened in 1969 by Dr. Enoch Arias and is again undergoing total reconstruction.

In 1972 the Hotel Playa de Loreto was opened by Ildefonso "Al" Green Garayzar and others. It later became the Hotel Presidente and then the Hotel La Pinta. Located north of town a few blocks, it features 29 haciendas and 20 villas, with private balconies facing the beach.

These days there are other choices for travelers to California's first settlement, including the five star adults-only Diamond Eden Loreto resort several miles south of town.

When it comes to a Loreto landmark, of course you can't beat the old mission. But for a landmark hotel in Loreto, it's hard to beat the one that has endured for 38 years, the Hotel Oasis. Plus, you get to visit Bambi.

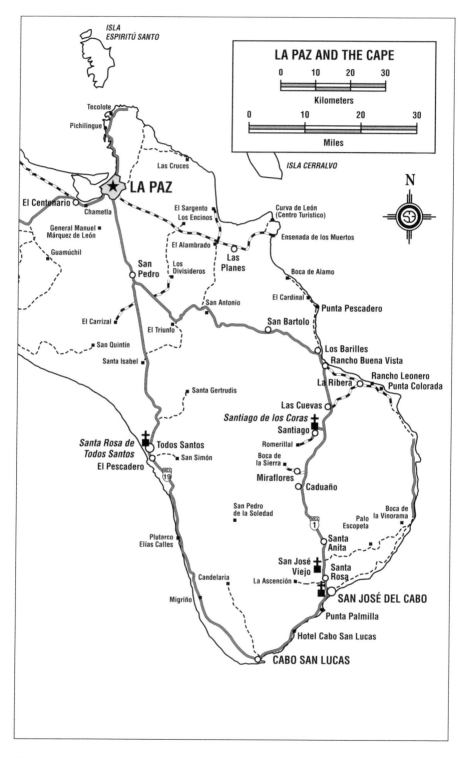

ISLA
ESPIRITÚ SANTO

LA PAZ AND THE CAPE

0   10   20   30
Kilometers

0   10   20   30
Miles

ISLA CERRALVO

N

Tecolote
Pichilingue

Las Cruces

★ **LA PAZ**

El Centenario
Chametla

El Sargento
Los Encinos

Curva de León
(Centro Turistico)

General Manuel
Márquez de León

El Alambrado

Ensenada de los Muertos

Guamúchil

San
Pedro

Los
Divisideros

Las
Planes

Boca de Alamo

El Cardinal

Punta Pescadero

El Carrizal

San Antonio

El Triunfo

San Bartolo

San Quintín

Santa Isabel

Los Barilles
Rancho Buena Vista

Santa Gertrudis

La Ribera

Rancho Leonero
Punta Colorada

Las Cuevas

*Santa Rosa de
Todos Santos*

Santiago de los Coras

Santiago

Todos Santos
San Simón

Romerillal

El Pescadero

Boca de
la Sierra

Miraflores

Caduaño

San Pedro
de la Soledad

Boca de
la Vinorama

Palo
Escopeta

Plutarco
Elías Calles

Santa
Anita

San José
Viejo

Santa
Rosa

Candelaria

La Ascención

Migriño

SAN JOSÉ DEL CABO

Punta Palmilla

Hotel Cabo San Lucas

CABO SAN LUCAS

Chapter 12: La Paz and the Cape

HOTEL PERLA, LA PAZ
The Pearl of Baja

It was *perlas* (pearls) that attracted Hernán Cortés to La Paz, but he was unable to sustain the colony of Spanish settlers he established there in 1535. For the next 185 years, until a mission was established at La Paz in 1720, the place was only visited by pearl hunters, some of whom forced the Indians to harvest pearls.

The Jesuit missionaries who arrived on the peninsula in 1697 did not allow their soldiers or Indians to labor for pearls. Instead they insisted that any work the Indians did would be for the greater glory of God, which meant Jesuit projects of building missions, roads, and infrastructure.

La Paz was noted for its black pearls (actually a metallic gray), and the pearls were harvested for over 400 years. Until 1874 when diving suits were introduced, Indians, often naked, free-dove to bring up the shells bearing the coveted pearls. In the late 1800s, the beautiful abalone shells themselves began to be harvested and shipped, almost rendering the pearl the second most important crop.

By decree of May 11, 1861, La Paz, with a population of about 800, was named a free port and was able to receive foreign goods. Pichilingue, nine miles away from La Paz, became the principal port, as no foreign goods were allowed to be landed elsewhere on the peninsula.

In 1868 Ross Browne reported in his book, *Explorations in Lower California*, that "the pearl fishery has greatly declined for several years past; the oysters having become scarce in the waters of the best fishing grounds, either in consequence of storms or other disturbances. The highest yield per annum for the past ten years has been about $20,000."

By 1941 the pearling industry had petered out entirely, as the pearl oyster, which attracted Cortés and hundreds of others, disappeared due to over-harvesting and disease. In 1941 Nobel Prize-winning writer John Steinbeck visited La Paz and based his book *The Pearl* on his experience.

Steinbeck became enamored of the town and reported in the *Sea of Cortez*, "...There is the genuine fascination of the city of La Paz. Everyone in the area knows of the greatness of La Paz. You can get anything in the world there, they say. It is a huge place —

217

View from the Hotel Perla, La Paz.

not of course so monstrous as Guaymas or Mazatlán, but beautiful out of all comparison. ...A cloud of delight hangs over the distant city from the time when it was the great pearl center of the world. The robes of the Spanish kings and the stoles of the bishops in Rome were stiff with the pearls from La Paz."

After the natural demise of the pearl, La Paz became the first site where experimental operations to artificially produce pearls was tried. The Japanese have since refined the process elsewhere.

The Pearl lives on

The Pearl of La Paz lives on, and not just in Steinbeck's book title, but in the form of a hotel and a mercantile company. In 1907 La Perla de la Paz, a mercantile company, was opened by Antonio Ruffo. The old La Perla de la Paz store is still in existence downtown, and I pop in for something every time I'm in town. It's a wonderful big colonial store, with thick walls, broad concrete pillars, wide aisles, an old yellowing tile floor, expansive shelving, and lots of merchandise, from furniture to food to clothing.

During the mid-1930s the economy of Baja California Sur was growing, but there was no place for the state capital and largest town to accommodate visitors. Lodging for distinguished guests had to be provided by local merchants and politicians.

This led to the government creating a semipublic fund to build a hotel. So the Hotel Perla de la Paz Corporation opened, and shares were sold to the citizens. Most of the shares were bought by the Castro family and the Ruffo family, which was operating the mercantile company, along with other enterprises. The Ruffos have since sold their interest in the hotel, but continue to operate the store.

By early 1940 construction on what was considered the first modern hotel in the State of Baja California Sur was underway. The legendary Hotel Perla, built in a simplified art nouveau style, opened in March, 1940 with 25 comfortable guest rooms and a grand ballroom named "Salón Madre Perla" (Mother Pearl Salon).

The inauguration ceremony was hosted by its founders: Col. Rafael Pedrejo (then Governor of Baja California Sur Territory), Juan Manuel Castro, Jorge Von Borstel, Miguel Cornejo, Salomón Tuchman, Arturo Canseco, and 15 other associates.

Steinbeck, who visited La Paz at the time, was partially prophetic in his reaction: "On the water's edge of La Paz a new hotel was going up, and it looked very expensive. Probably the airplanes will bring week-enders from Los Angeles before long, and the beautiful, poor bedraggled old town will bloom with a Floridian ugliness."

Center for important events

Fishermen can now fly into La Paz for weekends, but the ugliness projected by Steinbeck is for the most part still on hold. The Hotel Perla, which has graced the *malecón* (waterfront) and looked out over the bay for over 60 years, has hosted all the important events in the growing city for decades.

Following the 1941 attack on Pearl Harbor, a Mexican Air Force Squadron sent to defend Baja California Sur was housed in the Hotel Perla.

By the 1950s the oldest hotel in La Paz had already undergone extensive face-lifting, adding two more floors to the previous two. The Hotel Perla quickly became a favorite of American adventurers who drove the difficult journey down the peninsula. From *Solo Below* by Don Hugh (1958):

> "I drove my truck down the palm-lined *malecón* until I came to the La Perla Hotel. Hundreds of people were dining in the outdoor dining room bordering the street, and the Latin music, blaring forth from the innards of the building, voiced the fact that a dance was being held there. I parked my truck near the hotel and, with some misgivings as to whether they would accept a seedy-looking guest, I slinked my way past the formally clad joy-seekers to the reception desk.
>
> "I was greeted there by Señor José Cueli, the manager, with all the gusto of the Latin-American traditions, and I felt better about my importance."

The open-air restaurant on the ground floor of Hotel Perla had become the town's gathering place. During my visits there in the mid-1970s, I would sit over coffee and watch the parade of *paceños* (citizens of La Paz) pass by. In a few days one could meet virtually every tourist visiting the city from that comfortable perch in that outdoor restaurant.

The first time I stayed at the Hotel Perla, the state's premier hotel was showing her age. Carpets were worn, acoustics were bad, and walls were chipped and stained. On a subsequent visit when I stayed elsewhere, I saw the Hotel Perla draped in construction frenzy and covered with scaffolding. The major renovation was welcome, rendering a more modern, functional, and luxurious facility.

The current ownership of Hotel Perla results from a practical situation. Señor Adolfo Coronado Pimienta, an insurance salesman, lived in Mazatlán on the Mexican mainland and spent one week every month at Hotel Perla in La Paz. So when the opportunity arose in 1975, he bought the whole hotel! His daughter, Laura Coronado Pasas, is now the General Manager, his other daughter, Isabel Coronado Pasas, is Administrative Manager, and Adolfo himself is president. But his daughters run the show, as Señor Coronado still sells insurance!

The Coronados were the ones doing all those renovations during the 1970s, and they haven't stopped. The wonderful old hotel, now painted in café brown with lots of terra cotta trim, is resplendent with arches, tiles, and plants. During the year 2000, along with other modernizing and remodeling, an additional 50 rooms were added.

To prove her adroitness at renovating vintage hotels, Laura Coronado also bought the state's oldest hotel, Santa Rosalía's Hotel Francés.

The Hotel Perla in La Paz is second to none — the oldest, most historic, and still the center of the town's activities. Countless meetings between La Paz businessmen are held regularly in the dining room looking out over the bay.

According to one older guidebook, "The famous Perla Hotel, which has been the meeting place of the town aristocracy and tourists for years, is located right on the *malecón*. This venerable hostelry, so inextricable from the lore of La Paz, has had magnificent remodeling and additions of late.... Of course, there are any number of hotels and motels, but somehow the La Perla always seems synonymous with La Paz."

Los Arcos Hotel/Finisterra

Coppola on the *Malecón*

It seems fitting that the Los Arcos Hotel in La Paz would be on Avenida Alvaro Obregón, the *malecón* (waterfront) street named after a Mexican President. After all, that President's son, Mayo Obregón, played a role in the hotel's development.

But first came the Spaniards who built the hotel. The Spanish immigrants, Castro Verdayes Pinera and Sabino and Antonio Pereda, built the 12-room Los Arcos (the Arches) Hotel in 1950 on Avenida Alvaro Obregón, just a couple blocks down the *malecón* from the Hotel Perla.

Enter one of Baja's true legends, Luís Coppola Bonillas. Fresh from 35 European missions during World War II, the American pilot in 1949 had helped establish the region's only airline, Trans Mar de Cortez. The airline, started up and owned by Mayo Obregón, flew passengers, goods, and even livestock in surplus DC-3s between La Paz and mainland Mexico. Coppola helped Obregón manage the airline and was its only pilot.

Coppola's eye was also on the ground, and in 1952, he and his wife, Evangelina Joffroy, bought the Los Arcos Hotel. Coppola's father-in-law Alberto Joffroy was a major businessman in Sonora, owning Mexico's largest bread company, Sambo (this in the time before Bimbo Bread). He also imported supplies before the government agency *Conasupo* was established. With financial help from Joffroy and assistance from his friend Obregón, Coppola secured the deal. Coppola's best friend, Ignacio Sierra, became his partner and also served as the hotel's accountant.

During the 1950s the Los Arcos Hotel was managed by Bob and Estrella Elías, Estrella being the sister of owner Evangelina. For years, Mario Coppola, the son of Luís and Evangelina, managed the hotel. He still has an office there, but Rafael García is the Los Arcos Hotel manager today.

In 1956 the hotel expanded to 32 rooms by building the Cabañas Los Arcos, 10 duplex cabañas (20 rooms) next door. The original Los Arcos building was remodeled again in 1976, when it was enlarged to 182 rooms.

For years, the four distinctive arches of the original one-story building could be seen from way offshore. Today, integrated into the building's design, the original four arches are hard to spot.

The Cabañas Los Arcos offer seclusion in a tropical garden setting, with large laurel trees, bougainvillea, meandering cobblestone paths, and a swimming pool. Each bungalow is of hand-hewn stone topped with a palm thatch roof. On one side of the pool is a newer Mexican Colonial section, and the Cabañas now have 55 air-conditioned rooms.

Including the Cabañas section, there are 200 air-conditioned rooms and bungalows, two swimming pools, sauna, restaurant, cocktail lounge, coffee shop, boutique, convention center, travel and car rental booth, and fishing reservation desk.

One feature I appreciate is the hotel's big walk-in freezer. After your catch is filleted and bagged, you can tag it, and they will store it in their freezer. So it's no problem to go fishing one day, do other things for a few days, and then get your frozen catch just before you head for the airport.

On my last visit I caught my first *pargo*, which I had heard were great eating. As I was driving and did not want to preserve my catch, I gave most of it away. But I presented a *pargo* fillet to the hotel's Restaurant Bermejo cook, who did a top-notch job.

The Coppola presence in La Paz and the Los Cabos region lives on. In 1972, Luís Coppola went into partnership with Luís Bulnes Molleda. Together they built the dramatic Finisterra Hotel atop the crags that signify the end of the peninsula.

The children of Luís and Evangelina Coppola have taken over the family business. Sons Luís Coppola Jr. and Mario Coppola are no longer involved in the day-to-day operation, but oversee the family real estate and other holdings. Previously Luís Jr. and his brother Alberto Coppola managed the Finisterra, a job Alberto handles by himself today. A daughter lives in Hermosillo, where she and her family raise cattle.

Mario Coppola's office occupies one of the original Hotel Los Arcos guest rooms (#3), and he loves to talk to visiting guests. His knowledge could fill a book of "Baja Legends," and he admonished me not to forget this guy or that woman. For example, he referred me to the Gardenias, a businessman's hotel owned by a Mr. Portillo Fernández, the son of the contractor brought in by the Mexican government to build the original Hotel Perla.

Coppola also reflected on Baja California and its future: "We're already seeing the cape area booming. People are now renting more and more cars and driving a circle tour, like people do on the Hawaiian island of Oahu, here looping from Los Cabos to La Paz.

"We cannot stop progress," he added, "only control it. In that vein, hopefully we'll be seeing more and more ecotourism for Baja."

While all types of tourists have more options these days, with newer hotels opening up in La Paz on the road to Pichilingue, and resorts for fishermen farther out of town, there is something about staying right downtown where you can walk to restaurants and shops and stroll along the *malecón*, that I find the most appealing part of La Paz. And the Hotel Los Arcos fills the bill.

El Triunfo
The Largest Mill in Baja

The village of El Triunfo doesn't seem like much. Driving from La Paz to Cabo San Lucas, the little mining village catches your eye, a ghost town set amid old smelter ruins. The huge round brick chimneys jutting into the Baja sky are the only clues hinting at the town's former importance.

In 1862 rich silver deposits were discovered at nearby San Antonio, and the Triunfo Gold and Silver Mining Company came into being, giving birth to the mining town of El Triunfo. Within a few years it had a population of 10,000, mostly Yaqui Indians from Sonora, and was the largest city in the south.

It was noted that in 1868 the Triunfo district had some valuable silver lodes, especially the Mendocena, the Canoa, and the Mexican. Ores ranging in value from $70 to $120 per ton went down to a depth of 400 feet. Several hundred tons of ore had been taken out before the new mill was completed. It consisted of a battery of 24 stamps, 16 revolving barrels, and a series of capacious furnaces for chlorination. It was the only mill on the peninsula, except for a much smaller four-stamp mill at San Antonio. The small nearby village of San Antonio, by the way, briefly served as the capital of Baja California Sur in 1828 and 1829.

In 1874 a 36-stamp mill was in operation at El Triunfo and silver valued at $50,000 a month was being shipped to La Paz, but gradually the ore declined in quality. A 1918 hurricane flooded the mines, and after that, El Boleo Company from Santa Rosalía tried to resurrect the operation, finally abandoning the project in 1926. It was operated later on a smaller scale.

Today the village of El Triunfo has a population of about 800. The entire town feels like a western movie set, from the building facades downtown to the old smelters to the vintage two-tone church. No longer important as a mining center, the town is well known for the baskets made by the town's young people and sold there. If the store is open, they will often sell out of the handicrafts in one day.

The picturesque village is a reminder of the days of Baja's mining importance.

El Triunfo

OLD BEN THE MINER

The "First" Man of La Paz

Old Ben notched up a lot of "firsts" during his time in La Paz. A.W. Benseman was born in the late 1870s and migrated to La Paz during the first decade of the 20th century. Known simply as Old Ben, he was originally sent from San Francisco, California to install engines in the El Triunfo mines. But he fell in love *in* La Paz and *with* La Paz and decided to stay there, where he ran a machine shop.

He claimed a few "firsts" that nobody has challenged. He had the first automobile in La Paz, the first motorcycle, the first motorboat, the first *cine* or silent motion picture house, and the first internal combustion engine in Baja California Sur. He installed the first electric lights in La Paz and the first telephones in the El Triunfo mines. He helped install the original narrow-gauge mine railroad and was its engineer for four years.

Ben is like numerous other gringos who fell in love in Baja and settled there, becoming part of the folklore in the process. Old Ben was a busy guy; he definitely made his mark on a town he loved.

EL RANCHITO, LA PAZ

Daytime at the Cat House

Mention "El Ranchito" around La Paz and you'll always get a response. Women blush just hearing the words. Men roll their eyes, grin, and either knowingly, longingly, wistfully, or wishfully often murmur, "Ah, El Ranchito, sí, I have heard of this place."

223

Few in the La Paz area have not heard of El Ranchito, out in the desert just south of town. After all, it is one of the largest and most famous whorehouses in all of Baja.

The heart of the compound is a gravel courtyard with a fountain in its center. It is surrounded on all four sides by long one-story buildings like a motel. I discovered the place one bright sunny day about 25 years ago.

Looking around the four side buildings from inside the courtyard, I counted 66 closely-spaced doors facing the square. Small articles of clothing rested on the fountain's brick walls to dry in the tropic sun.

A few of the girls were up and about, performing their daily chores, laying out clothes, sweeping the gravel door stoops, or visiting with neighbor girls. It was a personal time, before the heavy makeup and provocative dresses that signified the long night ahead.

Anchoring the compound on one end was the restaurant and bar. The loud music piped throughout seemed especially inappropriate during the harsh bright reality of daylight. The place was virtually empty, with only a bartender behind the bar, a busboy mopping the floor, and two girls sitting with a couple of cowboys at one table.

Metal folding card tables and chairs, all adorned with brewery logos, filled the large, cavernous room. The concrete slab floor and general feeling of emptiness gave the place a sad, vacuous quality. The odor of spilled beer and wet cigarettes seemed stronger in an empty room with the music on too loud.

One could imagine that with the darkness of night, the place would put on its party face. The drabness would probably not be noticed when surrounded by scores of beautiful girls dressed to attract and lure.

With nightfall, I knew activity would increase until El Ranchito would become one of the more lively and engaging places in La Paz. All night long pickup trucks and cars from all over the area descend on the compound in the desert. When the rest of the town is waking up with the rising sun and the roosters crowing, El Ranchito is just going to sleep.

Even so, these days it must be even more active during the daytime hours than it was years ago. On a recent morning drive south from La Paz, I spotted the place and noted that taxi drivers were still shuttling clients down that dirt road, now fittingly hard-packed and well-used, to the famous whorehouse called El Ranchito.

Hotel El Palomar/Santiago Zoo

A Respite in the Shade

One of the most restful villages on the Baja California peninsula wasn't always that way. A mission established in 1723 in the verdant valley of Santiago south of La Paz had to be abandoned years later because of rebellions.

While the Indians to the north of Loreto were more passive and yielded to the ways of the padres, many of those to the south did not. Especially resentful were the Pericú witch doctors, who had lost their stature and continued to resist.

A decade after the mission was founded, a rebellion broke out over the entire south cape region, killing the padres at San José del Cabo and Santiago. The heart of the rebellion was at Santiago, where a group of Pericúes found Padre Lorenzo Carrancoa at prayer and dragged him outside where they ended his life with arrows, sticks, and stones.

Years later, after both La Paz to the north and San José del Cabo to the south gained importance, Santiago, which straddles the Tropic of Cancer, settled into a restful existence. Ross Browne noted in his 1868 journey: "Santiago occupies two sites, each on a picturesque eminence. On one of these stands the old Mission, still in a good state of preservation. The sugar crop in the valley gave promise of an abundant supply of cane."

In the following century Santiago changed very little. It was reputed to be "One of the most attractive towns in the peninsula," according to 1970's *Lower California Guidebook* by Gerhard and Gulick.

The town is built on two *lomas* (hills) with a valley in between. Enough water to irrigate about 1,500 acres comes from several springs. Between the two hills and the west side of the canyon is a former lake, which was drained and planted with sugar cane.

The 1971 *Sunset Magazine Guide to Baja California* says: "Santiago doesn't advertise its attractions, and the casual visitor is likely to miss them. The irrigated valleys around the town are green in the early spring with sugar cane and fruit trees. An old huge, *trapiche* (wooden sugar mill) crushes the cane and makes it into the *panocha* (brown-sugar cones) loved all over Mexico."

The entire Santiago area has about 4,000 residents, mostly involved in agriculture today. BCS Governor Leonel Cota Montaño is from Santiago, and the town has enjoyed a sprucing up, including a new plaza and a reinforced concrete access road.

Loma Norte is reached first, 1.7 miles from Highway 1, and contains the town's plaza, the town hall, a Pemex station, and a few stores. Loma Sur has a brick church and government offices, more homes, and one of the neatest little zoos I've ever visited. Just keep driving through town and you'll find it at the end of the paved road. While it's no San Diego Zoo, the only zoo in Baja California Sur is a delightful surprise.

Don and I were both amazed at the scope of the zoo, the only one south of the border town of Mexicali. In addition to the native indigenous animals, including rattlesnakes in a well-constructed pit, there were bears, monkeys, wolves, foxes, ostriches, tigers, and much more. The Parque Zoológico is open daily, 6 a.m. to 4 p.m., and is free. There is a receptacle for donations.

Perhaps the neatest surprise in Santiago is neither Loma Norte nor Loma Sur, but the heart of the wide, fertile palm-filled valley in between. There, on a shady lane among dates, mangoes, sugar cane, papayas, and bananas, is the El Palomar Hotel.

Until the El Palomar Hotel was opened in 1965 by Cirilo and Virginia Gómez, visitors to Santiago were put up for the night at the town hall. The El Palomar has long welcomed travelers and offers rooms, including meals. It is really more of a bed and breakfast, with only eight inexpensive rooms facing a fragrant garden. Through the years they have also offered guides, horses, and dove-hunting arrangements.

Gómez had previously worked at the nearby Rancho Buena Vista and built the El Palomar after it was suggested that the area would be ideal for a hunting lodge. The Rancho Buena Vista guest who made the suggestion was better known as the American crooner Bing Crosby.

El Palomar sustained considerable damage during the 1976 hurricane, but it was rebuilt and reopened in 1981 by the Gómez son, Sergio, and his wife Gloria. Sergio still proudly displays a photo of his mother with Bing Crosby.

A recent visitor was Barbra Streisand who, after a meal of fresh fish prepared *mojo de ajo* style, told Sergio it was unbelievably good and gushed over a new "favorite restaurant" of hers.

Not long ago, I arrived at the Loma Norte town plaza and took the left road down into the riverbed. In the valley floor I discovered the Palomar on the left. We enjoyed a wonderful lunch in their shaded patio overlooking all sorts of citrus and other fruit trees.

Before we left, another couple arrived. After they ordered lunch, they couldn't resist wandering the garden and touching the huge grapefruit, lemons, and bananas. They were from the East Coast and unfamiliar with citrus on trees, which we kind of figured out. But where they were from didn't make any difference. The lush tropical trees and plants surrounding the El Palomar can even impress a lot of jaded Californians, including the famous Bing Crosby.

Rancho Buena Vista/Hotel Buena Vista Beach Resort
Buena Vista on the East Cape

The oldest fishing resort along Baja's East Cape is the legendary Rancho Buena Vista, built back in 1952 by Herb Tansey and established as a fly-in resort. Paradoxically, a plane crash led to the development of the Rancho Buena Vista and a later plane crash took the life of its founder.

In 1946 Herb Tansey was captain of a TWA Constellation that crashed over Shannon, Ireland. Tansey and 37 passengers survived. The rest of the cockpit crew were among the 12 killed. Tansey himself had to have his leg amputated. It turns out that there was something wrong with the plane's altimeter, so Tansey sued and was paid a settlement by TWA.

On the ground, Tansey began teaching aeronautics in San Diego at a company that would one day become PSA airlines. One of his students, Enrique García, mentioned that he knew of a ranch for sale way down in Baja California. So Herb Tansey, García's father, José García, and student Olen Berger flew down to look it over. There was no landing strip, so they landed on the soccer field at the nearby village of La Ribera.

The goat ranch called the Buena Vista was on an East Cape bluff right on Las Palmas Bay. Immediately impressed, Herb Tansey suddenly knew how his settlement money would be spent. He bought the land, incorporated in 1951, built two cabins he named Rancho Buena Vista, and opened for tourists in 1952. He had José García manage the fledgling business, and arranged to have his guests picked up at the new airstrip by members of the Verdugo family.

During the 1950s Herb built his dream resort. Many guests flew private planes into the excellent 2,500-foot-long dirt strip less than a quarter mile away from the main ranch. Others arrived by either a three-hour taxi ride or a 20-minute charter plane ride from La Paz (75 miles). These days, most people fly into the international San José del Cabo Airport only 35 miles away.

Tansey built rooms duplex-style in a half moon concentration around the main dining/social center in the center. He hired Bobby Van Wormer, whose brother Frank was another of Tansey's students, as the manager.

The Buena Vista is a sportsman's paradise, with excellent fishing for tuna, marlin, wahoo, sailfish, and dorado right offshore. They offer super *pangas* or cruisers and a complete service to clean, freeze, prepare, and even smoke your catch.

Tansey continued to improve upon his dream throughout the 1950s. He was attracting fishermen to the East Cape, helped by the publicity generated by columnist Ray Cannon. Then on January 1959, Tansey, at 45 years of age, and one of his employees were killed when Tansey's private plane crashed between La Paz and the rancho.

Tansey's widow tried to run the operation, but sold Rancho Buena Vista to Colonel Eugene Walters in March, 1959. The Colonel kept Van Wormer as manager and later hired Ted Bonney, whose fishing interest and mechanical mind helped create the largest fishing fleet in the area.

Colonel Eugene Walters turned the rancho over to his son, Charles "Chuck" Milton Walters. Both Gene and his son have passed away, with Chuck buried next to Tansey on the hill above the Rancho Buena Vista. The hotel is now owned and managed jointly by Colonel Walters' grandson, Mark Walters (Chuck's son), and Eduardo Hermosillo, a member of the Hector Hermosillo Jr. family, which had acquired an ownership interest.

During its long tenure as the oldest fishing resort in the state of Baja California Sur, the Rancho Buena Vista has attracted worldwide sportsmen, from actors such as Chuck Conners to statesmen (President Dwight Eisenhower was a guest). As the original fishing resort on the East Cape, it has become one of Baja's legends.

Hotel Buena Vista Beach Resort

A short distance from the Rancho Buena Vista is an oasis fed by clear, natural hot springs. In 1976 Jesús "Chuy" Valdez opened a 12-room hotel that was originally called the Spa Buena Vista. Some of the buildings were built back in the 1940s as part of the residence of the territorial governor.

The Hotel Buena Vista Resort has grown to become one of the more popular on the East Cape and offers all sorts of fishing and hunting packages for guests. The Mediterranean-style bungalows with private patios and hammocks are hidden in the foliage of the lush grounds.

For non-fishing family members there's swimming, snorkeling, kayaking, hiking, tennis, biking, horseback riding, and even a massage therapist.

The Hotel Buena Vista Beach Resort is still owned by Chuy and his family; his son Esaul Valdez is general manager and Axel Valdez is the marketing director. Numerous fishing tournaments are held each year, including Chuy's Catch and Release Tournament, the Discover Baja Fishing Tourney, and the East Cape Big Game Blowout sponsored by Aero California and *Western Outdoor News*.

Big fish are being caught all year long at one of the East Cape's premier places. And that's the area called Buena Vista.

Palmas de Cortez/Playa del Sol/Punta Colorada

Van Wormer's Legacy

Bobby Van Wormer, one of the cape region's most colorful characters, is the owner of Palmas de Cortez, a popular fishing resort in Los Barriles. By now an East Cape legend, Van Wormer also owns the Hotel Playa del Sol next door and the Punta Colorada a few miles away.

The affable host was lured to the area by his brother Frank Van Wormer who had come down during the 1950s with Rancho Buena Vista's Herb Tansey. Frank kept regaling Bobby with the unspoiled beauty of the area. He kept talking about it. So Bobby finally relented, and the week after Christmas, 1956, the Lockheed aircraft worker went to see what it was all about. Bobby Van Wormer said those five days over the New Year's holiday, 1957 changed his life.

"I like to dive and came up with a mess of lobster. I thought, well there's one good thing about this place," Van Wormer recalled. "Then I went fishing and caught some nice *cabrilla* and *sierra*. Okay, great fishing, two things. I went dove hunting with equal success. Three. Then I looked up and down and saw nothing but unspoiled beaches for miles and realized at least four things make this a paradise. I knew then that this is where I belong."

He went back to Southern California and Lockheed, but his heart was already in Baja. In May 1957 he got away for two weeks and went right back to the East Cape, where he found himself helping Tansey at the Buena Vista. Somehow those two weeks stretched into a two-and-a-half month sojourn. When the 32 year-old Missouri native went back to California to work, he was encouraged by his sister, Dorothy, to be more responsible. But responsibility lies in the mind of the individual. Thus when Tansey visited Van Wormer to offer employment in Baja, Bobby decided that being a resort employee in Baja was responsibility enough.

Moving from California, Van Wormer even shipped his 21-foot outboard cruiser from Long Beach to La Paz in kit form and rebuilt it back down in Baja. Van Wormer worked for Tansey and became his assistant until money got tight and he laid himself off.

During that brief period in 1959, he helped owner John Mitre and manager Jorge Escudero, who were preparing to open the new Hotel Bahía de Palmas in Los Barriles. After Herb Tansey was killed in a plane crash, Tansey's widow called upon Bobby to return to the Rancho Buena Vista as manager.

She then sold the Rancho Buena Vista, and the new owner, Col. Eugene Walters, hired Van Wormer to continue as Buena Vista manager, a job he did with enthusiasm and devotion until 1966.

In 1965, Van Wormer married Rosa María "Cha Cha" Ruiz, who lived in the nearby village of Los Barriles. She worked at the local store owned by her father Eduardo Ruiz. The Ruiz family had owned the Los Barriles land where Mitre and Escudero built the Hotel Bahía de Palmas.

Opening the Hotel Punta Colorada

In 1966, Bob and Cha Cha Van Wormer wanted their own place, so they opened the Hotel Punta Colorada on a point just a few miles south of Los Barriles. This time Bob brought his brother Frank down to

Bobby Van Wormer

help him build the resort. Almost ninety miles south of La Paz, the inn was built high on a bluff in the comfortable old Baja style. Bob supervised the fishing and skin diving, and Cha Cha supervised what was reported by early guests as one of Baja's best kitchens.

Billed as the "Roosterfish Capital of the World" the friendly Hotel Punta Colorada opened with six rooms and two boats and today has 39 rooms and 15 boats.

The Punta Colorada oasis basks on a solitary point in a profusion of magenta bougainvillea, neatly trimmed laurel trees, and a myriad of palms. There's an indoor-outdoor bar full of photos of large fish and good times. Behind the hotel is a hard-packed 3200-foot airfield and in front, the sandy beach and the deep blue Sea of Cortez.

Hotel Palmas de Cortez

In 1973, Tito Ruiz (Cha Cha's brother) took over the Hotel Bahía de Palmas in town from Mitre and Escudero. The original hotel had opened in 1959 with just two *palapas*, one containing three guest rooms, while the other was the dining room, bar, and kitchen. After Tito passed away in 1983, the Van Wormers took title to the renamed Hotel Palmas de Cortez and set about creating an idyllic resort.

The beautiful Hotel Palmas de Cortez is right in the village of Los Barriles and now features over 50 air-conditioned rooms, plus suites and condos. The native-stone buildings, replete with tile, hammocks, and thatched roofs, blend gracefully with the tropical gardens and winding paths.

It is billed as a natural paradise with modern conveniences and has a spectacular seaside restaurant. Three meals a day are included in the room prices. Along with a large gift shop, there are complete workout facilities, swimming pool, tennis, racquetball, snorkeling, and scuba diving. There's a lot for the non-fisherman, and it's surprising how many families have come, making former male bastions like the East Cape fishing resorts into full-package vacation getaways.

Hotel Playa del Sol

A small hotel originally named the Hotel Playa Hermosa opened in Los Barriles in 1969, just to the north of the Hotel Palmas de Cortez. Bobby and Cha Cha have since bought that and renamed it the Hotel Playa del Sol (Beach of the Sun).

Along with the private beach in the sun, there are 26 air-conditioned rooms, swimming pool, and an indoor bar and entertainment center. It is often used for smaller groups or when the Palmas de Cortez is full. I stayed there recently and enjoyed my poolside room looking out over the Sea of Cortez. Meals are included, as in most of the fishing resorts. I took breakfast on the patio of the upstairs palapa, with a commanding view of the tropical gardens surrounding the hotel and the fishing fleet heading off across the sea.

Bobby and Cha Cha have three sons, one of whom, Bobby Van Wormer Jr., was appointed in 1999 to be Director of Tourism for the State of Baja California Sur. In this capacity, Bobby is on leave from helping the family run the hotel business, and is quickly making a name for himself in his new position.

"I don't mean to sound like a father bragging," Van Wormer said, "But I'm proud of some of the things Bobby is doing. He's really doing a great job." He went on to relate some incidents, including his dealing with agencies of the Federal Government that don't understand the fishing business. It sounded like the new Tourism Director handled some ticklish incidents with diplomacy, a sense of fairness, and firm resolve.

As State Tourism Director, Bobby meets regularly with the municipality directors like Mulegé's Diana Johnson, but it is not a full-time position for them.

"That reminds me," Van Wormer continued, "Don Johnson had three daughters and I had three sons. Early on I entertained the thought that maybe some of them would have gotten together, but I guess it was not to be."

Van Wormer's other two sons are an everyday part of the family business. Eddie, the second oldest, manages the Hotel Punta Colorada, and Carlos (Chucky) does everything. While Bobby and Cha Cha are still the hands-on managers of the two hotels in Los Barriles, their son Chucky is indispensable, overseeing much of the activity. Cha Cha, according to Van Wormer, "is the boss."

Bobby Van Wormer relocated to the East Cape of Baja California Sur almost a half-century ago because he found four things that made him realize he had found paradise. Of course, during his many years there he's found thousands of other reasons to liken his place to paradise. Interestingly, he still has four things that endear him to the area, his wife and three sons. The Van Wormers definitely will leave a legacy on the East Cape.

Coastline on the East Cape.

RANCHO LEONERO/PUNTA PESCADERO

East Cape Expansion

While the first few resorts in the Cape region were either fishing resorts or ultra-exclusive fly-in places, the addition of several hotels during the late1960s and early 1970s created the boom that would soon attract vacationers from around the world.

Two fishing resorts on the East Cape, Rancho Leonero and Punta Pescadero, were developed in the late 1960s.

Rancho Leonero — 1967

Back in 1950, wildlife cinematographer Gil Powell, a relative of actor William Powell, bought 300 acres on the beach to the south of Rancho Buena Vista. As he was always going off to Africa to shoot movies, the locals called him *El Leonero* (one who knows lions). His ranch, which he opened in 1967, became known as Rancho El Leonero, and later Rancho Leonero.

Powell enjoyed hosting his Hollywood friends, who used to fly in for fishing and relaxation. John Wayne, Bing Crosby, and Errol Flynn were guests at Rancho Leonero. Powell died in 1974 and the property languished.

Current owner John Ireland discovered it in 1979, finally purchased it in 1981, built the five original rooms, and opened the Inn at Rancho Leonero in 1986. Powell's old ranch itself had become the bar and office of the current resort.

In 1990 six more rooms were added, and the following year, a swimming pool. In 1992 the original six bungalows were finished. I found the resort a well-manicured delight.

231

Children romped in the pool, while I noted others snorkeling in the reef out front. Where only a decade ago, you almost never saw children, much less spouses, at the fishing resorts on the East Cape, Rancho Leonero regularly draws families to the area.

Punta Pescadero — 1968

One of the most remote of the East Cape resorts is Hotel Punta Pescadero, on a point of the same name about 10 miles north of Los Barriles. It's considered the most northern of the East Cape hotels and was established in 1968 by Johnny Mitre and Jorge Escudero, who had earlier built the Bahía de Palmas.

It's about a 1 and a half to 2 hour drive from either the Los Cabos or the La Paz airport, but there is a 3,500-foot airstrip runway with concrete run-up pads and tiedowns at Punta Pescadero. Peaceful and restful best describes this small resort, whose name translates to "Fisherman's Point." There are 21 suite-sized rooms, all with satellite TV, wood-burning fireplaces, minibars, private patios and spectacular views.

The grounds feature coconut palms, a swimming pool, and a broad beach. Some of the suites have private steps down to the beach. Adolfo Blanco, the hotel manager, says with pride, "Our staff will go out of their way to make our guests feel comfortable here."

Las Cruces/Hotel Palmilla
Pioneers of the Cape

Until a handful of visionary pioneers a half-century ago decided to invest in resorts near the tip of the Baja California peninsula, there had been little going on in the area since the Indians rebelled against the padres and the English and Dutch pirates way-laid Spanish galleons.

In fact, by 1950 Cabo San Lucas only had a population of 548, mostly fishermen and cannery workers. Even then the much larger town of San José del Cabo boasted fewer than 2,000 inhabitants.

The combined Los Cabos area today is a world-class resort area, thanks to just a handful of visionary men. Four of the most significant are Abelardo "Rod" Rodríguez Jr., William "Bud" Parr, Luís Coppola Bonillas, and Luís Bulnes. In the late 1940s and early 1950s, these men began buying land from small ranches. Among them, the four men, either independently or as partners, would build seven hotels or resorts: Los Arcos in La Paz, Club Rancho Las Cruces on the gulf east of La Paz, and farther south, the hotels Palmilla, Cabo San Lucas, Hacienda, Finisterra, and the Solmar.

Rancho Las Cruces

The first resort in Baja California Sur was built in 1950 by Rodríguez and Parr at Club Rancho Las Cruces, a private fly-in hunting and fishing resort on the gulf about 24 miles due east of La Paz. While there is a road to Las Cruces, it's never been very good, and once I had to turn a small rental car around before reaching the place.

Had the little car made it, upon my arrival on the hill overlooking the resort I would have found three restored *cruces* (crosses) which signify the area as the probable landing site of Hernán Cortés in 1535.

The remote location was selected by former U.S. pilot Rodríguez, son of Mexican President Abelardo Rodríguez (1932–34). Rodríguez had bought the former orchard property in 1948. He was joined by another American, Bud Parr. Parr served in WWII, came to La Paz in 1947 to "retire," and met Rodríguez; the rest is roughly the history of the cape region.

Their first project, Rancho Las Cruces, was so swank and exclusive that membership rosters read like a social register. Former President Dwight D. Eisenhower, Desi Arnaz, Bob Hope, and Bing Crosby were among the members, many luminaries enjoying ownership interests. In fact, when Parr later sold his interest in the Las Cruces, he sold it to Bing Crosby, who was a very frequent guest.

They built a swimming pool, tennis courts, driving range, and ultramodern bungalows set in a palm oasis. Early in its history, the Las Cruces became a hotel, but shortly reverted to being a private resort. Today the Las Cruces is still a private resort, managed by Abelardo Nicolás "Niki" Rodríguez, the son of "Rod" Rodríguez and grandson of the president.

Legendary Hotel Palmilla

The pioneers did not sit still. In 1956 Rodríguez and Parr opened up what was originally called the Hotel Las Cruces Palmilla, just a few miles south of the town of San José del Cabo. Considered by many to be one of the most beautiful cape resorts, the Hotel Palmilla has old-world charm in a spectacular setting.

Sprawling on an ocean point among 900 acres thick with palm trees, hibiscus, multicolored bougainvillea, ferns, bamboo, and tinkling fountains, the Palmilla has all the amenities one could think of: 4,500-foot airstrip, wedding chapel, tennis and croquet courts, horse stables, its own sportfishing fleet and private beach, and of course, swimming pool, restaurant, and bar. The Palmilla also boasts a 27-hole Jack Nicklaus-designed golf course with spectacular views of the Sea of Cortez from almost every hole.

Built by Rodríguez and Parr as an exclusive resort for international sportsmen, the Palmilla quickly became a secret hideaway for Hollywood celebrities.

The Spanish-colonial-style accommodations, which offer large air-conditioned rooms and suites, peek through tropical vegetation behind meandering cobbled walkways.

Nowadays on the drive from the highway into the Palmilla, you pass through the Villas del Mar, a planned resort community for 1,300 residential units, from the mountainside casitas "Las Bugambillas" to "Las Villas," private beach-front residences.

Grace and elegance are understated throughout the Palmilla. I walked through a small forest of king palms, their bright shiny-green trunks distinguishing them from their cousin palms. I reached the chapel, which rests serenely atop a small palm-covered knoll, and reveled in my tropical surroundings.

I was glad to see that the Palmilla has never lost its charm, even though it has changed owners and undergone a $13 million renovation in 1996, which included the addition of 62 spacious oceanfront suites. This year more rooms are currently being added on the north side of the property. While the Palmilla entered the new century with the heritage of excellence, its founders had shifted their interests elsewhere.

Both Parr and Rodríguez looked even farther south for their next ventures, the little village on the cape where there was a small fish-packing plant and little else. Their next enterprises would forever change Cabo San Lucas.

HOTEL CABO SAN LUCAS

Parr's Dream Begins Cabo Boom

After the successful 1956 opening of the Hotel Palmilla in San José del Cabo, founder William Mathew "Bud" Parr extended his vision south. He had a dream to build a private resort on the broad coastal lands between the town of San José del Cabo and the cannery down at the rocky promontory.

Just south of El Tule Arroyo was the broad, sandy Chileno Bay (Chilean Bay) named after a group of Chilean pirates. For 250 years, Spanish galleons laden with riches from the Philippines had to pass the tip of Baja on their way from the Orient to Acapulco. Pirates from other countries used the coves near land's end to hide while waiting to waylay the Spaniards. A group of Chileans were among those using the cove below El Tule.

During the late 16th and early 17th centuries, English pirates, encouraged by their queen, were the most successful looters. They even harassed their competition from other countries. So the Chileans constantly had to look over their shoulders for the English.

The British pirate Cromwell was so successful at looting ships it was said he had favorable winds during his every skirmish. The locals even named the winds after him. Breezes in the southern part of Baja California are still called "*coromuels*," as Cromwell might be called in Spanish, and Coromuel Beach at La Paz is reputedly named after them both.

Of course, any good pirate story involves buried treasure. It has been said that not only the Chileans but Cromwell left a fortune in buried treasure. Legend persisted that much of the treasure was buried in Chileno Bay.

After the era of the pirates, not much happened at the tip of Baja California for many years. There was little water, but in time a few hardy ranchos began with limited cattle grazing. A visitor to the area in 1868, J. Ross Browne wrote, "With a climate so warm and salubrious, water is the only desideratum."

By the 1950s, the Rancho El Tule at Chileno Bay was owned by a couple of elderly sisters, Josefina Reza Ojeda and Petronila Reza Ojeda. This is where Bud Parr's vision was to become a reality. He had found his ideal spot.

Parr, born in 1912, was an American who had worked for the OSS during World War II. He visited La Paz after the war and met Abelardo "Rod" Rodríguez, with whom he built the Las Cruces and the Palmilla. He sold his stake in the Club Las Cruces to singer Bing Crosby and later his stake in the Hotel Palmilla to Newport Beach developer Donald Koll.

This time Parr wanted to do it on his own. He and pilot friend Luís Coppola Bonillas, who earlier had acquired the Hotel Los Arcos in La Paz, bought the Rancho El Tule from the sisters in 1959. Coppola and Parr then formed a corporation, and Parr ended up taking over the corporation.

Parr had a dream, and he had a rancho, but he had a number of obstacles to overcome. First was water. Before he could build a 40-room hotel, he had to find water. Looking for the "staff of life," Parr had started digging wells on the beach. He ended up drilling eighteen holes before his workers found a well with enough water to support the hotel.

Treasure hunters on the beach

When people saw all this digging on the beach, rumors spread that Parr had good knowledge of the old pirates' treasure. For almost a decade afterward, people went to the beach at Chileno Bay with metal detectors and shovels and dug holes looking for treasure. Early employees told me that they were constantly finding evidence of some treasure seeker "digging up the beach."

There was no electricity, so Parr had to import his own power generators. He built a kitchen and a few cabins, had a few friends come to fish and hunt, and later a friend drew the hotel blueprint on a napkin. Architect Cliff May was called upon to enhance the original napkin design.

The Hotel Cabo San Lucas, with just the few rooms, opened for business on Sep. 30, 1959 and became the first hotel in Cabo San Lucas. (Even though it was almost 10 miles from land's end, the El Tule arroyo separated the Municipality of San José del Cabo from Cabo San Lucas, officially a Delegado or township.) It was 1961 before the main hotel was completed, marking the hotel's official opening.

Building a hotel in such a remote area called for innovation. Workers had to stay on the site, so accommodations had to be provided for them. From the Mexican mainland, Parr brought in 150 craftsmen: carpenters, masons, plumbers, stonecutters, and landscapers. Parr even brought in his own stone sculptor, the noted Carlos Gonzáles from Guadalajara, who carved 300 statues reminiscent of earlier Mexican cultures to grace the grounds.

In a 1992 *Baja Explorer* magazine article, Parr explains, "I built the Hotel Cabo more as a private club, a fun place. Members included Baron Hilton, Donald Douglas, and a group of executive friends of mine. It kept expanding and we decided to run it as a hotel because of the cost of keeping it up.

"This town (Cabo San Lucas) had just a few hundred people. The only source of employment was the cannery. They didn't even have a tavern. They had this town so sewn up they weren't even allowed to sell beer.

"We built the Hotel Cabo our way. There were plenty of employees, but they didn't have any skills. We had to teach them everything.

"The only supplies we brought in were cement, steel, and wood. All the furniture you see in these hotels (Hotel Cabo San Lucas and the Hacienda) we made ourselves. We brought in carvers and carpenters from Manzanillo, a carpenter town. I flew to Los Angeles and bought a woodshop.

"The Hotel Cabo San Lucas was a whole city we had to put in. We built a power plant, a reservoir, everything."

Creating an international resort

Even the hotel's housekeeping department had to be trained on premises. Parents entrusted their daughters to Bud and his wife Marion Parr to live at the site. The bedrooms for the single girls were all built around a patio with a single entrance to discourage men from entering. Some of the girls had never seen running water, much less fancy tile floors and other amenities like ice cubes. To help the workers with families, a Señor Foray was hired to care for and tutor young children.

Parr had to build an airstrip, and many of the early visitors arrived by private plane. During the 1960s the Hotel Cabo San Lucas became known internationally. Guests included John Wayne, Desi Arnaz, Lucille Ball, Phil Harris, Barry Goldwater, Ray Conniff, former President Dwight D. Eisenhower, actor Kirk Douglas and his son Michael, and many others. There, Ernest Hemingway's brother Gregory wrote *Papa — A Personal Memoir*, dedicating the book to Bud Parr.

Parr recalls, "John Wayne spent about six months with me after his lung cancer operation. We went with him to the Socorro Islands for fishing and hunting. He was the type of person who never said anything wrong, drunk or sober. I never saw a man like him in my life. He was a solid individual. I used him as a guide at the Hotel Cabo. At that time our clientele were all dove hunters and fishermen. Wayne would take groups out for *palomas* (white doves)."

A presidential brush-off

Mexican Presidents Miguel Alemán and Adolfo López Mateos were also guests at the Hotel Cabo San Lucas.

President López Mateos (1958–1964) was on hand for the official opening of the hotel on Nov. 26, 1962. He liked the hotel so well that he became a regular guest and even brought his own yacht.

It seems, however, that President López Mateos was a self-proclaimed ladies' man and known skirt chaser. He must have gotten a little frustrated at the Hotel Cabo San Lucas. He supposedly made a pass at Mrs. Marion Parr, who successfully managed to repel his sexual advances, and told her husband about it. Somehow, it just doesn't seem prudent to avenge one's honor when the person happens to be the president of the country you're doing business in. It is a testament to the diplomacy of the Parrs to have kept a good relationship with the president while keeping him at bay.

Before it was fashionable, Bud Parr was interested in the ecology of the area. He created an oasis on the 2,500 acres of the former Rancho El Tule. He brought in rubber trees from Mexico City, bougainvillea from California, banana trees and thousands of coconut palms from all over Mexico.

He built a resort that not only attracted fishermen and hunters, but one that would achieve worldwide prominence. The main building and lobby rest on a mesa, with the 125 private rooms and suites terracing down to the beach.

All the guest rooms are air-conditioned, with onyx bathrooms, stone fireplaces, private patios, and balconies. In addition, they are spacious, have mini-refrigerators, cable TV, and telephones with laptop computer jacks. There are studio rooms, junior suites, deluxe suites, and master suites. Several large villas are also available, from three-bedroom designs to a seven-bedroom villa with its own swimming pool and sauna. The villas range from 3,000 to 7,500 square feet, are terraced, and have glass walls facing the unobstructed ocean view.

The multi-tiered main swimming pool is on a terrace with columns, arches, a tumbling waterfall, and shallow ponds, all overlooking the Sea of Cortez. It is the setting for many photo shoots, including the popular *Sports Illustrated* swimsuit edition. One of supermodel Kathy Ireland's three *Sports Illustrated* covers was shot poolside at the Hotel Cabo San Lucas.

Chileno Bay is one of three safe swimming beaches in the area and offers miles of beaches and private coves. The recreational facilities the hotel offers are limitless.

Cary Grant mentioned that one thing he liked about the Hotel Cabo San Lucas was that nobody bothered him there. He was just one of many. Raquel Welch also liked to stay there for the same reason.

The Hotel Cabo San Lucas was the only Baja California resort named by *Condé Nast Traveler* magazine as one of the world's top 50 tropical resorts. It was voted Latin/Central America's Leading Resort at the October 1998 World Travel Awards ceremony held in the Bahamas, with over two million votes coming in from 181 countries.

Recently the interior of each room has been redesigned by noted Interior Designer Kathy Neidermeyer from Guadalajara. "Each interior is totally different," hotel manager Anina Louis told me enthusiastically. Artists and craftsmen were again brought in to render an original décor. The villas, for example, feature carved furniture and armoires, hand-loomed carpets and area rugs, and embroidered bed covers. The accessories are works of art, including basketry, ceramic work, and wood carvings.

Rodríguez starts Hacienda

After Parr got the Hotel Cabo San Lucas off the ground, "Rod" Rodríguez saw what his former partner was accomplishing at Chileno Bay and built a new hotel closer to the old cannery in the heart of Cabo San Lucas. He called it the Hacienda Cabo San Lucas and it opened in 1963. Rodríguez later sold it to a corporation, and Bud Parr ended up buying the Hacienda in 1977.

Bud and Marion Parr had four boys, Mike, Mitch, Mark, and Matt. The well-liked Mike, nicknamed *Zorrillo* (Skunk), has since passed away. Mitch, 40, and his wife Claudia now run the Hotel Cabo San Lucas. He's as active as his father, flies his own airplane, and loves to go diving.

His brothers Mark and Matt Parr run the family's Hotel Hacienda Beach Resort, originally built by Bud's old partner "Rod" Rodríguez. The Hacienda is unique in that it was the first resort hotel in downtown Cabo San Lucas. Its guest rooms appear to be bunkers or caves built into the hill.

Today there are numerous hotels, condos, and resorts to accommodate the growing legions of international tourists to the entire Los Cabos area. The classic resort, Hotel Cabo San Lucas, culminated the dream of Bud Parr.

Bud Parr, by all accounts, put the cannery village at the tip of the Baja California peninsula on the map. His vision and willingness to do what seemed impossible, carving a world-class resort out of a dry waterless rancho, has made him one of the top legends in recent Baja history.

RESORTS/HOTELS ON THE CAPE

Los Cabos Welcomes Jet Set

The addition of several hotels in the Los Cabos area during the late 1960s and early 1970s created the boom that would soon attract vacationers from around the world.

The 1970s saw other hotels join the earlier Hotel Hacienda (1963) in Cabo San Lucas. The Hotel Finisterra and the Mar de Cortez opened in 1972; the Solmar in 1974, and the opulent Twin Dolphin in 1977. Those first Cabo hotels, now a quarter of a century old, set the stage for others to follow.

In 1975 the first commercial air service began to Los Cabos. In 1978 the Mexican agency FONATUR chose the Los Cabos region for tourist development. Within years, the airport at Los Cabos was expanded and began service by international carriers.

Hotel Mar de Cortez — 1972

One of the best bargains in Cabo San Lucas is the Hotel Mar de Cortez, on the right side of the main street downtown — which now follows the contour of the water.

The charming colonial-style hotel is just a half block before what used to be Kilometer 0, the end of Highway 1. It was opened by Carlos Unsgon and Simon Yee, with a partnership interest by Bud Parr in 1972.

I've stayed there a couple of times, as for years it's been the best value in the area. The guest rooms are air-conditioned and have private baths. There's a wonderful restaurant, a good-sized swimming pool, a bar, small gift shop, and lots of information available at the front desk for fishing and other activities. It's ideal for those who like to stroll the downtown areas from their hotel.

Hotel Finisterra — 1972

For sheer drama, the Hotel Finisterra (end of land) nestled amid the crags at the tip of the peninsula, is hard to beat. I was there not long after it opened in the mid-1970s. At that time, the road leading up to the hotel was dirt. In fact, you had to take a dirt road leading from town to get to it.

The roads are paved now, and the Hotel Finisterra has not lost its impact. The view on one side toward town has become a real treat, with twinkling city lights on majestic display. The other side looks over the beach at the tip of Baja and out over the Pacific.

The Finisterra was the first hotel venture for Luís Bulnes Molleda, the manager of the Cabo San Lucas fish cannery at the bottom of the hill. Bulnes teamed with Luís Coppola Bonillas of the Los Arcos in La Paz to build the Finisterra.

According to Bulnes, "Before the Finisterra, the hotels were built by Americans. ...When we started the Finisterra, it was with a Mexican architect, Mexican engineer, and Mexican capital."

The Finisterra opened with 56 rooms, and was the first to stay open all year. Previously, the hotels were smaller when they opened for business and closed down totally during the summer months. The hotel is still managed by the Coppola family.

Solmar — 1974

The Solmar is a hotel built into the base of the rocks that signify land's end. From the long buildings fronting the Pacific Ocean, one can cross a broad sandy beach to the water. Swimming, however, is usually not advised there because of the strong undertow.

The Hotel Solmar was built by the pioneer Luís Bulnes Molleda, who had emigrated to Mexico from Spain as a young man. In 1954, he was hired to manage the local tuna cannery at Cabo San Lucas. At one time the cannery was the largest producer of tuna in Latin America and the third largest in the world.

During his years in Cabo, he began to acquire prime pieces of property near the tip of Baja and much of what would later become the Pedegral development in the hills. On part of his land he built the Finisterra with Luís Coppola Bonillas. He saved the quiet tranquility of the Pacific beach away from town for himself. There he built the Solmar, the beautiful two-story hotel built into the rocks at the extreme tip of land.

He said that the reason he bought that land is because "you're in town, but not in town." The Hotel Solmar is not only a favorite of many who seek the same isolated feeling, but is also where Bulnes still hangs his hat.

Twin Dolphin — 1977

The development of Los Cabos in the 1970s would not be complete without mentioning one of the area's most luxurious resorts, the Hotel Twin Dolphin, which opened in 1977. Sprawling over 135 acres on a secluded beach adjacent to Santa María Bay, the Hotel Twin Dolphin was named after the family yacht of its developer.

Texas oilman David J. Halliburton Sr. had visited the Cabo San Lucas area before WWII aboard the family's boat, *Twin Dolphin*. It would be almost 40 years before the hotel of the same name would be the area's new standard bearer for opulence.

While the hotel logo is a pair of leaping dolphins, the dolphins themselves play second fiddle to the décor patterned after the cave paintings found in Baja. The rock art is so powerful that after seeing it for the first time months after the hotel opened, I knew that one day I would have to visit the original paintings in the mountain caves.

The artist who depicted the rock art is Reisden Crosby Decker, the daughter of Harry Crosby, known for his exploration of Baja's famous caves and his classic book *The Cave Paintings of Baja California*.

The Twin Dolphin accommodations are 13 cabañas, which total 44 deluxe rooms and six suites that are more like private villas than hotel rooms. All the expected amenities of a world-class resort are available, including a putting green and a 1.6 mile jogging/walking trail.

The Hotel Twin Dolphin has been honored by *Travel & Leisure* magazine and *Condé Nast Traveler*, which named it the World's Best Latin Resort. Room rates are lower during the off-season and on the European-plan single. They are higher between November and May. The Twin Dolphin is still owned and operated by the Halliburton family, David Jr., Donald, and Elizabeth.

The 1980s brought continued prosperity and tourism to the former small cannery town. During the 1970s, choices were limited to those few pioneering hotels. The presence of those classic hotels heralded the advent of one of the world's top resort destinations. "Wanna buy a time share, anyone?"

CAPTAIN RITCHIE OF CAPE SAN LUCAS

A Character on the Cape

One of the earlier Europeans to jump ship and live among the *californios* was the English Captain Ritchie, the only European settler in the Cape region for some of the 19th century. A cabin boy in 1828, he became enamored with a San José del Cabo *señorita* and hid out until his ship sailed.

He raised some cattle and kept a supply of beef for the whalers who would make port at the cape. After the mines opened at El Triunfo and San Antonio, Ritchie made a business of transporting freight and passengers to the mines.

According to J. Ross Browne in his 1868 *Explorations in Lower California*, Ritchie

"Has been the host of all the distinguished navigators who have visited the coast during the past 40 years. Smuggling, stock-raising, fishing, farming and trading have been among his varied occupations. ...He has made and lost a dozen fortunes, chiefly by selling and drinking whiskey. No man is better known on the Pacific Coast than 'Old Ritchie.'

"He has suffered martyrdom at the hands of the Mexicans. They have robbed him, taxed him, imprisoned him, threatened to kill him, but all to no purpose; and they now regard him as an inevitable citizen of their country. At one time they confiscated his property, and carried him over to Mazatlán where they cast him into prison; but he survived it all.... The various injuries inflicted upon him would have destroyed any other man on earth. It will be a marvel if he ever dies.

"Captain Ritchie's house at Cape San Lucas is the home of adventurers from all parts of the world. Admirals, commodores, captains and mates inhabit it; pirates and freebooters take refuge in it; miners, traders and cattle-drovers make it their home. In short the latchkey is never drawn in. His hospitality is proverbial."

Of course, Captain Ritchie did die, but his legacy lives on. As an adventurer, his chosen refuge of Baja California was a perfect venue for his independent spirit. Others who made Baja their home have generally shared that same sense of adventure no matter when they arrived: the pirates, the early Spaniards, the 19th century vagabonds, and even the Baja aficionados of today.

JANOS XANTUS RECORDS HIS FINDS

Surveyor Measures More than Tides

The Cape region is rich in the folklore of its characters. Today some foreigners join the Mexicans loitering in the streets to regale the tourists with deeds, misdeeds, and adventures. But a century and a half ago, only a couple of outsiders lived in the area of Cabo San Lucas. One of these visitors ensured that his name would enter the annals of history, by dabbling in ornithology and botany, which resulted in several species of birds and plants being named after him.

He was the Hungarian naturalist Janos Xantus, who lived at Cabo San Lucas for two years (1859 to 61), where he was employed by the United States Geological Survey for the purpose of measuring tides. He had also agreed to collect specimens of the uncharted flora and fauna of the area to send to the Smithsonian Institute.

He began his adventure by getting a small boat to take him from La Paz to Cabo San Lucas. Near there he set up his camp some seven miles from his nearest neighbor, the Englishman Captain Ritchie, and 30 miles from San José del Cabo, then the nearest town.

Xantus had to haul his drinking water in a goatskin bag those seven miles from a brackish well near Captain Ritchie. Camped on a remote beach where he set up his tide gauge, Xantus was almost completely isolated, receiving irregular news reports from occasional whalers.

Xantus wrote, "The winds blow hard all the time and upset everything in my tent, as there is nothing but quicksand to fasten the pegs in. ...There is a great quantity of birds, and what is most astonishing — an infinite variety of snakes and lizards of enormous size."

It has been widely acknowledged that, in his considerable spare time, Xantus had observed and collected some 100 new species of animals from the gulf region. Some examples of these firsts include:

— The Xantus Hummingbird (*hylocharis xantusii*), normally only found in Baja California, although in recent years a nest was found in southern California;

— The Xantus' Murrelet (*synthliboramphus hypoleucus*), a small bird with a habitat on rocky ocean islands and the open ocean. It has a highly restricted breeding range; the world population is concentrated in four major colonies.

He is also known to herpetologists, since he named a gecko (*phyllodactylus xanti*) and the genus *Xantusia (*night lizards*)*.

Flora to which the name Xantus is affixed includes, the plants *Xantus chaenactis*, *Xantus clarkia*, and Xantus' spineflower.

For all his discoveries, Xantus was a controversial naturalist. He has been called a "picturesque liar" and was accused of mislabeling some of his finds. Xantus also appropriated other people's stories of interesting adventures and works previously published in English, passing them off as his own. He thus entertained his fellow Hungarians with "his" exciting life and times in Mexico and the western U.S.

One would think that discovering 100 new species with which he is credited would be more than a lifetime of success, but Xantus boasted that he had collected 3,829 new species totaling 92,000 specimens. He didn't need to exaggerate or enhance his interesting life. Being one of just a handful of foreigners in Baja at the time was more adventure than most people would ever experience.

As if trying to survive on a remote beach wasn't daunting enough, Xantus found himself a pawn in a political struggle between the conservatives in San José del Cabo and the liberals in La Paz. He was forced to pay a license fee for his tide gates by the conservatives, while the liberals accused him of supporting their enemies' cause. To punish the foreigner, they confiscated one of his guns and a keg of gunpowder, and killed and ate one of his cows.

Xantus may have had a few run-ins with the political machinery, but apparently he did not have problems with the Mexican women.

This was documented by John Steinbeck, who arrived in the cape area 80 years later, in 1941. In his book *Sea of Cortez*, Steinbeck gently rebukes the social biases of the time by openly honoring Xantus thusly,

> "And we do not feel we are injuring his reputation, but rather broadening it, by repeating a story about him. Speaking to the manager of the cannery at the Cape, we remarked on what a great man Xanthus [sic] had been. Where another would have kept his tide charts and brooded and wished for the Willard Hotel, Xanthus had collected animals widely and carefully.
>
> "The manager said, 'Oh, he was even better than that.' Pointing to three little Indian children he said, 'Those are Xanthus's great-grandchildren,' and he continued, 'In the town there is a large family of Xanthuses, and a few miles back in the hills you'll find a whole tribe of them.' There were giants in the earth in those days....
>
> "We wonder what modern biologist, worried about titles and preferment and the gossip of the Faculty Club, would have the warmth and breadth, or even the fecundity for that matter, to leave a 'whole tribe of Xanthuses.' We honor this man for all his activities. He at least was one who literally did proliferate in all directions."

In many cultures people hope to have at least one son to carry on the family name. The prodigious Hungarian certainly did better than that. Not only did he leave a "tribe," but also plants and animals named Xantus.

The Hotel California occupies a colonial building.

HOTEL CALIFORNIA, TODOS SANTOS

Did the Eagles Soar Here?

"Welcome to the Hotel California. Such a lovely place (such a lovely place) such a lovely face. Plenty of room at the Hotel California. Any time of year (any time of year) you can find it here."

So went the lyrics of the Eagles' hit song "Hotel California." According to local legend, the rustic Hotel California in Baja's Todos Santos is the venue for the song. But is there really a connection? Has there ever been?

In recent years the hotel had begun to capitalize on an alleged connection, even selling Eagles T-shirts and other paraphernalia in the lobby. Carloads of folks on day trips from Cabo San Lucas could be seen roaming around the place, snapping up souvenirs like they were Elvis Presley's underwear.

Many have doubted any connection. There are certainly other Hotel Californias; in fact gone now is a small motel near the second Pemex in Guerrero Negro called the Hotel California. Another example is the Hotel California in Palm Springs, California. In addition, most Eagles fans thought the lyrics to be symbolic of a culture; after all, that's what the Eagles had said all along.

According to Don Henley of the Eagles, "I was looking at the American culture and when I called that one song 'Hotel California' I was simply using California as a microcosm for the rest of America and for the self-indulgence of our entire culture. It was, to a certain extent, about California, or about the excesses out here. But, in many instances, as California goes, so goes the nation."

Henley penned the lyrics to the song, and he should know. Don Fender wrote the music and "Hotel California," released Thanksgiving 1976, became the signature number of what was already one of the 1970's hottest groups. The album "Hotel California" sold 15 million copies, making it an all-time best seller. It should come as no surprise for establishments to attempt to cash in on the fame of the name.

The village of Todos Santos, which straddles the Tropic of Cancer near the Pacific about midway between La Paz and Cabo San Lucas, has long been an agricultural oasis, with mangos, avocados, and citrus trees. The vast sugar cane fields provided employment for the several sugar mills that thrived for over a century. By the late 19th century the picturesque community enjoyed numerous municipal buildings and even theaters for live performances.

In 1950, Antonio "El Chino" Tobasco opened a small hotel in one of the older colonial-style two-story buildings at Calle Juárez and Márquez de León, not far from the town's plaza. It would later be called the Hotel California.

Back in the 1970s, when Don Henley was purported to have been part-owner, or wrote the lyrics to the song while sequestered there (take your pick, both versions have made the newspapers and magazines), the hotel catered to backpackers and other itinerant travelers. For just a few bucks, long-haired gringos found solace. Rooms were only $2 a night and instead of beds, guests slept on hammocks. A shared bathroom was down the hall.

Long-time Todos Santos resident/artist Pablo Domingo claims that during the mid-1980s it was called the Mission Hotel and rooms went for only $6 per night.

Americans bought the hotel in 1987 and began extensive remodeling. They restored the original Spanish tiles and arches. They added a swimming pool of cobalt-blue tile, a restaurant, and a curio shop. The 16 rooms were all refurbished with private baths. The rooms are huge, with shower stalls you could hold a party in, and some rooms (#5, upstairs, for example) have additional sitting rooms and private balconies. Some have views of the plaza or out to the ocean.

By summer 1998 the place dripped with charm, not to mention magenta bougainvillea, adding contrasting splashes of color as it seemingly dripped into the deep blue pool. The curio shop took up more room than the old café, and the signature song "Hotel California" played constantly in the background. One would think employees might tire of the constant refrain.

Hotel managers Manuel and Sylvia Valdez did a bang-up job helping to create a "piece of history" for visitors from the upscale Cabo San Lucas developments only an hour or so away. The entire town of Todos Santos had become an artists' enclave in recent years, and according to Janet Howey, proprietor of Tecolote Libros, "The town is packed with rental cars from about 11 a.m. to 3 p.m. each day."

Many of the visitors, looking about for some type of Disneyana, not realizing the charms of a town like Todos Santos are what you don't see, have been quick to grab the Eagles myth propagated by the hotel owners. And if they run into a local in the know, they become disillusioned. They want to believe the fantasy and often get upset with those who might use facts to burst the bubble.

Domingo said sometimes people get downright mad when they're told that the Eagles had nothing to do with Todos Santos' historic hotel. "One woman angrily told me that the next thing I'd be telling her was that there was no Santa Claus. I told her I didn't know about that, but did know the Eagles had no connection with the Hotel California. She stormed off in a huff," he bemusedly recalls.

In March 2000 I visited Todos Santos again, looking forward to spending a night in the historic hotel, Eagles connection or not. I was surprised to find it closed, locked up, shut tight. I learned it was sold in May 1999 to some Americans, who put a sign out front saying, "Hotel Closed For Remodel. Will Open June 1." It never opened again. It's now for sale again, at a price reputed to be just under $1 million.

Across the street I noticed a new gift shop that devoted its entire stock to Hotel California and Eagle merchandise. There were T-shirts, ashtrays, pencils, cups, and caps. They even had postcards with the words "Hotel California" emblazoned in old-style calligraphy below the balcony arches of the closed building across the street. The myth lives on.

I found a delightful new-old place to stay in — the Plaza Inn, recently opened by Lisa Nelson in an old colonial building. It was the old home of the Jorge Santana family, who ran the sugar mill. The pastel building with arched doorways and three-foot-thick walls faces the plaza and is just across from the church and next door to the old theater.

There're only four very moderately priced rooms, all off the central *sala*. The *sala*, or entry/living room, is inviting, with big wooden tables and chairs, hand-carved furniture, thick tile floors, and languorous ceiling fans. My large sleeping room had its own huge private patio and view out over the lush green valley to the ocean beyond. While the Hotel California may be closed, I discovered an even more authentic place to stay.

Other writers tried to validate the claim of the Eagles to the Hotel California in Todos Santos. Joe Cummings, author of *Baja Handbook* and *Cabo Handbook*, recently dug up Don Henley's number and sent him a fax. The very next day he received a fax back, signed by Don Henley himself, in which he stated that, "neither myself nor anyone in the Eagles has ever had any association, either business or pleasure, with the Hotel California in Todos Santos."

You can't get any more definitive than that. But then again, try telling that to the lady who just bought a T-shirt across the street.

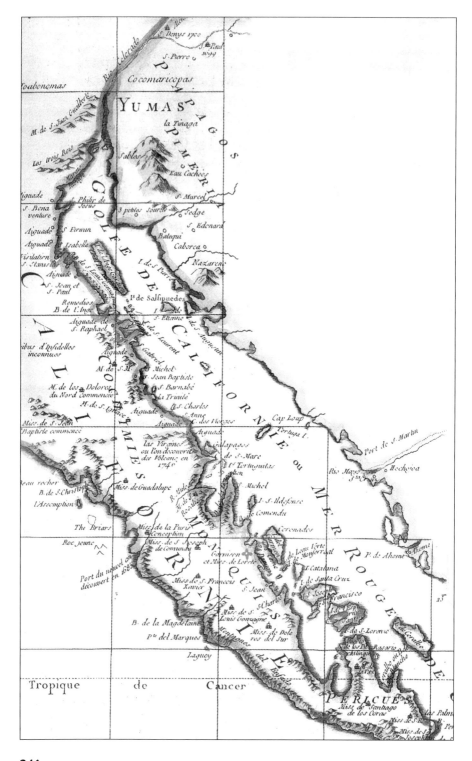

Epilogue

The People Are the Legacy

With this book, we have now explored Baja California from many angles. We've looked into some fascinating stories about explorers who first set foot on what would become Mexico's two most remote states, been entertained by tales of pirates who lay in wait for richly-laden Spanish galleons, and examined numerous anecdotes from the days of the padres, including missions lost and missions restored.

We've visited many Baja establishments, from vintage fly-in resorts to venerable old bars to incongruous and impressive restaurants to gold, copper, and onyx mining enterprises to old casinos and racetracks. We've looked behind the scenes at the peninsula's most upscale resorts and some of its most down-to-earth ranchos.

We've been introduced to many of the characters of Baja. There was naturalist Janos Xantus, who discovered 100 new species, but claimed thousands. There was William Walker, who with his band of outlaws tried to "take over" Baja California. There was Doc McKinnon, who traveled the countryside performing rudimentary dentistry. We've met the "Clam Man of San Felipe" and Francisco Muñoz, the best bush pilot the peninsula has ever known, and we've been introduced to some of the writers like John Steinbeck and Erle Stanley Gardner, who have told the world about this wondrous land called Baja.

Baja California, at over 800 miles in length and about 75 miles wide, is by all accounts a harsh land of deserts, high mountains, and very little water. The few oases have been peopled for years by hardy *bajacalifornios* who have eked out an existence in almost impossible conditions. The people of Baja California are their own greatest legacy.

At fewer than three million people in the entire peninsula, about 90 percent live in the northern state of Baja California. Over half of those live in Tijuana and Mexicali. With Ensenada and the Rosarito area also heavily populated, the vast reaches of Baja are home to but a few. In fact, Baja California Sur is the country's second-least populated state.

The *bajacalifornios* remain different from the rest of Mexico, both in isolation and in attitude. They are extremely sturdy and have learned to make the difficult commonplace. They are proud, and many consider surviving under such harsh conditions their badge of honor.

Their heritage is somewhat different too, as in addition to Spanish and Indian, many are the descendants of Englishmen and other Europeans who found Baja California to their liking and jumped ship or did whatever it took to remain. They raised families, and a more diverse blood now flourishes throughout the land.

Some are descendants of those who, like Nicolás Márques, landed with Salvatierra in 1697, or even in the immediate years following, like the soldier Juan de Arce, who had English lineage along with his Spanish surname.

Some are descendants of later arrivals, like those of Thomas Smith or Peter Davis or Richard Daggett or Frank Fischer or Eugenio Grosso or Don Johnson or Bob Van Wormer, all adventurous and hardy men who have left their progeny in Baja. To find a common thread, the *bajacalifornios* share an adventurous and laborious heritage.

The Transpeninsular Highway, which opened in 1973, has been the biggest catalyst for change the peninsula has ever seen. It opened doors not only for economic development, but also the attendant tourism that followed.

The remote reaches have become more accessible, bringing change to those hardy mountain men, ranchers, fishermen, and their families. By all accounts, it was a mixed blessing, forever changing the needs and wants of those who had lived in a frontier time warp.

The ways of the city folk slowly infiltrated into the mountains, and radios and televisions began to obliterate the silence or muffle the soft sounds of goat bells tinkling or wind rustling through the meager trees.

While he has coveted, and even acquired, a few items to ease a difficult life or provide a little entertainment, the *bajacalifornio* has himself changed very little. The *bajacalifornio* is by nature a devout family man, a loyal ally to his friends, and helpful and friendly to strangers beyond expectations, and progress has not diminished those qualities.

Those of us who have traveled extensively in Baja know what I mean. When you're far from a town or highway and experience a car problem, you hope that the next car will be that of *bajacalifornios*. The locals will not only stop, but will go about rendering assistance, even if it takes them all day.

In addition, almost all Baja drivers are natural mechanics. They are used to making on-the-spot repairs with seemingly no available parts, crafting something that might work and usually does.

The *bajacalifornio* lives by the phrase "*Mi casa es su casa*" (my house is your house). Many times I've been a reluctant recipient of hastily crafted meals that I'm sure have been ill-afforded. It's almost impossible to refuse, so I got in the habit of bartering, finding out what they might use — a tool, canned food, matches, coffee, or something.

When I return to the States, I know what I miss most about Baja. Sure, I miss the harsh yet beautiful and intriguing land. I miss those idyllic unpeopled beaches and the deserts and mountains. I miss the solitude, where a reluctant nature provides the only sounds, such as a startled covey of quail exploding from cover with a furious flapping of wings, or the possessive cawing of a seagull, or the gentle lapping of waves upon a cobbled beach.

But most of all I miss the people. I've been fortunate enough to have traveled the world, yet I've found the friendliest, most gentle, most giving people right in my own backyard, right in the remote areas of Baja California. The people of Baja California are themselves the greatest legends of all.

Selected Bibliography

The accompanying books and reference materials will help the reader learn more about
Baja California:

Allen, Col. D.K. *Field Notes of Lower California (San Vicente Basin)*. International Company of Mexico, 1887.

Ames, Bette and Wilma Knox. *Through Baja by RV*. Los Angeles: Travel Treasures, 1975.

Automobile Club of Southern California. *Baja California*. Los Angeles: Guidebooks and Maps from 1940s to present.

Baegert S.J., Johann Jakob. *Observations in Lower California, a 1771 report*. Berkeley and Los Angeles: University of California Press, 1952.

Bairstow, Lynne. *Frommer's Portable Los Cabos & Baja*. New York City: Macmillan, 2001.

Baja Peninsula — Insight Pocket Guide. New York: Houghton Mifflin, 1995.

Bales, Mike. *Launch Ramps of Baja California*. Torrance: Launch Ramp Publications, 1992.

Bancroft, Margaret and Griffing. *Flight of the Least Petrel*. New York: Putnam & Sons, 1932.

Barbosa, Lupita E. and Martín E. Barrón. *From Velicatá to San Diego: Fr. Junípero Serra* Tijuana: Luz Y Arte Editorial, 1984.

Belden, L. Burr. *Baja California Overland* Glendale: La Siesta Press, 1968.

Benchley, Peter. *Girl From the Sea of Cortez* New York: Doubleday, 1982.

Berger, Bruce. *Almost An Island* Tuscon: University of Arizona Press, 1998.

Blaisdell, Lowell L. *The Desert Revolution: Baja California, 1911* Madison, Wisconsin: University of Wisconsin Press, 1962.

Blanco, Fierro (Walter Nordhoff). *Journey of the Flame* New York: The Literary Guild, 1933.

Botello, Judy. *The Other Side* San Diego: Sunbelt Publishing, 1998.

Brenton, Tadeo. Ed. *Baja California Yearbook* Ensenada: Las Californias Publishing, 1963.

—. Ed. *The West Coast of Mexico* San Ysidro: Grace Loftin, 1969.

Brow, Dix. *Sea of Cortez Guide* Ventura: Western Marine Enterprises, 1970.

—. *Boating in Mexico* Tuscon: Aztec, 1976.

Browne, J. Ross. *Explorations in Lower California* New York: Harper & Bros., 1868.

Bush, Wesley A. *Paradise to Leeward: Cruising the West Coast of Mexico* New York: D. Van Nostrand, 1954.

Cahill, Rick. *Border Towns of the Southwest* Boulder: Pruett Publishing, 1987.

Cannon, Ray. *How To Fish The Pacific Coast*. Palo Alto: Lane Book Co., 1953.

—. *The Sea of Cortez* Palo Alto: Lane Book Co., 1966.

Carroll, Richard. *The Motor Camper's Guide to Mexico and Baja California*. San Francisco: Chronicle Books, 1975.

Carmony, Neil B. and David E. Brown. *Tales From Tiburón, An Anthology of Adventures in Seriland*.

Southwest Natural History Association, 1983.

Carter, Pel. *Trails and Tales of Baja*. Southwest Arts Foundation, 1967.

Cepek, Dick and Walt Wheelock. *Rough Riding*. Glendale: La Siesta Press, 1968.

Chance, Lisbeth. *Baja Run*. Walker Publishing, 1986.

Coyle, Jeanette and Norman Roberts. *A Field Guide to Plants of Baja California*. La Jolla: Natural History Publishing Co., 1975.

Crosby, Harry. *Antigua California*. Albuquerque: University of New Mexico Press, 1994.

—. *Cave Paintings of Baja California*. San Diego: Sunbelt Publications, 1997.

—. *The King's Highway in Baja California*. San Diego: Copley Books, 1974.

—. *Last of the Californios*. San Diego: Copley Books, 1981.

Cross, Cliff. *Baja California*. Tuscon: HP Books, 1974.

Crow, James T. *New Baja Handbook for the Off-Pavement Motorist in Lower California*. Newport Beach: Bond/Parkhurst Books, 1973.

Cummings, Joe. *Baja Handbook*. Chino: Moon Publications, 1992.

Demaris, Ovid. *Poso Del Mundo*. Boston: Little, Brown & Co., 1970.

DeMente, Boye. *Insiders Guide*. Phoenix Books, 1975.

Dunne, S.J., Peter Masten. *Black Robes in Lower California*. Berkeley & Los Angeles: University of California Press, 1952.

Eiler, Dorothea M. *Baja Gringos*. San Leandro: Bristol Publishing, 1993.

Ellsberg, Helen. *Los Coronados Islands*. Glendale: La Siesta Press, 1983.

—. *Doña Anita of El Rosario*. Glendale: La Siesta Press, 1985.

Enea, Sparky. *With Steinbeck in the Sea of Cortez*. Los Osos: Sand River Press, 1991.

Espinosa, Rik. *Espinosa's Guide to Baja*. Santa Monica: Roundtable Publishing, 1989.

Espinoza, Anita Grosso de. *Reflections*. Tijuana: Arte y Publicidad Gráfica, 1994.

Fischer, Paul. *Adventure to Land's End*. Los Angeles: ARS Publications, 1975.

Fisher, Richard, D. *National Parks of Northwest Mexico*. Tuscon: Sunracer Publications, 1988.

Fogel, Daniel. *Junípero Serra, the Vatican, and Enslavement Theology*. San Francisco: ISM Press, 1988.

Fons, Valerie. *Keep It Moving*. Seattle: The Mountaineers, 1986.

Francez, Padre James Donald. *The Lost Treasures of Baja California*. Chula Vista: Black Forrest Press, 1996.

Gardner, Erle Stanley. *The Hidden Heart of Baja*. London: Jarrods Publishers, 1964.

—. *Host With The Big Hat*. New York: Morrow & Co. 1969.

—. *Hovering Over Baja*. New York: Morrow & Co. 1961.

—. *Hunting The Desert Whale*. New York: Morrow & Co. 1960.

—. *Land of Shorter Shadows*. New York: Morrow & Co. 1948.

—. *Mexico's Magic Square*. New York: Morrow & Co. 1968.

—. *Off The Beaten Track In Baja*. New York: Morrow & Co. 1967.

Garrison, Chuck. *Offshore Fishing; Southern California and Baja*. San Francisco: Chronicle Books, 1981.

Gerhard, Peter. *Pirates on the West Coast of New Spain*. Glendale: Arthur Clark Co., 1960.

Gerhard, Peter and Howard Gulick. *Lower California Guidebook*, 4th Ed. Glendale: Arthur Clark Co., 1970.

—. *Maps of Baja California*. Glendale: Arthur Clark Co., 1962.

Gessner, Lotti. *Hotel Cabo San Lucas — The Man Behind the History*. Los Cabos: Gessner, 1999.

Goldbaum, David. *Towns Of Baja California: a 1918 report*. Glendale: La Siesta Press, 1971.

Goldman, Edward. *Plant Records of an Expedition to Lower California* (Washington, D.C., Smithsonian Institute, U.S. National Museum,1916.

Gotshall, Daniel W. *Marine Animals of Baja California*. Ventura: Western Marine Enterprises, 1982.

Gudde, Erwin G. *1,000 California Place Names*. Berkeley: University of California Press, 1947.

Hager, Anna Marie. Ed. *The Filibusters of 1890*. Los Angeles: Dawson's Book Shop, 1968.

Hall, Douglas Kent. *The Border: Life on the Line*. New York: Abbeville Press, 1988.

Hancock, Ralph, Ray Haller, Mike McMahan, and Frank Alvarado. *Baja California*. Los Angeles: Academy Press, 1953.

Hale, Howard. *A Long Walk To Mulegé*. Spring Valley: Pinkerton Publications, 1980.

Harris, Richard. *Hidden Baja*. Berkeley: Ulysses Press, 1998.

Hazard, Ann. *Cartwheels in the Sand*. San Diego: Renegade Enterprises, 1999.

Higginbotham, Patti and Tom. *Backroad Baja*. Sparks: Something's Fishy Publications, 1996.

Hittell, Theodore H. *El Triunfo de la Cruz — The First Ship Built in The Californias, an 1880 report*. San Francisco: California Historical Society, 1984.

Hoctor, Fred. *Baja Haha*. San Diego: Backside Press 1984.

Howey, Janet and Lee Moore. *The Todos Santos Book*. Todos Santos: El Tecolote Libros, 1998.

Hugh, Don A. *Solo Below, A Guide Book to Lower California*. San Bernardino: AAA Publishing, 1958.

Hunter, Ben. *The Baja Feeling*. Ontario: Brasch & Brasch, 1978.

Hunter, Jim. *Offbeat Baja*. San Francisco: Chronicle Books, 1977.

Jackson, Everett Gee. *It's a Long Road to Comondú*. College Station: Texas A & M Press, 1987.

Janovy Jr., John. *Vermillion Sea*. Boston-New York: Houghton Mifflin, 1992.

Johnson, William Weber. *Baja California*. New York: Time-Life Books, 1972.

Jones, Fred and Gloria. *Baja Camping*. San Francisco: Foghorn Press, 1994.

Jones, Jack. *Baja*. New York: Fawcett Gold Medal, 1982.

Jordan, Fernando. *El Otro Mexico*. La Paz: State of Baja California Sur, 1976.

Kira, Gene. *King of the Moon*. Valley Center: Apples & Oranges, 1996.

—. *The Unforgettable Sea of Cortez*. Torrance: Cortez Publications, 1999.

Kira, Gene and Neil Kelly. *Baja Catch*. Valley Center: Apples & Oranges, 1988.

Kirchner, John A. *Baja California Railways*. San Marino: Golden West Books, 1988.

Klink, Jerry. *The Mighty Cortez Fish Trap*. London: A.S. Barnes & Co., 1974.

Krutch, Joseph Wood. *Baja California and the Geography of Hope*. San Francisco: Sierra Club, 1967.

—. *The Forgotten Peninsula*. New York: William Sloane, 1961.

Kulander, Charles. *West Mexico, From Sea to Sierra*. Ramona: La Paz Publishing, 1992.

Landeros, Alberto Tapia. *En El Reino de Califia Universidad Autónoma de Baja California*. Mexicali: 1998.

Langewiesche, William. *Cutting for Sign: One Man's Journey along the U.S.-Mexican Border*. New York: Vintage Books, 1995.

Lindsay, Lowell E. Ed. *Geology of the Imperial and Mexicali Valleys*. San Diego: San Diego Association of Geologists, 1998.

Lingenfelter, Richard. *The Rush of 1889 — Baja California Gold Fever*. Los Angeles: Dawson's Book Shop, 1967.

Lucas, Lois. *Baja Sand Castle*. San Ysidro: LBL Publishing, 1984.

Martínez, Pablo L. *A History of Lower California*. Mexico, D.F.: Editorial Baja California 1960.

Mathes, Dr. W. Michael. *A Brief History of the Land of Calafia: the Californias, 1533–1795*. La Paz: Patronato del Estudiante Sudcaliforniano, 1977.

—. *Las Misiones de Baja California*. La Paz: Editorial Aristas S.A. de VC.V., University of San Francisco, 1968.

—. (Transcriber). *The Capture of the Santa Ana at Cabo San Lucas: November 1587* (The Accounts of

Francis Pretty, Antonio de Sierra and Tomás de Alzola). Los Angeles, Dawson's Book Shop, 1969.

Mayoral, Francisco A. Fierro. *Remembranzas de un Bajacaliforniano*. Tijuana: Talleras Gráficos, 1963.

Mackintosh, Graham. *Into a Desert Place*. England: Unwin Hyman, 1988.

—. *Journey With a Baja Burro*. San Diego: Sunbelt Publications, 2001.

Meigs, Peveril and Carl Sauer. *Lower California Studies: Site and Culture at San Fernando de Velicatá*. Berkeley: University of California Press, 1927.

Mexicali Tourist Guide. Mexicali: Baja California, 1997.

Mexico's Baja. New York: Fodor's Travel Publications, 1987.

Miller, Max. *California's Secret Islands*. New York: Ballentine Books, 1959.

—. *The Cruise of the Cow*. Richmond: E.P. Dutton & Co., 1951.

—. *Land Where Time Stands Still*. New York: Dodd, Mead & Co., 1943.

Miller, Tom. *Anglers Guide to Baja California*. Huntington Beach: Baja Trail Publications, 1982.

—. *Eating Your Way Through Baja*. Huntington Beach: Baja Trail Publications, 1986.

Miller, Tom and Elmer Baxter. *The Baja Book*. Huntington Beach: Baja Trail Publications, 1974.

—. *The Baja Book II*. Huntington Beach: Baja Trail Publications, 1987.

Miller, Tom and Carol Hoffman. *Baja Book III*. Huntington Beach: Baja Trail Publications, 1991.

Minch, John, Edwin Minch, and Jason Minch. *Roadside Geology and Biology of Baja California*. Mission Viejo: Minch and Assoc., 1998.

Morrison, Wilbur H. *The Adventure Guide to Baja California*. Edison: Hunter Publishing, 1990.

Murray, Spencer. *Cruising The Sea of Cortez*. Palm Desert: Desert Southwest, 1963.

McDonald, Marquis & Glenn Oster. *Baja: Land of Lost Missions*. San Antonio: The Naylor Co., 1968.

McDonald, Paula. *Crosing the Border Fast and Easy*. San Ysidro: Borderline, 1992.

McMahan, Mike. *There It Is: Baja*. Northridge: Brooke House, 1973.

McMahan, Mike, Ralph Hancock, Ray Haller, and Frank Alvarado. *Baja California*. Los Angeles: Academy Press, 1953.

Navarre, Monty and Harry Merrick. *Baja Traveler*. Long Beach: Airguide Publications, 1974, 1988.

Niemann, Greg. *Baja Fever*. La Crescenta: Mountain N' Air Books, 1998.

Nordhoff, Walter. (Blanco, Fierro). *Journey of the Flame*. New York: The Literary Guild, 1933.

North, Arthur Walbridge. *Camp and Camino in Lower California*. Glorieta: Rio Grande Press, 1910.

—. *The Mother of California*. San Francisco & New York: Paul Elder & Co., 1908.

Off-Road Racing Handbook. Westlake Village: SCORE International 1987.

O'Neil, Don and Ann. *Loreto, Baja California: First Mission and Capital of Spanish California*. Los Angeles: Tio Press, 2001.

Otterstrom, Kerry G. *Mulegé*. Mulegé: AMAC Impresos, 1992.

Palacios Roji, Alma. *Tijuana-Ensenada*. Tijuana: Litografica Limón, 1981.

Patchen, Marvin and Aletha. *Baja Adventures*. Huntington Beach: Baja Train Publications, 1981.

Pendleton, Don. *Baja Blitz*. Ontario: Worldwide Gold Eagle, 1993.

Pepper, Choral. *Baja California: Vanished Missions, Lost Treasures, Strange Stories Tall and True*. Los Angeles: Ward Ritchie Press, 1973.

—. *Desert Lore of Southern California*. San Diego: Sunbelt Publications, 1999.

Peterson, Walt. *The Baja Adventure Book*. Berkeley: Wilderness Press, 1987.

—. *Diving and Snorkeling Baja California*. Melbourne: Lonely Planet, 1999.

Peterson, Walt and Michael Peterson. *Exploring Baja By RV*. Berkeley: Wilderness Press, 1996.

Phillips, Norman. *Baja Highway One*. North Hollywood: Four Wheeler Publications, 1974.

Phleger, Marjorie. *Pilot Down, Presumed Dead*. New York: Harper & Row, 1963.

Pierce, Paul Panther. *A Baja Love Song*. Huntington Beach: Baja Trail Publications, 1985.

Polk, Dora Beale. *The Island of California — A History of the Myth*. Lincoln: University of Nebraska Press, 1991.

Pourade, Richard F. *The Call To California*. San Diego: Copley Books, 1968.

—. *The Explorers; The History of San Diego*. San Diego: Copley Books, 1960.

Pryor, Alton. *Little Known Tales in California History*. Roseville: Stagecoach Publishing, 1997.

Reseck, John Jr. *We Survived Yesterday: Kayaking From San Diego to Cabo San Lucas*. Glendale: Griffin Publishing, 1994.

Reveles, Daniel. *Enchiladas, Rice, and Beans*. New York: One World/Ballentine, 1994.

Rice, Larry. *Baja to Patagonia*. Golden: Fulcrum Publishing, 1993.

Richmond, Doug. *Baja*. Sierra Madre: Bagnall Publishing, 1970.

Robinson, John W. *Camping and Climbing in Baja*. Glendale: La Siesta Press, 1983.

Roberts, Norman. *Baja California Plant and Field Guide*. La Jolla: Natural History Publishing Co., 1989.

Robertson, Tomás. *Baja California and its Missions*. Glendale: La Siesta Press, 1978.

—. *Historical Notes on Baja California*. Ensenada: San Miguel, 1972.

Rocha, Dr. Ernesto Sosa. *Reseña Histórica de la Pesca en el Puerto de San Felipe*. San Felipe: 2000.

Romano-Lax, Andromeda. *Sea Kayaking in Baja*. Berkeley: Wilderness Press, 1993.

Rovirosa, Lic. A. Salazar. *Cronología de Baja California*. Mexicali: 1957.

Sadil, Scott. *Angling Baja*. Portland: Frank Amato Publications, 1996.

Salvadori, Clement. *Motorcycle Journeys Through Baja*. North Conway: Whitehorse Press, 1997.

Sanborn, Don. *Mexico Travelogue*. McAllen: Sanborn Travel, 1974.

Scott, Annette. *Cruising and Sketching Baja*. Flagstaff: Northland Press, 1974.

Secretaria de Educación Pública. *Baja California; Historia y Geografía*. Mexicali: 1993.

Senterfitt, Arnold. *Airports of Baja California*. San Diego: Arnold D. Senterfitt, 1966.

Shedenhelm, W.R.C. *Rockhounding in Baja*. Glendale: La Siesta Press, 1986.

Smith, Don. *The Baja Run: Racing Fury*. Washington, D.C.: Troll Associates, 1976.

Smith, Jack. *God and Mr. Gómez*. New York: Readers Digest Press, 1974.

Smith, Kacey. *Baja GPD Guide*. Denver: Lizard lady Publications, 2000.

Smothers, Marion. *Vintage Baja*. Campo: In One Ear Publications, 1993.

Snyder, John Otterbein. *The Trout of the San Pedro Mártir, Lower California*. Berkeley: University of California Press, 1926.

Stanton, Larry. *Glory Days of Baja*. Camden, S.C.: Culler & Sons, 1996.

Statler, Ruan L. *El Gringo Invisible*. New York: Carlton Press, 1988.

Steinbeck, John. *Log From the Sea of Cortez*. New York: Penguin Books, 1941.

Steinbeck, John and Edward F. Ricketts. *The Sea of Cortez: A Leisurely Journal of Travel and Research*. New York: Viking Press, 1941.

Stephens, Bascom A. *Annual Publication of the Historical Society of Southern California*. Los Angeles: 1888–1889.

—. *The Gold Fields of Lower California*. Los Angeles: Southern California Publishing, 1889.

Sunset Travel Guide to Baja California. Palo Alto: Lane Books, 1971.

Thomson, Donald A, and McKibbin, Nonie. *Gulf of California Fishwatcher's Guide*. Tuscon: Golden Puffer Press, 1981.

Tijuana Map and Guide. Tijuana: Turismo del Estado, 1969.

Tilton, Willis G. *Baja California: The Last New Frontier*. Topeka: Central OK Printing, 1971.

Timberman, O.W. *Mexico's Diamond in the Rough*. Los Angeles: Westernlore Press, 1959.

Tomson, Tommy. *Jesuit Gold of Lower California*. New York: Vantage Press, 1983.

Venegas, S.J., Padre Miguel. *A Natural and Civil History of California (2 Volumes), 1758*. Washington D.C.: Library of Congress, 1966.

—. *Obras Californias* (Introduction by Dr. W. Michael Mathes). University of San Francisco, 1978.

Vogel, Randy. *Climbers Guide to Valle Azteca, Baja California*. Laguna Beach: Bonehead Publishing, 1995.

Warren, Sam. *Having Fun in Tijuana*. San Diego: Warren Communications, 1988.

Warren, Roger. *Red Lights of Baja Mexico*. San Diego: Warren Communications, 1992.

Washburn, Elizabeth H. *Assault on Baja*. Lynwood: Fred Press, 1966.

Waterman, Jonathan. *Kayaking the Vermilion Sea*. New York: Touchtone, Simon & Schuster, 1995.

Wayne, Scott. *Baja California, A Travel Survival Kit*. Berkeley: Lonely Planet, 1985.

Weber, Msgr. Francis J. *The Peninsular California Missions 1808-1880. (Three reports translated and annotated)*. Los Angeles: 1979.

West, Carolyn and Jack. *Cruising the Pacific Coast*. Princeton: Sea Publications, 1966.

Wheelock, Walt. *Beaches of Baja*. Glendale: La Siesta Press, 1968.

Wibberley, Leonard. *Yesterday's Land: A Baja California Adventure*. New York: Ives Washburn, 1961.

Wilde, Jocelyn. *Bride of the Baja*. New York: Pocket Books, 1980.

Williams Jack. *Baja Boaters Guide* (2 Volumes). New York: H.J. Williams Publications, 1996.

Williams Jack and Patty Williams. *The Magnificent Peninsula*. New York: Publishers Press, 6th Ed., 1998.

Willoughby, Lee Davis. *The Baja People*. Sausalito: Dell, 1983.

Wong, Bonnie. *Bicycling Baja*. San Diego: Sunbelt Publications, 1988.

Wortman, Bill and Orv. *Bouncing Down to Baja*. Los Angeles: Westernlore Press, 1954.

Zwinger, Ann. *A Desert Country Near the Sea*. New York: Harper & Row, 1983.

Publications and Newsletters:

Baja Almanac: California Norte and *Baja Almanac: California Sur*. Baja Vision.

Baja California. Robin Cox, Editor, AeroCalifornia.

Baja Explorer Magazine. Landon Crumpton, Publisher, 1991, 1992.

Baja Life Magazine. Baja Communications Group, Eric Cutter, Publisher, 1994–2000.

Baja Times. Roberta Ridgley and John Utley, Editors, 1979–1994.

Baja Traveler. Mayte Rodríguez Cedillo, Editor/Publisher, 1999–2001.

Baja Traveler Magazine. Landon Crumpton, Publisher, 1988, 1989.

Chubasco. Vagabundos del Mar, Fred and Gloria Jones, Editors.

Discover Baja. Lynn Mitchell, Editor, Discover Baja Travel Club, Hugh & Carol Kramer.

El Calendario de Todos Santos. Grupo de Cabo L. Bruce S. de R.L. de C.V., 2000.

El Correcaminos. Los Cabos, Lloyd Kahn, Editor, 2000.

Mexico West Travel Club. Shirley Miller, Publisher.

Mexico's West Coast Magazine. Grace Loftin, Editor.

Pacific Discovery. California Academy of Sciences, 1965.

San Felipe Magazine. Bruce Barber, Editor, October 1991.

Sea of Cortez Review. Jennifer Redmond, Ed. San Diego: Sunbelt Publications, 2000.

SUNBELT PUBLICATIONS
"Adventures in the Natural and Cultural History of the Californias"

Baja Legends: Historic Characters, Events, and Locations, 2nd edition
Greg Niemann

A long-time Baja California journalist shares his extensive knowledge of the peninsula, its colorful past and booming present, in this easy-to-read reference book including its world-famous faces and still-famous places that keep this long finger of the continent in the international spotlight.

Baja California Plant Field Guide, 3rd edition, (SDNHM)
Jon Rebman & Norm Roberts

This widely acclaimed guide which includes over 715 species in 111 plant families in Baja California. Useful also for over 50% of the plants of the entire Sonoran Desert and southern California.

Cave Paintings of Baja California:
Discovering the Great Murals of an Unknown People
Harry W. Crosby

Central Baja hosts one of the five greatest sites in the world for the Great Mural style and ranks with those of the Pyrenees, northwest Africa, and outback Australia. These ancient giant, ghostly figures are only accessible by arduous days-long trekking or with this lavishly illustrated full-color account.

Las Vegas Legends: What Happened in Vegas...
Greg Niemann

Tells the stories behind the headlines and history of "The Entertainment Capital of the World" aka "Sin City"— Vegas! From the first explorers and early founders to the famed entrepreneurs and entertainers to shape this unique city.

Oasis of Stone: Visions of Baja California Sur
Miguel Angel De La Cueva & Bruce Berger

Striking images and text showcase southern Baja coastal, desert, and mountain ecosystems and the geology that created this "oasis of stone."

The Other Side: Journeys in Baja California
Judy Botello

This travel memoir spans twenty years, covers much of the peninsula, and tells of a journey between two diverse lands and cultures.

Palm Springs Legends: Creation of a Desert Oasis
Greg Niemann

From the original Cahuilla inhabitants of the area, to the settlers who were drawn to the therapeutic waters of the original hot springs, you will get to know the stories that made Palm Springs famous.

Tequila, Lemon & Salt: From Baja Tales of Love, Faith, & Magic
Daniel Reveles

The border town of Tecate comes to colorful life and the lives of its inhabitants unfold, full of surprises and a few broken dreams in this new collection of stories.

Also available by Daniel *Guacamole Dip: From Baja... Tales of Love, Faith, and Magic*

Sunbelt produces and distributes publications about "Adventures in the Natural History and Cultural Heritage of the Californias," including guidebooks, regional references, maps, pictorials, and stories that celebrate the land and its people.